LAW AND SOCIAL STATUS IN CLASSICAL ATHENS

Law and Social Status in Classical Athens

EDITED BY

VIRGINIA HUNTER

AND

JONATHAN EDMONDSON

OXFORD
UNIVERSITY PRESS

OXFORD
UNIVERSITY PRESS
Great Clarendon Street, Oxford OX2 6DP

Oxford University Press is a department of the University of Oxford.
It furthers the University's objective of excellence in research, scholarship,
and education by publishing worldwide in

Oxford New York

Athens Auckland Bangkok Bogotá Buenos Aires Calcutta
Cape Town Chennai Dar es Salaam Delhi Florence Hong Kong Istanbul
Karachi Kuala Lumpur Madrid Melbourne Mexico City Mumbai
Nairobi Paris São Paulo Singapore Taipei Tokyo Toronto Warsaw

with associated companies in Berlin Ibadan

Published in the United States
by Oxford University Press Inc., New York

First published 2000

British Library Cataloguing in Publication Data

Data available

Library of Congress Cataloging in Publication Data

Law and social status in classical Athens / edited by Virginia Hunter and Jonathan Edmondson.
p.cm.
Includes bibliographical references and index.
1. Status (Law)—Greece—Athens—History. 2. Social status—Greece—Athens—History.
I. Hunter, Virginia J. II. Edmondson, J. C.

KL4127.L39 2000
346.495'12013—dc21 99-054992

ISBN 0-19-924011-6

1 3 5 7 9 10 8 6 4 2

Typeset in Bembo
by Regent Typesetting, London
Printed in Great Britain
on acid-free paper by
Biddles Ltd., Guildford and King's Lynn

Preface

In the last ten years or so, one of the most fruitful developments in Athenian history has been the increasing dialogue that has taken place between social and legal historians. A steady flow of books and important articles has considerably advanced our understanding of Athenian law and society (Osborne 1985; Cartledge, Millett, and Todd 1990; Cohen 1991; Gagarin 1992; Todd 1993; Hunter 1994; Cohen 1995; Foxall and Lewis 1996; Thür and Vélissaropoulos-Karakostas 1997; Hunter 1997). The orations that were written to be delivered in the Athenian courts in the late fifth and fourth centuries BC have also received much recent attention in the form of editions and translations (for example, Gagarin 1989 and 1997; MacDowell 1990; Carey 1992; Carey 1998; Gagarin and MacDowell 1998). This work has moved away from the study of the law *per se*, whether procedural or substantive, and has aimed instead to situate Athens' legal institutions in their broader social context and to clarify the manner in which law and legal institutions helped to define Athenian social organization and social relations.

Despite this recent work, one key issue that has gone relatively unexplored is the intersection between law and social status. It has long been recognized that the Athenian polis of the fifth and fourth centuries was a composite of slave and free. But these two broad classes represented only polar opposites in a society that was in fact immensely complex. For there were others of varying social status who counted among the free and who, to one degree or another, experienced marginalization. These included resident aliens or metics, transient foreigners, bastards, and the disenfranchised (that is, citizens who were debarred from participating in the political, legal, and religious life of the city). Inferior in status, all these groups lacked the rights and privileges enjoyed by full citizens. Some of these groups are now receiving attention after a long period of neglect (for bastards, for example, see now Patterson 1990;

Ogden 1996). As for slaves, they too were stratified into private, owned by individuals, and public, the property of the state. In addition, there were a number of manumitted slaves who were granted the status of metics. How was this mosaic sustained? One answer is through the law. For the law served to empower and privilege some, while marginalizing others, sometimes even setting out differential rights and treatments. Penalties, for example, could differ according to status: slaves were routinely punished more severely than citizens for the same offence. And slaves were not adjudged competent to act as witnesses in lawsuits, a symbolic and very public demonstration of their inferior status. Resident aliens (metics), on the other hand, were—in theory—able to use the full legal machinery of the Athenian polis. They could sue and be sued in private suits and probably in public ones too; they could act as witnesses in the courts. But in actual practice metics seem not to have been able to exercise these privileges to the full. The law, it can be argued, thus played a crucial role in constructing social status at Athens. Status groups, whether citizens, resident aliens, or slaves, were defined at least in part juridically, by the manner in which they were treated by Athenian law and judicial practice.

It was the desire to explore further the interplay between law and social status that led the editors of this volume to organize an international conference at York University, Ontario, in the spring of 1997. The Department of History (Faculty of Arts) immediately welcomed our proposal, and provided significant financial support. The conference became part of a sequence of major international conferences sponsored annually by the department, some of which have resulted in important publications, especially in the area of social history (Lovejoy and Rogers 1994; Rogers and Shubert 1996). Osgoode Hall Law School, the Law Faculty at York University, co-sponsored the conference. We are very grateful to the then Dean, Marilyn Pilkington, and to Douglas Hay for their support and we are hopeful that this will mark the beginning of increased interaction between the department and the law school. A number of other units at York University helped to make the conference possible and we are grateful too for their support: the Programme in Classical Studies, the Division of Humanities, Founders College, Vanier College, the Faculty of Arts, the Office of the Vice-President (Academic), and the Office of the President. An impasse in local labour-relations meant that it was not in the end possible to hold the conference on the York campus, but we were grateful for the considerable efforts of Alison Keith, which enabled us to hold the two-day conference at Victoria College, University of Toronto. All the papers have been extensively revised following the conference, and we are most grateful to the Press's anonymous readers for their comments.

J.E.

References

CAREY, C. (ed.) 1992. *Greek Orators*, vi: *Apollodorus, Against Neaira. [Demosthenes] 59*. Warminster.

——(tr.) 1998. *Trials from Classical Athens*. London and New York.

CARTLEDGE, P. A., P. MILLET, and S. C. TODD (eds.) 1990. *Nomos: Essays in Athenian Law, Politics, and Society*. Cambridge.

COHEN, D. 1991. *Law, Sexuality, and Society: The Enforcement of Morals in Classical Athens*. Cambridge.

——1995. *Law, Violence, and Community in Classical Athens*. Cambridge.

FOXALL, L. and A. D. E. LEWIS (eds.) 1996. *Greek Law in its Political Setting: Justification and Justice*. Oxford.

GAGARIN, M. 1989. *The Murder of Herodes: A Study of Antiphon 5*. Studien zur klassischen Philologie 45. Frankfurt am Main.

——(ed.) 1992. *Symposion 1990: Vorträge aus griechischen und hellenistischen Rechtsgeschichte*. Cologne.

——(ed.) 1997. *Antiphon: The Speeches*. Cambridge.

GAGARIN, M. and D. M. MACDOWELL (tr.) 1998. *Antiphon and Andocides*. Austin.

HUNTER, V. J. 1994. *Policing Athens: Social Control in the Attic Lawsuits, 420–320 BC*. Princeton.

——1997. 'The Prison of Athens: A Comparative Perspective', *Phoenix* 51: 296–326.

LOVEJOY, P. E. and N. ROGERS (eds.) 1994. *Unfree Labour in the Development of the Atlantic World* (= *Slavery and Abolition* 15/2). London.

MACDOWELL, D. M. (ed.) 1990. *Demosthenes, Against Meidias (Oration 21)*. Oxford.

OGDEN, D. 1996. *Greek Bastardy in the Classical and Hellenistic Periods*. Oxford.

Osborne, R. G. 1985. 'Law in Action in Classical Athens', *JHS* 105: 40–58.

Patterson, C. B. 1990. 'Those Athenian Bastards', *Cl. Ant.* 9: 40–73.

Rogers, N. and A. Shubert (eds.) 1996. *Spectacle, Monument, and Memory*. Ottawa (*Histoire sociale/Social History* 29/58).

Thür, G. and J. Vélissaropoulos-Karakostas (eds.) 1997. *Symposion 1995*. Cologne.

Todd, S. C. 1993. *The Shape of Athenian Law*. Oxford.

Contents

Notes on Contributors

Edward E. Cohen: Chairman of the Executive Committee, Jeffbanks Inc., Philadelphia.

Jonathan Edmondson: Associate Professor of History and Classical Studies, York University, Toronto.

Mark Golden: Professor of Classics, University of Winnipeg, Manitoba, Canada.

Virginia Hunter: Professor Emerita of History, Glendon College, York University, Toronto.

David Mirhady: Lecturer in Ancient History and Classical Studies, University of Calgary, Alberta, Canada.

Robin Osborne: Professor of Ancient History and Fellow, Corpus Christi College, University of Oxford.

Cynthia Patterson: Associate Professor of History, Emory University, Atlanta, USA.

Bruce Robertson: Assistant Professor of Classics, Mount Allison University, New Brunswick, Canada.

Stephen Todd: Senior Lecturer in Classics, University of Keele, Staffordshire, England.

Illustrations

Abbreviations

Ancient authors and their works are cited in abbreviated form according to the list of abbreviations found in *The Oxford Classical Dictionary* (3rd edn., 1996). The following abbreviations are used for academic journals, collections of inscriptions and papyri, and standard handbooks.

ABSA	*Annual of the British School at Athens*
AJA	*American Journal of Archaeology*
AJP	*American Journal of Philology*
Ant. Cl.	*L'Antiquité classique*
ASNP	*Annali della Scuola normale superiore di Pisa*
BICS	*Bulletin of the Institute of Classical Studies*
C&M	*Classica et Mediaevalia*
CB	*The Classical Bulletin*
Cl. Ant.	*Classical Antiquity*
CP	*Classical Philology*
CQ	*Classical Quarterly*
CR	*Classical Review*
CRAI	*Comptes rendus de l'Académie des Inscriptions et de Belles-lettres*
Davies *APF*	J. K. Davies, *Athenian Propertied Families 600–300* BC (Oxford, 1971)
EMC/CV	*Echos du Monde classique/Classical Views*
G&R	*Greece and Rome*
GRBS	*Greek, Roman, and Byzantine Studies*
HSCP	*Harvard Studies in Classical Philology*
IG	*Inscriptiones Graecae*
Inscriptions Juridiques Grecques	*Recueil des inscriptions juridiques grecques*, ed. R. Dareste, B. Haussoullier, and T. Reinach (Paris, 1892–1904)
JHS	*Journal of Hellenic Studies*
ML	R. Meiggs and D. M. Lewis (eds.), *A*

	Selection of Greek Historical Inscriptions to the End of the Fifth Century BC, rev. edn. (Oxford, 1988)
Num. Chron.	*Numismatic Chronicle*
OCD	*The Oxford Classical Dictionary*, 3rd edn., ed. S. Hornblower and A. J. S. Spawforth (Oxford, 1996)
OGIS	*Orientis Graeci Inscriptiones Selectae*, ed. W. Dittenberger (Leipzig, 1903–5)
PCPS	*Proceedings of the Cambridge Philological Society*
P Hal.	*Dikaiomata: Auszuge aus alexandrinischen Gesetzen und Verordnungen in einem Papyrus des philologischen Seminars der Universität Halle (Berlin, 1913)*
P Oxy.	*The Oxyrhynchus Papyri*
RE	*Realencyclopädie der classischen Altertumswissenschaft*
SEG	*Supplementum Epigraphicum Graecum*
TAPA	*Transactions of the American Philological Association*
Tod *GHI*	M. N. Tod, *A Selection of Greek Historical Inscriptions*, 2nd edn. (Oxford, 1946)
ZPE	*Zeitschrift für Papyrologie und Epigraphik*
ZRG	*Zeitschrift der Savigny-Stiftung für Rechtsgeschichte. Romanistische Abteilung*

I

Introduction: Status Distinctions in Athenian Law

Virginia Hunter

The subject of this collection is the articulation of law and social status in classical Athens.[1] How, it asks, did the law of Athens construct and sustain social status? In posing this question, the papers assembled here have made no effort to solve or even to enter seriously into the definitional debate around class and status initiated by Finley (1973) and de Ste Croix (1981). Nor does the term status, as used here, derive from a Weberian definition equating it with the social estimation of honour or prestige (de Ste Croix 1981: 89; Giddens and Held 1982: 65–8; Harris 1988: 602).[2] For while it could be argued that resident aliens, for example, were distinguished from Athenian citizens by their lack of honour or prestige, in fact what divided them was much more fundamental: each was a juridically defined group with privileges, on the one hand, and disabilities, on the other, enshrined in law. These two social groups together with a class of slaves represent the three 'orders' of Athenian society, to use Finley's terminology (1973: 45; cf. de Ste Croix 1981: 94–5; Hansen 1991: 86).[3] In this collection, status groups refer to these juridically defined orders, and status to the standing of each group within the resultant social hierarchy,

[1] Works on status and status distinctions in classical Athens include Grace 1973; Finley 1973: 35–61; 1981a and b; de Ste Croix 1981: 81–98; Hansen 1991: 86–8; Todd 1994; Cohen 1994; Fisher 1995; and Todd 1997.

[2] Such prestige might be based on a number of factors, including birth, wealth, or high office. Like de Ste Croix (1981: 92–3), Harris (1988: 602) is critical of this kind of analysis of society, which derives from contemporary sociology. In his view, it blurs 'radical inequalities in the distribution of wealth, power and . . . amenities'.

[3] For a discussion of order (*ordo*) in Rome, see Harris 1988: 600–1, with bibliography *ad loc.* Ober (1991) analyses Aristotle's use of the concepts of class, status, and order in the *Politics*.

together with its attendant privileges and disabilities, honour or lack thereof.[4]

For the most part too, this collection does not enter into the controversy about status and contract that has recently engaged Todd (1994) and Cohen (1994). I say 'for the most part', because Cohen's chapter in this volume, 'Whoring under Contract', rejects the idea that prostitution in Athens was based on considerations of status. Instead, he believes, it sprang from consensual arrangements, often set forth in a written contract. The profession, moreover, embraced all segments of the population, including citizens, thus being an early example of 'market egalitarianism'. In fact, Cohen's views are part of a larger market approach which informs his paper and which sees considerations of status or order (a term he rejects) as in practice essentially irrelevant in the 'monetarized economy' of fourth-century Athens. Challenging—and iconoclastic—Cohen's thesis may be, but a reading of other chapters in this volume reveals that he has not made many converts. As a whole, the contributions reinforce the notion of order and the reality of juridically defined groups whose social and economic roles and whose personal lives were deeply affected by their place in the prevailing hierarchy.

The legal system, of course, is not alone in sustaining privileges for some, liabilities for others. As Garnsey and Saller point out in their discussion of the social hierarchy at Rome (1987: 109), three processes maintain inequality: (1) the property system, where control of productive property (or land, which constituted the means of production in ancient society) is in the hands of a ruling group, (2) the legal system, which legitimates that control, and (3) the occupational system, which, through a division of labour, reinforces the social hierarchy.[5] While Garnsey and Saller make it clear that all three processes are interconnected, it is only the second that is the focus of this collection. Indeed, if one were to

[4] Todd (1994) also interprets status as legal status. In Athens, of course, the law also circumscribed the rights of groups like *nothoi* and *atimoi*. They have not been included here because the collection as a whole concentrates on the three major status groups. For distinctions within the class of slaves and for intermediate states 'between slavery and freedom', see Finley 1981a and b and Todd 1994. The latter concludes (137) that, although status boundaries 'remained at all times flexible in certain contexts and rigid in others', there is 'very little evidence for any supposed breakdown in the system within the fourth century'.

[5] The three processes derive from Karl Marx, who, Garnsey and Saller believe, 'developed conceptual tools for identifying the fundamental processes producing and reproducing inequalities in society over time'.

attempt a thorough analysis of status and its concomitants, 'claims, privileges, immunities, powers, and their opposites' (Finley 1981a: 148), one would have to adopt an approach similar to that advocated by M. I. Finley in his discussion of the servile statuses of ancient Greece (1981a). There Finley suggests the following categories of analysis (149): (1) claims to property, (2) power over one's own and others' labour and movements, (3) power to punish, (4) privileges and liabilities in legal action, (5) privileges in the area of the family, (6) privileges of social mobility, and (7) privileges in the sacral, political, and military spheres.[6] Again it is clear that privileges and liabilities that inhere in the law itself and in the legal system are only part of a larger picture, manifestations, as it were, of other more fundamental rights and privileges or their opposite that the law serves to legitimate.

Let me now turn to status distinctions in Athenian law. I begin with Trevor Saunders's recent study of Plato's penology, in particular, his discussion of class distinctions in the penal code Plato envisioned for his utopian society, Magnesia (1991: 334–48). There Saunders analyses a series of penalties differentiated according to social class.[7] That is, the penalties were based on whether one was a citizen, a foreigner, or a slave. Let me cite two examples. The Magnesian code prescribes a variety of punishments for passers-by who fail to go to the aid of a parent assaulted by a son (881b–d). Natives of Magnesia are liable to a curse from Zeus, the guardian of kin and parents, resident aliens are sent into permanent exile, and itinerant aliens are reprimanded. The penalty for slaves is 100 strokes of the lash. Elsewhere the code deals with offences committed in the market-place (764b). These include damage to temples and fountains, the security of which falls under the jurisdiction of the *agoranomoi*. The latter have the responsibility of punishing offenders. A slave or a foreigner they whip and chain, a citizen they fine.

Saunders ends his analysis of class distinctions by suggesting that Plato's historical inspiration may be Cretan and derive from the law code of Gortyn. One part of the code, on rape and seduction, does indeed prescribe a series of penalties differentiated by social status. Fines for rape, for example, vary according to the status of

[6] Cf. Finley 1981b: 131.

[7] Cf. Morrow 1939: 66–71 and Hunter 1994: 159–62. The terms 'class distinctions' and 'social class' are Saunders's.

both the victim and the perpetrator, with the highest amount, 400 drachmas (200 staters), prescribed for the rape of a free person (man or woman) by a slave and the lowest, 5 drachmas, for the rape of a male or female slave by a free man. These are the extremes. In addition, if a free man rapes an equal, that is, a free man or woman, he is fined 200 drachmas, while for the rape of an *apetairos* (a free person of inferior rank), only 20 drachmas is prescribed (col. 2, ll. 2–10). As Saunders rightly comments (347), not only do penalties in the law code of Gortyn differ according to 'social position', but an offence against a free person is more serious than that committed against one of inferior rank, whether a slave or an *apetairos*. Conversely, an offence perpetrated by a slave is more serious than one committed by a free person, where the victim is the same.[8] In fact Gortyn's law code is not unique. Other Greek codes of the classical and Hellenistic eras also prescribed penalties that differ according to social status. They include the codes of Rhodes, Syrus, Andania, Pergamum, and Ptolemaic Egypt. Pergamum is typical. A law from the second century BC prescribes that a slave who pollutes a well without the knowledge of his master is to be placed in the pillory and given 100 lashes. Subsequently, he is bound in the stocks for ten days. At the end of that time, he is whipped again, no less than fifty lashes. A free man, by contrast, forfeits the animals, the clothing, and/or the utensils he brought to the well and is fined 50 drachmas (*OGIS* 483, ll. 168–84).[9] It appears then that Plato's code was not unusual in being 'drenched in considerations of status' (Saunders 1991: 342). Historical Greek codes can also be so characterized.

[8] The text is that of Willetts 1967, who differentiates *oikeus* (serf) from *doulos* (slave) (13–15). Both Finley (1981a: 136) and Cole (1984: 108 n. 53) reject this view, arguing that the two servile groups are synonymous. On the other hand, Cole (108) follows Willetts (12)—as does Saunders (347 n. 35)—in conjecturing that an *apetairos* was a free person without political rights. For a full and recent bibliography on the law code of Gortyn, see Morris 1990.

[9] For other Greek codes preserved in inscriptions and on papyri, see Glotz 1908: 579–87 and Morrow 1939: 67–9.

SLAVES

To turn now to Athens, let me begin with slaves. Since space does not permit me to analyse the legal position of slaves in detail,[10] what I propose instead is to highlight several of the more obvious legal liabilities slaves experienced *vis-à-vis* the free. This will serve as background to my major concern, penal law. First and foremost, a slave could not, with one exception discussed below, sue or be sued in the courts. He was a perpetual legal minor under the authority of his master, who as *kyrios* represented the slave in public if ever such representation were needed. In practice, of course, slaves might assume considerable responsibility. Midas, the slave of Athenogenes, for instance, managed a perfume business for his master and allegedly ran up debts amounting to 5 talents. Hyperides' lawsuit *Against Athenogenes* makes it clear that his master, not Midas himself, was legally liable for these debts (3. 6, 21; Harrison 1968: 175; MacDowell 1978: 82). In fact, Hyperides cites a law attributed to Solon to the effect that any damages incurred or offences committed by a slave were to be the responsibility of the master who owned him at the time the offence took place (3. 22; Mactoux 1988: 335–6).[11] In the spirit of this law, a master was himself sued for any wrongs done by his slave (Dem. 53. 20). There is one significant exception: if a slave acted on his own with no instructions from his master, he could be sued in his

[10] For the legal position of slaves, see Morrow 1939: 73–89; Harrison 1968: 163–80; MacDowell 1978: 79–83; and Todd 1993: 184–94.

[11] In referring to damages or offences (i.e. delictual acts) on the part of slaves, the law does not cover contractual obligations into which they might have entered. It is generally agreed that at least some of Midas' debts arose from such obligations (Gernet 1955: 161; Harrison 1968: 175; Cohen 1991: 246–7). As Harrison notes (175): 'it is only by a sort of analogy that the law can be applied to contractual debts'. Given the law's silence on this matter, Cohen (1991: 247) suggests that slaves who entered into business contracts as independent entrepreneurs might have been responsible for their own debts. This case, however, offers no confirmation of such a view. For, while Midas and his sons worked independently, Athenogenes owned the business and had accounts submitted to him monthly (Hyp. 3. 19). In addition, Epicrates' whole argument rests on the liability of Midas' original owner, whom he accuses of dishonest dealings in concealing the extent of the debts run up by his slave (12, 20–1, 26). For more on the law cited at 3. 22, see Gernet 1955: 155–6 and Harrison 1968: 173 n. 2, both of whom accept Revillout's reading of the text (ἀ[ναλώμ]ατα, losses) rather than Jensen's (ἀ[δικήμ]ατα, offences). In fact, the law is not really applicable here, since, in his contract with Athenogenes, the speaker had assumed liability for Midas' debts (3. 7–12).

own name. Callarus, the slave of the son of Tisias, the speaker of Demosthenes 55, is our sole extant example of this procedure. Callarus was sued several times by Callicles, a neighbour, who brought the suits, the speaker alleges, as part of a policy of harassment aimed at himself and his farmland (55. 31–5). For although Callarus was the defendant in these cases, the lawsuit makes it evident that his master was the real target and so was liable (cf. Dem. 37. 22 and 51; Harrison 1968: 174). On the other hand, there is a hint dropped by the speaker that he might be forced to surrender the slave to his opponent. 'Noxal surrender', as this procedure has been termed, has not found wide acceptance among scholars. But if, as Gernet believes (1955: 156), it was part of Athenian legal practice, it had the effect of making slaves responsible for their own actions.[12]

The cases of Midas and Callarus, while immensely valuable as evidence for social practice in respect of the responsibilities assumed, property held, and debts incurred by slaves, indicate nonetheless that slaves were not *sui iuris*.[13] Hence Plato could state unequivocally of the slave that 'when he is treated with injustice or contempt, he is unable to defend himself or anyone else for whom he feels concern' (*Gorgias* 483b). This is a succinct description of the slave's legal incapacity. On the other hand, the statement may also allude to the slave's inability to call upon the network of kin and friends needed to function in a society where quasi-legal forms of self-help, sanctioned by the judicial system, were the rule. (Cf. Patterson, in this volume.)

My second major point is that slaves were not competent to

[12] Harrison (1968: 174) has serious doubts about this practice, given the paucity of direct evidence apart from *Lexica Segueriana* 187 (ἐγγυῆσαι. ὅταν τις κρινόμενος παράσχῃ δοῦλον ἀνθ' ἑαυτοῦ τιμωρηθῆναι, to hand over as a pledge: when one who is on trial surrenders a slave for punishment in place of himself). Indirect evidence includes Pl. *Leg*. 936d, the provisions of which, as Gernet points out (1955: 156), approximate the Roman practice of noxal surrender. See too Morrow 1939: 60–1 and Beauchet 1897: 2. 456. The latter accepts the practice in Athens.

[13] Here again there is an exception. By the fourth century slaves had judicial rights in commercial suits (*dikai emporikai*) and could appear as parties (Gernet 1955: 162–3; Harrison 1968: 175–6). Cf. Cohen 1973: 114–21; 1991: 248–9. The evidence for these rights is drawn from Demosthenes 34 (5, 10, 18–20, 31, 46), where Lampis, who is both a shipmaster (*naukleros*) and a slave (*pais, oiketes*), appears as a party to a commercial suit. On Lampis, see Harrison 1968: 167 n. 6 and Hunter 1994: 217 n. 33. Not all have been so sure as Gernet (1955: 163) that Lampis was 'certainement de condition servile'. See now Todd 1994: 135–6, who suggests that Lampis might be a freedman and questions whether slaves had such rights. Patterson (in this volume) believes he was a foreigner living in Athens.

testify as witnesses in court. Such testimony was the prerogative of the free. Instead, a slave's evidence was extracted under torture. Nor could this be voluntary or even volunteered by his master. The master had to challenge an opponent to accept the evidence of his slave or in turn himself agree to accept the latter's challenge. If such a challenge were accepted, the case might hinge on the body of the slave. Whether resorted to or not—a challenge could always be refused—judicial torture was a device for turning a slave's evidence into legal testimony. It is thus a concomitant of the slave's incapacity to testify in court. This, at least, is a view to which David Mirhady would subscribe, though it is a view now vigorously contested.[14] In this volume, Mirhady analyses the Athenian rationale for torture, unearthing, both in the lawsuits and in drama, a consistent mentality. What did Athenians think about judicial torture? It was deemed not only an appropriate way of eliciting the truth, Mirhady argues, but also a means of 'confirming their own social hierarchy and cohesion'. Given too their familiarity with the practice of submitting slaves to violence, they believed that torture, if properly administered, worked. By contrast, citizens were immune from torture: under a decree passed in the late sixth century in the archonship of Scamandrius, it was forbidden to submit the free to judicial torture (Andoc. 1. 43; Isoc. 17. 14; Lys. 4. 14; 13. 27 and 59; MacDowell 1962: 92–3). Here then is a significant status distinction between slave and free embedded in the law of Athens and in the procedures of the judicial system.

There was, of course, an exception to the rule that slaves could not testify except under duress. *Menusis* (denunciation) was a procedure under which slaves might, in very specific circumstances, inform against their masters. Hitherto it has generally been accepted that those circumstances included treason, sacrilege, and theft of public property (Harrison 1968: 171; MacDowell 1978: 181–3). Here Osborne reviews the evidence for slave denunciation and comes to the conclusion that in Athens (unlike Ceos) its use was restricted to religious crimes. Only where the gods were implicated, could slaves be permitted to impugn the honour of citizens and thus disrupt existing social relations. Osborne con-

[14] See Mirhady 1996, a survey of the primary evidence. By contrast, a new orthodoxy would see the procedure as 'predominantly a legal fiction' (Gagarin 1996: 1; cf. Thür 1996). I myself reject this view. Indeed, elsewhere I reached the same conclusion as Mirhady (1991a and b), that torture served as an alternative to a jury trial (Hunter 1994: 89–93).

cludes that the solidarity of the citizens of Athens in the face of slaves was even stronger than previously suspected.

Within the framework of these general distinctions, let me now turn to penal law. I shall begin with the law on silver coinage promulgated by the *nomothetai* in 375/4 and preserved in an inscription first published in 1974 (Stroud 1974; *SEG* XXVI. 72). In this inscription, the penalty laid down for servile offences is fifty strokes of the lash, to be administered in public and meted out to two groups of slaves, one public, the other private. The central figure in the inscription is the *dokimastes*, a public slave who tested coins for their silver content. If he failed to test in accordance with the law, the penalty of fifty lashes was prescribed (ll. 13–16). The law also sets out penalties in the event that a retailer refused to accept the silver coins tested by the *dokimastes*. They differ according to status. Free persons, if convicted, were fined, while slaves, both male and female, received fifty lashes (ll. 30–2). Depending on the location of these offences, a series of magistrates was responsible for administering the penalties.

In what follows, I shall consider the two categories of slaves, private and public, in turn, beginning with the former. First, however, it is worth noting that the law on silver coinage is not the only public document that differentiates penalties according to status. In two other inscriptions of the fourth century, slaves similarly received fifty strokes of the lash, while the free paid a fine. The amount of the fine is specified in the edict of the priest of Apollo Erithaseus (*IG* II^2 1362), forbidding the cutting of wood in the sacred precinct: a free man caught breaking this rule paid 50 drachmas (l. 15). Unfortunately, the second inscription (*IG* II^2 380), concerning the duties of the *agoranomoi* in maintaining order and cleanliness in public spaces in the Piraeus, is defective. While it is clear that the two groups of offenders, free and slaves, are differentiated, with slaves receiving fifty lashes for littering or fouling such spaces (ll. 40–2), the penalty imposed on the free is missing. We can only assume that it was 50 drachmas. On the other hand, it is probably safe to say that fifty strokes of the lash was a common penalty for slaves guilty of public offences. It recurs in a decree cited by Aeschines as the penalty prescribed for a slave who was the lover of a free boy or who pursued him for sexual purposes (1. 139).[15]

[15] Yet another status distinction occurs in the law on *hubris*, the provisions of which

While the law on silver coinage and the decrees discussed above refer to slaves who were privately owned, their provisions about such slaves are very different from those permitted in private suits. As we have already seen, the offences (delicts) of slaves were in the end the responsibility of their masters. Thus a suit (*dike*) involving a slave became in effect a dispute between his or her owner and another Athenian. As for the slave at the centre of the dispute, his or her fate was in the hands of his master, who, if he was fined or suffered a loss of some kind because of the slave, was quite within his rights to punish the latter as he saw fit. Since slaves were members of the *oikos*, any punishment they received was administered in private. Examples of whipping and confinement and other forms of violence against slaves are not lacking.[16] Indeed, slaves were even submitted to private torture in the search for information (Dem. 48. 14–18; cf. Dem. 40. 14–15; Lys. 1. 16–18). In other words, the punishment of slaves was a matter of private practice and left to the discretion of the master.

A variation on the procedure resorted to in the case of the private offences of slaves is set forth in a third-century Alexandrian law concerning assault (*P Hal.* 1 ll. 186–202), which specifies the following. If a slave (male or female) strikes a free person, he or she shall receive no less than 100 lashes. But if his/her master acknowledges the deed, he may pay, on the slave's behalf, twice the amount prescribed as a penalty for a free person (probably 200 drachmas). The law goes on to prescribe even more serious financial penalties for a master who disputes the charge against his slave. He himself is to be indicted and, if he loses the case, must pay 300

extended to slaves. Anyone fined for this offence was imprisoned until the fine was paid, provided that the victim was a free person (Dem. 21. 47). Cf. Aeschin. 1. 16, a version of the law that does not mention the status of the victim. Most scholars accept the authenticity of the former text, but not of the latter. MacDowell (1990: 263–4), for example, believes that a forger invented the text of Aeschin. 1. 16 to fit the context, part of which (1. 15) is 'plainly based' on the text of Dem. 21. 47. Cf. Fisher 1992: 36 n. 1. It is worth noting that Harris (1992: 77–8) reverses MacDowell's reconstruction, arguing that Dem. 21. 47 is a forgery, 'stitched together' from Aeschines' quotation of the law. I have accepted the arguments of MacDowell and Fisher. For more on this law and the paradoxical nature of a provision offering slaves protection from *hubris*, see Fisher 1995, who concludes that the law assumed a 'limited degree of humanity, honour and capacity for good action' on the part of slaves. Nonetheless, he believes that it remained 'a classic case of tokenism within the framework of slavery' (75) and a legal provision seldom used. By contrast, Mactoux (1988: 336–7) sees nothing humane in this law but considers it a means of protecting 'une propriété animée par laquelle se définit le maître'.

[16] See Hunter 1994: 162–73 for the private punishment of slaves.

drachmas for one blow and considerably more if there was more than one blow.[17] By contrast, in the cases cited above, which concern public offences, Athenian law does not allow a master to assume liability on behalf of his slave. Instead, it draws a firm distinction between a public and a private offence on the part of a slave. The law on silver coinage offers an example of the former: the suit under which retailers who refuse the currency tested by the *dokimastes* are to be indicted is a 'denunciation' or *phasis*, a public procedure akin to a *graphe*, which any Athenian could bring before the courts or, as here, before a series of magistrates. In this and other cases that were equivalent to *graphai*, the slave was wrested from the *oikos* and from the authority (*kyrieia*) of his or her master and made fully liable for his/her actions. The right of the polis to override the authority of the slave's owner in such cases stands in contrast to the limitations embodied in the procedures employed in judicial torture. For while torture also drew slaves from the privacy of the *oikos* into the public realm to testify for or against a master, the acquiescence of the latter was required and solicited through the institution of the challenge. In other words, in the disputing process the courts did not have the power to override an Athenian's authority as *kyrios* by forcing him to relinquish a slave or slaves for torture. Again there was a significant exception. In a major emergency such as the one that followed the mutilation of the Herms, the normal rules were suspended and special powers conferred on the Boule. Among its emergency measures, the Boule arrested female slaves in the house used as a headquarters by the alleged conspirators (Andoc. 1. 64). Presumably, the women were tortured for information.[18] In this case, however, no permission was sought from their master. Here the public good transcended the authority of an individual *kyrios*, as it did not in a dispute between individual Athenians. The same principle holds in respect of the public offences of slaves.

A question worth asking about the public punishment of slaves is, why the whip? As we have seen, it is prescribed in all the public documents cited above, as well as in other contemporaneous Greek codes. Saunders suggests that 'whipping, though it shames, is simply the *counterpart* of fines'. Appropriate as it is for slaves as opposed to free persons, he believes that it 'does not in

[17] For a convenient text, see Hunt and Edgar 1934: no. 202.

[18] Cf. MacDowell 1962: 79.

itself demonstrate an intention to punish them more severely' (1991: 344 n. 23). It seems to me that the practice of whipping needs further thought. Certainly, no one would deny that whipping was the counterpart of fines. Indeed, one explanation of its use is simple and obvious: legally, slaves did not have the right to own property (Harrison 1968: 236; MacDowell 1978: 80). Hence, any income they earned or any wealth they accumulated—anything that was 'theirs'—belonged by law to their master. It stands to reason then that as legal minors they could not be fined in their own right. In effect, any fine would redound to a master. This explanation certainly holds for the mass of Athenian slaves. On the other hand, in the fourth century there were some notable exceptions, the result of changes in the practice of slavery. Some slaves lived apart from their masters, paying the latter a regular fee (*apophora*) out of their earnings (Aeschin. 1. 97; Men. *Epit.* 330). Otherwise, they were independent and able to earn and accumulate savings of their own. Midas, whom we met above managing one of Athenogenes' perfume shops and who incurred enormous debts in the name of the business, was surely one of this group. No doubt too some of the servile retailers mentioned in the law on coinage were among these slaves who 'lived apart'. Whatever independence and responsibility such slaves enjoyed and however much wealth they accumulated, their status was not one acknowledged by the law (Perotti 1974: 55–6). Here law and social practice diverged.[19] For as we have already seen, even in the late fourth century the law made a master liable for the damages and debts incurred by his slaves (Dem. 53. 20; Hyp. 3. 6, 21–2). Similarly, penal law made no exception for slaves whose independence was acknowledged privately by their owners. Ability to pay notwithstanding, they too faced the whip. Clearly, there is more involved here than simply the appropriate counterpart of a fine.

If we turn to public slaves, we are drawn to the same conclusion.

[19] Perotti (1974: 55) concludes that the *choris oikountes* 'ne jouissent d'aucune capacité juridique', except in commercial suits (discussed above, n. 13), '. . . leur *status* d'esclaves reste inchangé'. In fact, one of the slaves denounced and sold as the property of Adeimantus in the Attic Stelai (stele 6. 31–46) was a *skytotomos* (shoemaker) who lived apart and had possessions of his own. They were sold with him as legally belonging to Adeimantus. (The text is that of Pritchett 1953: 271, with brief commentary in Pritchett 1956: 279–81; cf. Lewis 1966: 182 and Todd 1993: 188.) See also Perotti 1976 for the distinction between slaves who were *choris oikountes* and *andrapoda misthophorounta*. The latter did not enjoy the independence of the former but were hired out as a form of investment by their master.

As we noted above, the law on silver coinage prescribed a penalty of fifty lashes for the *dokimastes* if he failed to test in accordance with the law. The whipping was to be administered by the *syllogeis tou demou*, who were probably his supervisors. Again this law is not the only public document that prescribes a penalty of whipping for public slaves. Other *demosioi* punished in this way include slaves on the Acropolis (*IG* II^2 333. 6–7) and three custodians of weights and measures stationed in different locations in Athens (*IG* II^2 1013. 5, 45–9). The latter inscription decrees a punishment of fifty lashes for a slave producing false measures. The use of the whip in these instances is curious. After all, public slaves were a privileged group (Jacob 1928: 146, 191; Harrison 1968: 177; Todd 1993: 194). In a sense, they were the ancient equivalent of civil servants, and as such received a salary from the state. Hence, specific provisions for remuneration are set forth in the law on coinage. Both the *dokimastes* in Athens and his counterpart in the Piraeus are to receive the same salary, with that of the former to come from the same exchequer as paid the salary of the mint workers (ll. 49–55). There is some evidence as well that public slaves had the right to own property other than land. The name (or half the name, [. . .]leides) of a *demosios* is included in a manumission inscription dated *c.* 330 (*IG* II^2 1570. 78–9). He was the former owner of a newly freed slave.[20] Finally, if we may judge from the example of Pittalacus, a *demosios* whose peccadilloes Aeschines recounts in his oration against Timarchus, public slaves could be quite well off and had considerable freedom of movement. Pittalacus had a house of his own (probably rented), where he ran a gambling establishment, and money enough to pay for the favours of the young Timarchus (1. 54–9). If any slaves came close to crossing the bounds that separated free and slave, it was the *demosioi*. Yet in spite of their privileged status and their financial independence, they too faced the whip. Under penal law they remained 'conceptually' slaves

[20] For the property of public slaves, see Harrison 1968: 236, citing Beauchet 1897: 2. 463–4, whose speculations are mostly groundless. Apart from the inscription cited, the evidence for property is scanty, based mainly on the example of Pittalacus (Aeschin. 1. 54–68), which some have questioned. Jacob (1928: 149), for example, believes he was a freedman. Cf. Todd 1993: 194. I myself am not prepared to dismiss Aeschines' evidence so readily but would apply to it the same criterion—verisimilitude—as one usually applies to unverifiable statements of fact made by the orators. The description of the style of life of Pittalacus, about whose status as a public slave (mentioned three times at 54 and 62) Aeschines is both emphatic and contemptuous, must have rung true to an Athenian jury.

(Todd 1993: 194). I would suggest that we are dealing with something structural in the nature of slavery that required the public acknowledgement of status distinctions through representations and symbols.

The symbolism of the whip is perhaps most succinctly expressed by Herodotus in a brief tale told in the opening chapters of the Scythian Logos (4. 1–4). The Scythians, he tells us, were absent from their own land for twenty-eight years on an expedition of conquest. On returning, they discovered that their slaves had usurped their place, having married their wives and produced a new generation now come to manhood. The latter successfully resisted their former masters in battle after battle until someone came up with an idea that led to the slaves' defeat. He argued that it was pointless to fight slaves in a conventional manner with spears and bows, since this only made them think that they were the equal of the free. Instead, he urged each man to seize his horsewhip and use it. When the slaves see the whips, he predicted, they will recognize that they are our slaves and submit. His prediction came true, or so Herodotus alleges. The slaves were terrified and submitted to their former masters. Herodotus, who was not an Athenian but an exile from Greek Asia Minor, wrote his *Histories* sometime in the mid-fifth century. It seems that by that time the whip had already distinguished itself as a marker of the slave condition, the symbol, on the one hand, of the master's authority and, on the other, of the slave's degraded and cringing nature.[21] This image of master and slave would surely resonate with Herodotus' Athenian listeners, who would understand all too well the paradox inherent in owning and disciplining another human being. For the use of the whip was not foreign to the slave-owners among them: it was commonly used to punish slaves in the privacy of the home. In addition, individual violence against slaves was the source of much mirth on the Athenian stage.[22] Aristophanes tells us that he tried to avoid the worst excesses of his competitors in this regard

[21] On this passage, cf. Finley 1980: 118. Other instances of whipping occur at Hdt. 1. 114. 3; 3. 16; 7. 22. 1, 35, 54. 3, 56. 1, 103. 4, 223. 3; 8. 109. 3. None refers to its use against slaves. Instead, the whip serves to express the contempt and even arrogance of its wielder, usually the king of Persia, and, in some cases, the slavishness of its victim. (Cf. Hartog 1988: 332–5.) See too Plut. *Arist.* 23. 2, an account of Pausanias' harsh and arrogant treatment of the Greek troops in Asia Minor in 478. Among the charges for which he was later recalled to Sparta was the fact that he had had free men flogged as punishment.

[22] For violence against slaves, including the use of the whip, see Hunter 1994: 162–73.

(*Peace* 742–9). Yet his comedies uniformly depict slaves being beaten, whipped, and threatened with chains and shackles. Even in the less ribald drama of Menander, the whip could still raise a laugh. (See, for example, Men. *Sam.* 320–7, 677–80.)

Herodotus' tale is, of course, pure ideology, an illustration of the way in which slaves were culturally constructed.[23] If drama served to reinforce that construction, so did the law, by delineating activities from which slaves were barred, thus suppressing the development of the full human capacities identified with the free. It also did so by submitting slaves to physical violence while leaving the free inviolate. The public nature of this violence is also significant. As in Plato's *Laws*, the whipping of slaves took place in public areas like the Agora, where they were administered by an appropriate official or officials. The actual whipping was probably the task of a public slave.[24] In other words, whippings were public spectacles, which served, on the one hand, as 'moral-degradation ceremonies' for those punished (Beattie 1986: 468) and, on the other, as a way of affirming the authority of masters as a class. Laden with ideological overtones, public whippings were no simple counterpart of fines. Through such whippings and the ritual that attended them, the law sustained status distinctions between slave and free. The law also reinforced such distinctions in the method of execution it inflicted on slaves. According to Todd (in this volume), slaves were submitted to *apotumpanismos* (death on the 'plank'), which, unlike the drinking of hemlock, seems to have been a public spectacle and, as much as whipping, a form of theatre.[25]

The notion of ideology, in this case the ideology of the body, is also at the core of Robertson's chapter in this volume, on the scrutiny of new citizens. Beginning with the question of how age was assessed at the *dokimasia*, Robertson concludes that neither councillors nor jurors judged according to a chronologically determined date of birth but by the physical appearance of the nude

[23] See Hunter 1992 for the cultural construction of slaves together with a discussion of both the notion of ideology and the ideology of slavery.

[24] On public whippings, see Hunter 1994: 156–8.

[25] Slaves, of course, were not the only ones executed by *apotumpanismos*. Free persons, among them citizens (e.g. traitors), also died on the plank. In his chapter, which explores the question of whether there was a consistent principle behind forms of the death penalty, Todd concludes that *apotumpanismos* was reserved either for those like slaves who had no standing in the community or for those who had forfeited such standing. Held outside the city wall, *apotumpanismos* symbolized the expulsion of the outsider from the community.

youths. Their criterion was the ideal body depicted in art and formed in the palaestrae and gymnasia. Viewed in this way, the body was not neutral but an ideological production appropriate only to those of citizen status. By appealing to this ideal, the *dokimasia* reinforced the distinction between citizen and slave. In presenting his argument, Robertson adverts to a further status distinction embedded in Athenian law. According to Aeschines, slaves were barred from Athens' palaestrae and gymnasia, where it was illegal for them to exercise or rub themselves dry with oil (1. 138; cf. Plut. *Solon* 1. 3). Slaves were thus prohibited from moulding their bodies into the ideal form admired by the Athenians. Mactoux also discusses this law, which she believes was fundamental in the formation of citizens and their opposites, slaves. For it was in the palaestrae and gymnasia that Athenians prepared themselves not only for the Panhellenic games, but also for hoplite warfare, both activities crucial to their identification as members of the polis. The law thus enforced a 'definitive differentiation' of slave and citizen (Mactoux 1988: 341).

METICS AND FOREIGNERS

In addition to slaves, Plato's *Laws* also differentiated foreigners as a separate status with its own structure of penalties that were often very different from those of either slaves or citizens. Did Athenian law embody similar status distinctions in respect of foreigners? In answer to this question, I shall again consider penal law and what it prescribed for foreigners resident in Attica (metics). Here two points are worth observing at the outset. First, where metics are concerned, we should not expect the same sharp differentiation as existed between slaves and free. Metics were after all free persons, mostly Greeks, attracted to the polis because of its economic prosperity or cultural amenities. If put at too great a disadvantage, they could always desert Athens, as they did a number of times in her history, most particularly in the mid-fourth century when Xenophon proposed a series of concessions meant to induce metics to return to Athens (*Vect.* 2). Secondly, we must keep in mind that the prescriptions of penal law offer only a partial picture of the way the social hierarchy was maintained at Athens. Underpinning the legal position of metics were substantial liabilities, which the law perpetuated and legitimized. In what follows, I shall adumbrate the most significant of these liabilities.[26]

Aristotle characterizes the metic as 'one who is excluded from *timai*' (*Pol.* 1278ª38). That is, he was excluded from all magistracies and priesthoods and could not sit on the juries or in the assembly. To the individual metic, however, non-participation in public life may have been far less worrisome than the economic disability he experienced in being unable to own real property either in land or in houses. Unless granted *enktesis* by popular decree, he could invest only in movable property.[27] Even his home and working quarters were rented (Xen. *Vect.* 2. 6). Finally, a metic could not marry an Athenian citizen. By the fourth century it was an indictable offence punishable by sale into slavery (Dem. 59. 16 and 124). In addition to these major disabilities, there are two institutions that an alien had to accept in order to become and remain a permanent resident of Attica. As status markers, they distinguish the metic from the citizen. First, a metic was required to have a citizen 'protector' or *prostates*, a requirement that Aristotle believed in itself differentiated the metic's legal status from that of the citizen (*Pol.* 1275ª12–13). And although we remain uncertain what role the *prostates* played in the life of the metic, there is no doubt that he was essential. To be without a *prostates* was an offence indictable under the law and harshly punished. (See below, p. 19.) Secondly, the metic paid an annual poll tax, the *metoikion*, amounting to 12 drachmas for a man and 6 for a self-supporting woman (Harpocration s.v. *metoikion*; Whitehead 1977: 75; Todd 1997: 113–14). Again, the punishment for non-compliance was extremely harsh. In characterizing these two institutions as status markers, I agree with David Whitehead, who describes the *metoikion* as 'the stamp of metic-status, and a constant reminder of

[26] Works consulted on metics include Clerc 1893; Gauthier 1972; and Whitehead 1977.

[27] *Enktesis*, the right to own real property in Attica, was not the only privilege to which a metic might aspire. See MacDowell 1978: 78–9 for a list of these privileges, including *isoteleia* (equality in taxation), the privilege of paying the same taxes as a citizen and/or exemption from the *metoikion* (the annual poll tax on metics). A metic might also receive the honorary title of *proxenos* or *euergetes*. *IG* II² 287, an honorary decree of the fourth century (cited by MacDowell), confers all these privileges together. Cf. Whitehead 1977: 28–30 for a list of thirteen inscriptions honouring individuals believed to be metics. In them the major privileges of *proxenia*, *enktesis*, and *isoteleia* appear in different combinations. See too Todd 1993: 173–4, who believes that, far from blurring the distinction between metics and citizens, metics with special privileges, like privileged slaves, served 'to highlight the depth of the gulf between the main statuses'.

the citizen/metic divide' (1977: 76; cf. Finley 1973: 164). I am confident that Whitehead would agree that the institution of the *prostates* had the same practical effect and ideological implications.

Before turning to penal law, I propose to offer a brief sketch of the legal position of the metic.[28] Unlike the slave, the metic could sue and be sued in the Athenian court. Certainly this was the case in private suits (*dikai*), which generally fell under the jurisdiction of the polemarch (Arist. *Ath. Pol.* 58. 2–3). Scholars disagree about public suits (*graphai*). Fortunately, however, there are several actual cases extant in the orators indicating that at least some public suits could be initiated by metics and were tried in the same manner as those of citizens. (See, for example, Dem. 59. 66.)[29] Also unlike slaves, resident aliens were competent to appear in court as witnesses.[30] Thus in some ways the metic enjoyed a legal position not far different from that of the citizen, a fact that has persuaded many scholars to see the position as one of privilege.[31] But as Patterson shows (in this volume), this is a myth. Here Patterson reconsiders the metic's legal status and his/her rhetorical representation within the Athenian system of justice, as revealed in the Attic orations. Without tribe, or deme, or, for the most part, *anchisteia*, the metic's access to the law and to the protection it afforded was severely limited. Legal rules alone, she concludes, did not provide the metic with either status or security.

[28] Works consulted on the legal position of the metic include Harrison 1968: 187–99; MacDowell 1978: 76–9; Todd 1993: 194–9.

[29] It is generally believed that metics could indict only in matters of personal concern, never in the interest of a third party or the state (Whitehead 1977: 94). On the other hand, Aristotle tells us that public suits against sycophants (*probolai*) were introduced to the Assembly in the sixth prytany and that the number was limited to six, three against citizens, three against metics (Arist. *Ath. Pol.* 43. 5). Like Rhodes (1981: 527), I find it surprising that the polis put metic sycophancy on a par with that of citizens, since citizen sycophants who brought *graphai* must have outnumbered metics. Christ (1992: 341–3), who discusses this passage and earlier explanations of it, suggests, reasonably, that the term sycophant need not apply only to persons bringing *graphai* but to anyone involved in 'legal chicanery' of the sort attributed to sycophants. (For legal chicanery, see Harvey 1990.)

[30] Whether they might be tortured to extract information remains a moot point. Elsewhere I have argued that extant instances of torture or the threat of torture are so few in number as to be insignificant and, like the rare examples of the torture of citizens, exceptional (Hunter 1994: 175–6). Lysias 4 seems to me conclusive. The slave involved in this case, one of her co-owners pleaded, could not be tortured because he had set her free (4. 12 and 14; cf. Isoc. 17. 14). (Legally her status would be that of a metic.) The implication is that not only citizens but all free persons were immune from judicial torture. (Cf. Carey 1988.)

[31] See Whitehead 1977: 1–2 for the 'privilege model'. Whitehead challenges this 'modern orthodoxy' (95), arguing against those who would maximize the gulf between metic and *xenos* and minimize that between metic and citizen.

Against this background, let me turn again to penal law, where most commentators have noted an obvious status distinction between citizen and metic. The murder of a resident alien (or a *xenos* or slave) was tried by the court of the Palladium along with cases of unintentional homicide (Arist. *Ath. Pol.* 57. 3). As a result, the punishment was correspondingly lighter than the death penalty inflicted by the Areopagus for the murder of a citizen: the accused, if found guilty, went into exile (Dem. 23. 45, 71–2). As Clerc observed many years ago (1893: 99): 'La personne du métèque était donc moins précieuse, aux yeux de la loi, que celle du citoyen, on ne peut le nier.' Let us consider the person of the metic further. As we have seen, the major distinction between free and slave was the use of corporal punishment to punish the latter. Was there an analogous penalty that distinguished metic from citizen? There was: for certain public offences metics faced the penalty of sale into slavery, citizens never did. The most detailed evidence for this penalty is found in Demosthenes 59, *Against Neaera*, a lawsuit dated *c.*340. The suit is a *graphe xenias*, under which aliens or alleged aliens could be indicted for usurping the rights of citizens. In it Demosthenes cites a law prohibiting marriage between aliens and citizens (59. 16–17). Under the law any alien convicted of living as a husband with an Athenian woman was sold into slavery and his property confiscated. The law makes no mention of the fate of the woman. On the other hand, it does prescribe a penalty for an Athenian man convicted of living as a husband with a foreign woman. He paid a fine of 1,000 drachmas. In this case, the law also mentions the woman: like her male counterpart she was sold into slavery. Nor is this all Athenian law had to say about marriage. It also prescribed that if a man gave a foreign woman in marriage to a fellow citizen as if she were related to him, he faced the penalty of *atimia*, disfranchisement, along with the confiscation of his property (59. 52–3).[32] Clearly, this was a very serious offence, demanding the heaviest penalty the courts could inflict short of death. Why not enslavement? Because in the fifth and fourth centuries enslavement was not a penalty prescribed by law or handed down by the courts for the offences of citizens. In general, no Athenian had to fear enslavement in Athens, although he or she

[32] On these laws, see Harrison 1968: 26–9. Harrison dates them after 403/2 but sometime before *c.*340, the date of Demosthenes 59.

might be made a slave by being captured in war or by pirates.[33] While there is no law extant prohibiting the enslavement of Athenians, the practice probably originated in the early sixth century with the reforms of Solon, which abolished debt slavery and even freed those who had been sold into slavery for debt (Arist. *Ath. Pol.* 6. 1, 9. 1; Plut. *Solon* 15. 3–5; Harrison 1968: 164; Ober 1989: 62). Whenever the practice originated, this was a significant right enjoyed by all Athenians. It was not one that they were prepared to share with aliens, including metics.

In general, slavery threatened any metic who appeared to step outside the bounds of his or her status by ignoring the markers of status noted above. For example, a metic convicted of being without a *prostates* faced a penalty of enslavement (*Suda* s.v. *poletai*; Harrison 1968: 165). So did one who failed to pay the metic tax. About the second offence, Demosthenes provides some interesting details in one of his orations against Aristogiton (25. 57–8). There he alleges that Aristogiton, having grown weary of, and annoyed at, his former benefactor, the metic Zobia, arrested her for not paying the metic tax. Using a form of self-help known as *apagoge*, he seized her 'with his own hands' and took her to the office of the *poletai*, the officials who were responsible for the tax. Had her tax not been paid, she would have been sold into slavery. If nothing else, the incident reveals 'the precariousness of metic status' (Patterson, in this volume). The same features, somewhat garbled, recur in the story of Xenocrates, the philosopher. He too was saved from slavery, even though he had been arrested and, in one version, had already been sold as a slave to Demetrius of Phalerum, who promptly freed him (Diog. Laert. 4. 14; cf. Plut. *Mor.* 842b). Harrison (1971: 169) believes that enslavement was the penalty for offences that could not be committed by a citizen, a view that has some merit. For slavery was also the penalty for anyone convicted under a *graphe xenias* of masquerading as a citizen (Dem. 24. 131; *Ep.* 3. 29; Harrison 1971: 193 n. 1; Scafuro 1994: 172, 178–81).[34]

[33] One exception is an Athenian ransomed by a fellow citizen. If he did not repay the debt, he became the property of his ransomer (Dem. 53. 11). According to Plutarch (*Solon* 23. 2), an Athenian father might sell his daughter if he discovered she was no longer a virgin. No examples of this penalty are extant.

[34] He/she was not enslaved at once but held in prison pending the outcome of a trial for false witnessing. Other references to the *graphe xenias* include Dem. 39. 18; 40. 41; Isae. 3. 37; Hyp. fr. B26 and 28–9. The latter also mentions a *graphe doroxenias* in the case of the bribery of a jury by an alien acquitted in a *graphe xenias*. See too Arist. *Ath. Pol.* 59. 3 (with

This included an Athenian, putatively a citizen, who was struck off the deme register because he could not establish his legitimacy under official scrutiny in a *diapsephisis* (Dem. 57; Isae. 12).[35] Similarly, a young man of eighteen who failed at the *dokimasia* to gain entry into the ranks of the ephebes because he was deemed not to be of citizen parentage was also sold into slavery (Arist. *Ath. Pol.* 42. 1).[36]

In my view, Harrison has only partially understood this penalty. After all, in the case of a suppositious marriage between a citizen and an alien or metic, the actual offence was precisely the same for both parties. Yet the onus of blame was on the alien, resulting in widely divergent penalties: on the one hand, enslavement, on the other, a relatively light fine of 1,000 drachmas, and that for the male alone. Here again is a genuine status distinction in Athenian law. Here too we can state unequivocally that a suppositious marriage entered into by an alien or a metic was viewed more seriously than the same offence committed by a citizen and correspondingly punished more severely (cf. Hansen 1991: 118). Indeed, for this and other offences that concern status boundaries the very harshness of the penalty was meant not just to differentiate the metic from the citizen in some symbolic way, as the whip differentiated the slave, but, by reinforcing status boundaries, to control the metic population. In fact, the concern to control outsiders masquerading as citizens reached a height in 346/5, when the demes of Attica scrutinized the qualifications of their members to ensure that all were genuine citizens. Demosthenes describes the procedures and the results in a lawsuit composed for a man struck off the register of the deme of Halimous (Dem. 57; cf. Isae. 12). By this time, the polis had probably already adopted the law prohibiting marriages between citizens and aliens. In essence, both the law about marriage, with its clearly articulated penalty of enslavement, and the *diapsephisis* were a warning to metics that membership in the community of Athenian citizens was closed to all outsiders except those few individuals on whom the demos chose to confer

Scafuro 1994: 180) and Harpocration s.v. *doroxenia*. Since no examples are extant, it is unclear what the penalty might have been. (Cf. Todd 1993: 106–7 and 111; 1994: 134.)

[35] For the *diapsephisis*, see also Aeschin. 1. 77 and 86.

[36] Again enslavement was not automatic but followed an unsuccessful appeal to the jury-court. If the young man won the appeal, the members of his deme were required to register him (Arist. *Ath. Pol.* 42. 1).

citizenship as a reward for outstanding service or benefactions. In his prosecution of the metic courtesan Neaera, Apollodorus, himself a naturalized Athenian, expresses the harsh reality of the 340s with all the fervour of a new citizen. He alleges that, by living as the wife of a citizen, Neaera had arrogated Athenian citizenship, a gift that only the demos could confer on those who were eminently worthy. As punishment, he calls for the enslavement of both Neaera herself and her children (Dem. 59. 124).

Several of the examples cited above allude to another distinction between metics and citizens: the resort to summary arrest. *Apagoge* recurs in both anecdotes concerning the *metoikion*. In fact, summary arrest was a significant 'procedural difference between the treatment of metics and citizens' (Whitehead 1977: 93). The first step in the prosecution of a metic was to take him or her, by force if necessary, to the office of the polemarch and demand sureties, i.e. three citizen guarantors, up to the sum involved in the dispute. Isocrates' *Trapeziticus* (17. 12) is an excellent source for this procedure. According to the speaker, who is a metic and the son of Sopaeus of Pontus, Pasion the banker accused him of spiriting away his slave. Having made the accusation, Pasion haled him before the polemarch, demanding sureties, and did not release the man until he had provided them to the total of 6 talents. What would the speaker's fate have been, had he not been able to round up citizen guarantors for this enormous sum? He would have been thrown into prison and remained there until his trial (Dem. 32. 29; Gauthier 1972: 138). Gauthier (136) includes this and three other examples under the rubric *dikai*, private suits, though he later suggests (144) that the same procedure was employed in public suits. In fact, we do not know if the triad of summary arrest, sureties, and prison was sanctioned in all or only in some cases. What we do know is that in private suits a citizen was never arrested but summoned by his opponent. Nor was a citizen required to produce sureties, let alone to remain in prison until his case came before the court.[37]

The usual explanation of this complex of procedures is a func-

[37] In certain public suits, however, Athenian citizens were obliged to provide sureties. One example is an *endeixis* followed by an *apagoge* (summary arrest). If the arrested man offered sureties, and his prosecutor was willing to accept them, he did not have to remain in prison until his trial. On these procedures, see Hansen 1976 and, for a simplified account, Hunter 1994: 134–6. See also Hunter 1997: 300–1.

tional one: they were designed to protect the plaintiff in case the metic should disappear or even flee Attica (Whitehead 1977: 93; MacDowell 1978: 76). This is a perfectly reasonable explanation as far as it goes, but it fails to grasp the complexity of the liabilities imposed on the metic. Let us probe a little deeper. In practical terms, summary arrest and sureties make sense in the case of aliens temporarily resident in Athens. Where metics are concerned, however, there is far less justification for such measures. Metics were after all not transients but individuals who had succeeded in acquiring a citizen *prostates* and had registered in a deme of residence.[38] Indeed, some, like Lysias and Apollodorus, were not immigrants at all but had been born in Athens. Apollodorus, as we have seen, was eventually naturalized as a result of the benefactions of his father, Pasion. Lysias was not, though he made every effort to become a citizen. Both were businessmen with large slave holdings. Only their wealth distinguished them from other metics who had businesses and professions of all kinds that provided them with a livelihood in Athens (Whitehead 1977: 116–17). Not only did they have a stake in the city but many ended their days there, as is revealed by the corpus of Attic inscriptions, which includes hundreds of epitaphs commemorating the death of individual metics (Whitehead 1977: 33–4 and 111).[39] Either they themselves or their families had chosen to set up stelae in their adopted homeland. Finally, one category of metic had never immigrated at all and perhaps had lost all contact with, or even memory of, a place of origin. Freed slaves, having no family or country to which to

[38] Cf. Lévy 1988, who defines the metic as a person definitively established in Athens, where 'un droit de résidence perpétuel' distinguished him/her from a *xenos* pure and simple (56).

[39] On the basis of *IG* II^2 7882–10530 and inscriptions in *SEG* 1–24, Isager and Hansen 1975: 217–19 tabulate a total of 490 metics buried in Attica in the fourth century. Nielsen et al. (1989: 419), who include *IG* II^2 10531–13085, raise the total to 650 metics 'all with ethnics instead of demotics as an indication of their status as foreigners'. Unfortunately, there is a serious problem here which neither of these works acknowledges: with the exception of *isoteleis* (*IG* II^2 7862–81 and 8650), metics do not proclaim their status but provide only their ethnic identity (the *ethnikon*), making it impossible to distinguish between resident aliens and *xenoi* (Whitehead 1977: 33–4). Dating of the inscriptions is also a problem, with many or even most (Gauthier 1972: 124 n. 55) belonging to the Hellenistic or Roman period. As a result, Gauthier objects to using the evidence of the tombstones. His arguments are summarized and mostly refuted by Whitehead (1977: 110–11). I would agree with Whitehead's conclusion: impossible as it may be to distinguish resident aliens from *xenoi* on the basis of the *ethnikon*, it is unlikely that many of the latter 'happened to die in Athens'. This would mean that the vast majority of tombstones dated to the fourth century belong to metics. In other words, one can use the evidence collectively rather than individually.

return, remained in Attica as resident aliens. Athenian law lumped all these individuals together with transients (*xenoi*). Why? Whitehead (93) provides a partial answer in linking the demand for sureties with a major status distinction experienced by the metic. 'The procedure doubtless had its roots in the metic's inability to own land—unlike the citizens he could leave and take his property with him—and it illustrates the restrictions on metics which themselves stemmed from other restrictions such as the lack of *enktesis*.' In other words, the procedures were a concomitant of other liabilities imposed on the metic and as such a status distinction in the law. Thus the law constructed the metic as an outsider without the solid roots in the polis that came from land-ownership and lineage. This construction is as much a part of the ideology of the metic as those aspects that Whitehead has documented.[40]

I have ended both parts of this paper with the notion of ideology in the belief that ideology affords both a reflection of, and a justification for, the inequalities experienced by slaves and metics, including those embedded in the law of Athens. In my view, ideology maintains inequality and social hierarchy as much as the three processes noted for Rome by Garnsey and Saller (1987: 109) and outlined at the beginning of this chapter (see above, pp. 2–3).

GENERAL CONCLUSIONS

It is probably correct to state that in respect of status distinctions in the law the difference between Plato's Magnesia and classical Athens is only one of degree. In addition, Athenian law approximated codes extant from other parts of the Greek world. Nonetheless, Athens' example could be deemed curious, given its proud claims to equality before the law. Consider the words of Theseus in Euripides' *The Suppliant Women* (ll. 433–7). Having lauded the city of Athens as a place where the people and not a king governs, Theseus turns to the legal system and states:

With written laws,
People of small resources and the rich
Both have the same recourse to justice. Now
A man of means, if badly spoken of,

[40] On the ideology of the metic, see also Citti 1988.

Will have no better standing than the weak;
And if the little man is right, he wins
Against the great.[41]

This eulogy of the law of Athens and the equality it afforded its citizens may be anachronistic in the mouth of Theseus, but it is matched by a host of similar claims, among them, the stirring words the historian Thucydides attributes to Pericles in his Funeral Oration (2. 37. 1–2; cf. Aeschin. 1. 5; Dem. 21. 67, 188; 23. 86; 24. 59; 25. 15–16). Such eulogies reflect a true and rather remarkable reality. For foremost among the many rights Athenians enjoyed was equality through and before the law, that is, the right to participate as equals in the political process and the right of equal access to the judicial system, whether as disputants or as jurors. The former went under the name of *isonomia*, a word that had its origins in the late-sixth-century struggle of aristocrats against the rule of the Peisistratid tyrants. In the classical era, *isonomia* together with *isegoria*, the equal right to speak in the assembly, were among the hallmarks of political democracy. (Cf. Finley 1981c: 83–4; Hansen 1991: 81–5.)[42]

If it is true that eulogies like that of Theseus reflect Athenian reality, it is just as true that they are illusive in the reality they construct. In the first place, they represent an ideal that was never reached in practice, for Athenian citizens were never more than theoretical equals. Finley (1981c: 86) describes the equality they shared as 'artificial'. Josiah Ober has gone further, documenting economic inequality in what he calls the 'egalitarian state' (1989: 192; cf. Roberts 1996: 189). Apart from their greater access to political power, the wealthy also enjoyed the advantages of an élite education, which provided training in rhetoric and with it skill in addressing the courts and the assembly.[43] Secondly, such eulogies often contribute to yet another level of illusion by representing the law as 'something magical', even 'God-given'. The description is that of Colin Sumner in his discussion of the ideology of law (1979: 275). While numerous examples of this kind of ideology are to

[41] Tr. Frank Jones.

[42] In addition to Finley and Hansen, recent discussions of *isonomia* and *isegoria* include Sinclair 1988: 13–17; Ober 1989: 72–5, 78–9; Sealey 1994; Raaflaub 1996.

[43] For equality in democratic Athens, see Ober and Hedrick 1996. I have found the papers of Morris, Raaflaub, and Roberts especially useful. The last, for instance, criticizes the tradition that 'cohesiveness, homogeneity, and equality' were characteristics of the Athenian demos (197).

be found in the Attic orations, none is perhaps so telling as Demosthenes' discourse on law in *Against Aristogiton 1* (25. 15–16):

> the laws desire what is just and honourable and salutary; they seek for it, and when they find it, they set it forth as a general commandment, equal and identical for all. The law is that which all men ought to obey for many reasons, but above all because every law is an invention and gift of the gods, a tenet of wise men, a corrective of errors voluntary and involuntary, and a general covenant of the whole State, in accordance with which all men in that State ought to regulate their lives.[44]

Demosthenes' discourse serves to mystify the nature of law, giving 'universal legitimacy' to what are actually the policies and principles of a ruling élite (Sumner 1979: 275). It is noteworthy that his words also play on the notion of equality.

In sum, the notions of equality, of equality before the law, and of the law itself all share in a certain mystification. They are ways in which the citizens of Athens constructed their world and are thus every bit as ideological as their analogous construction of the slave and metic. This construction was reinforced by the belief that Athenians shared a common lineage extending back to heroes and even gods and that as a people they were autochthonous, sprung from the soil of Attica itself. By its very nature, this kind of equality excludes others. *Isonomia* and *isegoria*, for instance, are political rights enjoyed only by those who shared in the political process, while autochthony and lineage essentially exclude outsiders.[45] Equality, like democracy, in other words, extended to

[44] Tr. J. H. Vince. Cf. Dem. 25. 11 and 26. 25–7. For a lengthy disquisition on the law, which also shares in a certain mystification, see Pl. *Crito* 50a–54c. Another form that the discourse on law took in the fourth century was the image and eulogy of the ancient lawgiver (for the most part, Solon), recently analysed by Thomas 1994. As Thomas points out, the appeal to a single lawgiver undermines the notion that laws were made and upheld by the demos (127). For Solon's laws were often seen as 'unchanging and unchangeable' (129). As a result, the image has 'clear anti-democratic overtones' (126). In my view, the image also envelops the law in a mystique and is thus another aspect of the ideology of law. Cf. the related appeal to the ancestral constitution (*patrios politeia*), noted by Thomas 1994: 122 n. 11 and brilliantly discussed by Finley 1975, who characterizes it as an image of the past that is not just traditional but 'mythical' (57).

[45] For autochthony as an aspect of the Athenian 'imaginary', see Loraux 1986. As Loraux points out (149): 'according to the needs of the moment, the purity of an unalloyed birth provides the basis for hegemony or the city's hatred of barbarians'. She also notes (331): 'In the epitaphioi, it is an essential characteristic of the city that it has no periphery: those "strangers within" (16), that is, metics and slaves, are ignored by the official oration with a consistency that cannot be accidental.' See too Connor 1994, who argues that the Athenians were 'far from autochthonous'. Autochthony, he believes, was an ideology in conflict with

some and not to others. In no sense did it embrace a humankind perceived as having inalienable human rights. (Cf. Finley 1981c: 92; Hansen 1991: 84–5.) That is a notion that awaited an entirely different and a later material reality, a fact that in itself may go some way to explaining why the Athenians, like other Greeks, promulgated and upheld penalties differentiated by social class.

References

Beattie, J. M. 1986. *Crime and the Courts in England 1660–1800*. Princeton.

Beauchet, L. 1897. *Histoire du droit privé de la république athénienne*, ii. Paris.

Carey, C. 1988. 'A Note on Torture in Athenian Homicide Cases', *Historia* 37: 241–5.

Christ, M. R. 1992. 'Ostracism, Sycophancy, and Deception of the Demos: [Arist.] *Ath. Pol.* 43. 5', *CQ* 42: 336–46.

Citti, V. 1988. 'The Ideology of Metics in Attic Tragedy', in T. Yuge and M. Doi (eds.), *Forms of Control and Subordination in Antiquity*. Leiden. 456–64.

Clerc, M. 1893. *Les métèques athéniens*. Paris.

Cohen, E. E. 1973. *Ancient Athenian Maritime Courts*. Princeton.

—— 1991. 'Banking as a "Family Business": Legal Adaptations Affecting Wives and Slaves', in M. Gagarin (ed.), *Symposion 1990*. Cologne, Weimar, and Vienna. 239–63.

—— 1994. 'Status and Contract in Fourth-Century Athens: A Reply to Stephen C. Todd', in G. Thür (ed.), *Symposion 1993*. Cologne, Weimar, and Vienna. 141–52.

Cole, S. G. 1984. 'Greek Sanctions against Sexual Assault', *CP* 79: 97–113.

Connor, W. R. 1994. 'The Problem of Athenian Civic Identity', in A. L. Boegehold and A. C. Scafuro (eds.), *Athenian Identity and Civic Ideology*. Baltimore and London. 34–44.

Finley, M. I. 1973. *The Ancient Economy*. London.

—— 1975. *The Use and Abuse of History*. New York.

—— 1980. *Ancient Slavery and Modern Ideology*. New York.

—— 1981a. 'The Servile Statuses of Ancient Greece', in M. I. Finley, *Economy and Society in Ancient Greece*, ed. B. D. Shaw and R. P. Saller. New York. 133–49.

'the social reality Athenians saw around them' (37). He concludes that civic identity itself was a construct that had to be reconstructed in every generation (41).

—— 1981b. 'Between Slavery and Freedom', in M. I. Finley, *Economy and Society in Ancient Greece*, ed. B. D. Shaw and R. P. Saller. New York. 116–32.

—— 1981c. 'The Freedom of the Citizen in the Greek World', in M. I. Finley, *Economy and Society in Ancient Greece*, ed. B. D. Shaw and R. P. Saller. New York. 77–94.

FISHER, N. 1992. *Hybris: A Study in the Values of Honour and Shame in Ancient Greece*. Warminster.

—— 1995. '*Hybris*, Status and Slavery', in A. Powell (ed.), *The Greek World*. London and New York. 44–84.

GAGARIN, M. 1996. 'The Torture of Slaves in Athenian Law', *CP* 91: 1–18.

GARNSEY, P. and R. SALLER 1987. *The Roman Empire: Economy, Society and Culture*. London.

GAUTHIER, P. 1972. *Symbola: Les étrangers et la justice dans les cités grecques*. Nancy.

GERNET, L. 1955. *Droit et société dans la Grèce ancienne*. Paris.

GIDDENS, A. and D. HELD (eds.) 1982. *Classes, Power, and Conflict: Classical and Contemporary Debates*. London.

GLOTZ, G. 1908. 'Les esclaves et la peine du fouet en droit grec', *CRAI*: 571–87.

GRACE, E. 1973. 'Status Distinctions in the Draconian Law', *Eirene* 11: 5–30.

HANSEN, M. H. 1976. *Apagoge, Endeixis and Ephegesis against Kakourgoi, Atimoi and Pheugontes: A Study in the Athenian Administration of Justice in the Fourth Century* BC. Odense.

—— 1991. *The Athenian Democracy in the Age of Demosthenes: Structures, Principles and Ideology*, tr. J. A. Crook. Oxford and Cambridge, Mass.

HARRIS, E. 1992. Review of MacDowell 1990. *CP* 87: 71–80.

HARRIS, W. V. 1988. 'On the Applicability of the Concept of Class in Roman History', in T. Yuge and M. Doi (eds.), *Forms of Control and Subordination in Antiquity*. Leiden. 598–610.

HARRISON, A. R. W. 1968–71. *The Law of Athens*, 2 vols. Oxford.

HARTOG, F. 1988. *The Mirror of Herodotus*, tr. J. Lloyd. Berkeley and Los Angeles.

HARVEY, D. 1990. 'Sykophant and Sykophancy: Vexatious Redefinition?', in P. Cartledge, P. Millett, and S. Todd (eds.), *Nomos: Essays in Athenian Law, Politics and Society*. Cambridge. 103–21.

HUNT, A. S. and C. C. EDGAR (tr.) 1934. *Select Papyri*, ii. Cambridge, Mass. and London.

HUNTER, V. J. 1992. 'Constructing the Body of the Citizen: Corporal Punishment in Classical Athens', *EMC/CV* 36: 271–91.

HUNTER, V. J. 1994. *Policing Athens: Social Control in the Attic Lawsuits, 420–320 BC*. Princeton.

—— 1997. 'The Prison of Athens: A Comparative Perspective', *Phoenix* 51: 296–326.

ISAGER, S. and M. H. HANSEN 1975. *Aspects of Athenian Society in the Fourth Century BC*, tr. J. Hsiang Rosenmeier. Odense.

JACOB, O. 1928. *Les esclaves publics à Athènes*. Liège and Paris.

LÉVY, E. 1988. 'Métèques et droit de résidence', in R. Lonis (ed.), *L'Etranger dans le monde grec*. Nancy. 47–67.

LEWIS, D. M. 1966. 'After the Profanation of the Mysteries', in E. Badian (ed.), *Ancient Society and Institutions: Studies Presented to Victor Ehrenberg*. Oxford. 177–91.

LORAUX, N. 1986. *The Invention of Athens: The Funeral Oration in the Classical City*, tr. A. Sheridan. Cambridge, Mass.

MACDOWELL, D. M. (ed.) 1962. *Andokides: On the Mysteries*. Oxford.

—— 1978. *The Law in Classical Athens*. Ithaca.

—— (ed.) 1990. *Demosthenes, Against Meidias (Oration 21)*. Oxford.

MACTOUX, M.-M. 1988. 'Lois de Solon sur les esclaves et formation d'une société esclavagiste', in T. Yuge and M. Doi (eds.), *Forms of Control and Subordination in Antiquity*. Leiden. 331–54.

MIRHADY, D. C. 1991a. 'The Oath-Challenge in Athens', *CQ* 41: 78–83.

—— 1991b. 'Non-Technical *Pisteis* in Aristotle and Anaximenes', *AJP* 112: 5–28.

—— 1996. 'Torture and Rhetoric in Athens', *JHS* 116: 119–31.

MORRIS, I. 1990. 'The Gortyn Code and Greek Kinship', *GRBS* 31: 233–54.

—— 1996. 'The Strong Principle of Equality and the Archaic Origins of Greek Democracy', in J. Ober and C. Hedrick (eds.), *Demokratia: A Conversation on Democracies, Ancient and Modern*. Princeton. 19–48.

MORROW, G. R. 1939. *Plato's Law of Slavery in Its Relation to Greek Law*. Urbana.

NIELSEN, T. H., L. BJERTRUP, M. H. HANSEN, L. RUBINSTEIN, and T. VESTERGAARD 1989. 'Athenian Grave Monuments and Social Class', *GRBS* 30: 411–20.

OBER, J. 1989. *Mass and Elite in Democratic Athens: Rhetoric, Ideology, and the Power of the People*. Princeton.

—— 1991. 'Aristotle's Political Sociology: Class, Status, and Order in the *Politics*', in C. Lord and D. K. O'Connor (eds.), *Essays on the Foundations of Aristotelian Political Science*. Berkeley and Los Angeles. 112–35.

OBER, J. and C. HEDRICK (eds.) 1996. *Demokratia: A Conversation on Democracies, Ancient and Modern*. Princeton.

PEROTTI, E. 1974. 'Esclaves *choris oikountes*', in *Actes du colloque 1972 sur l'Esclavage*. Annales littéraires de l'Université de Besançon 163. Paris. 47–56.

—— 1976. 'Contribution à l'étude d'une autre catégorie d'esclaves attiques: *Les andrapoda misthophorounta*', in *Actes du colloque 1973 sur l'Esclavage*. Annales littéraires de l'Université de Besançon 182. Paris. 181–91.

PRITCHETT, W. K. 1953. 'The Attic Stelai', *Hesperia* 22: 225–99.

—— 1956. 'The Attic Stelai', *Hesperia* 25: 178–317.

RAAFLAUB, K. A. 1996. 'Equalities and Inequalities in Athenian Democracy', in J. Ober and C. Hedrick (eds.), *Demokratia: A Conversation on Democracies, Ancient and Modern*. Princeton. 139–74.

RHODES, P. J. 1981. *A Commentary on the Aristotelian Athenaion Politeia*. Oxford.

ROBERTS, J. T. 1996. 'Athenian Equality: A Constant Surrounded by Flux', in J. Ober and C. Hedrick (eds.), *Demokratia: A Conversation on Democracies, Ancient and Modern*. Princeton. 187–202.

DE STE CROIX, G. E. M. 1981. *The Class Struggle in the Ancient Greek World from the Archaic Age to the Arab Conquests*. Ithaca.

SAUNDERS, T. J. 1991. *Plato's Penal Code: Tradition, Controversy, and Reform in Greek Penology*. Oxford.

SCAFURO, A. C. 1994. 'Witnessing and False Witnessing: Proving Citizenship and Kin Identity in Fourth-Century Athens', in A. L. Boegehold and A. C. Scafuro (eds.), *Athenian Identity and Civic Ideology*. Baltimore and London. 156–98.

SEALEY, R. 1994. *The Justice of the Greeks*. Ann Arbor.

SINCLAIR, R. K. 1988. *Democracy and Participation in Athens*. Cambridge.

STROUD, R. S. 1974. 'An Athenian Law on Silver Coinage', *Hesperia* 43: 157–88.

SUMNER, C. 1979. *Reading Ideologies: An Investigation into the Marxist Theory of Law and Ideology*. London and New York.

THOMAS, R. 1994. 'Law and the Lawgiver in Athenian Democracy', in R. G. Osborne and S. Hornblower (eds.), *Ritual, Finance, Politics: Athenian Democratic Accounts Presented to David Lewis*. Oxford. 119–33.

THÜR, G. 1996. 'Reply to D. C. Mirhady: Torture and Rhetoric in Athens', *JHS* 116: 132–4.

TODD, S. C. 1993. *The Shape of Athenian Law*. Oxford.

—— 1994. 'Status and Contract in Fourth-century Athens', in G. Thür (ed.), *Symposion 1993*. Cologne, Weimar, and Vienna. 125–40.

—— 1997. 'Status and Gender in Athenian Public Records', in G. Thür and J. Vélissaropoulos-Karakostas (eds.), *Symposion 1995*. Cologne, Weimar, and Vienna. 113–24.

WHITEHEAD, D. 1977. *The Ideology of the Athenian Metic*. Cambridge.

WILLETTS, R. F. (ed.) 1967. *The Law Code of Gortyn*. Berlin.

2

How to Execute People in Fourth-Century Athens

S. C. Todd

ACT I: CONSTRUCTING THE PLOT

This chapter is written at a time of continuing debate about the future management of prisons.[1] Its starting-point is a story which would gladden the heart of the most ardent of penal privatizers, but which took place at Athens in 318 BC: the story of the man who was invited to sponsor his own execution.

Phocion, one of Plutarch's heroes, was an Athenian politician and general, active in the second half of the fourth century. Throughout his career he had supported accommodation with the power of Macedon, even when the Macedonian regent Antipater abolished the democracy in 322. When the democracy was briefly restored four years later, Phocion was predictably impeached before the Assembly and sentenced to death for treason.[2] Plutarch alleges that this was at an unconstitutional meeting, packed out and intimidated by slaves, foreigners, and those members of the lower orders who had been deprived of the vote by Antipater, but he gives no indication that there was anything improper about the manner of execution, which was by hemlock-poisoning. The manner of death is reminiscent of the account in Plato's *Phaedo* of

Versions of the paper on which this chapter is based have been delivered at seminars in Amsterdam, Cambridge, Chapel Hill, New York, Oxford, and Toronto. My thanks are due to those present on each occasion for their comments and suggestions, and to the British Academy for supporting my trip to the Netherlands.

[1] Particularly in the English-speaking world, as is emphasized by Harding (1997: 2–10), who analyses the growth of private prisons in the USA, Australia, and the UK over the past decade, and discusses the likelihood of future developments in New Zealand and Canada. (I owe this reference to Richard Sparks.)

[2] Plut. *Phoc.* 34–6.

the execution of Socrates in 399, and Plutarch is clearly conscious of the parallel, though his account of Phocion's death draws attention to a number of distinctive features.[3]

Whereas Socrates was the only person to be executed in Plato's account, for instance, four other Athenians were sentenced to death at the same time as Phocion. Their names are given as Nicocles, Thudippus, Hegemon, and Pythocles, but we know little more about them than that they were his *philoi* (political allies and/or personal friends). To demonstrate their devotion to their leader, they all claimed from him and received the dubious privilege of drinking the poison before he did. Plutarch remarks in the course of this story that a single fatal dose of hemlock cost 12 drachmas to prepare, which is quite expensive.[4] It is therefore hardly surprising that, as Socrates had been told by his executioner, 'we only prepare [presumably at state-expense] the minimum dose that is necessary'.[5] Unfortunately, however, in our case the four *philoi* each took too large a swig from the bowl, so that when it came to Phocion's turn, there was no hemlock left. The executioner refused to mix up any more unless he was paid the cost of it; and so Phocion himself had to call on another of his friends to provide the necessary money.[6]

Phocion, of course, was a stickler for routine: the sort of man who would insist on an execution being carried out decently and in good order even if it killed him (as in this case it did). But here let us relax for a moment into the world of fantasy. What would have happened if Phocion had refused to produce the 12 drachmas, or if for that matter Phocion (or any other prisoner) had refused to drink the poison? There used in English law to be a macabre custom that three successive failed attempts to hang somebody

[3] The extent of the parallel (which is made explicit at Plut. *Phoc.* 38) is unclear, though the distinctiveness of the details outlined below suggest that it is not total. In theory, even the hemlock could be an invention by Plutarch to match Socrates—a hypothesis which would change but not resolve the problem analysed in Act IV of this chapter; it would mean that all the securely attested cases of execution by hemlock could be dated within the period 404–399, but that would not help to explain the putative abandonment of this method of execution thereafter.

[4] Unskilled building labourers in Athenian temple-accounts in the 320s received typically 1½ drachmas per day: for this and other data on wage-levels at Athens, see Markle 1985: 293.

[5] Pl. *Phd.* 117b8–9.

[6] This detail may be intended to demonstrate Phocion's genteel poverty, or it may imply that his property has been confiscated (but his wife retains house and slaves: Plut. *Phoc.* 37), or simply that he is not given to carrying cash on his person.

would lead to the sentence being commuted to life imprisonment,[7] but that is a function of circumstances outside the victim's control. We can hardly suppose that if Phocion had refused to drink the hemlock, he would thereby have escaped his death-sentence. Presumably therefore he would still have been executed, but in an alternative and less pleasant manner. We have, indeed, a fairly good idea of what that alternative would have been; and it is the existence of these alternatives that will supply the focus for this chapter.

For the moment, however, we may draw one preliminary conclusion from our story. Hemlock-poisoning, admittedly, is not a particularly nice way to die. It causes a range of unpleasant side-effects, most notably vomiting and muscular spasms, and it has plausibly been suggested that Plato in the *Phaedo* is deliberately suppressing these symptoms to avoid detracting from the philosophical significance of Socrates' death.[8] On the other hand, Plutarch's account of Phocion clearly implies that hemlock was a privileged death: the alternative was something worse. To that extent, therefore, Gernet is justified in describing the use of hemlock as 'permitted but controlled suicide'.[9] Phocion, like Socrates, is being left in a room with the equivalent of a pearl-handled revolver, and invited to behave like an officer and a gentleman (a point to which we shall return at the end of Act IV).

ACT II: ASSEMBLING THE PROPS

Our sources are rarely specific about details of executions, and it is hard to be sure how many methods of execution coexisted in classical Athens. The use of hemlock is clearly attested, anecdotally and otherwise, at least from 404/3 onwards. Less certain is precipitation into the *barathron* or *orugma*: both words denote a pit, but the two may or may not have the same location. It is generally[10]

[7] This happened to John Lee in 1885, when the trapdoor repeatedly failed to open: later accounts of the case are discussed by Priestly 1985: 246–50.

[8] Thus Gill 1973: 27.

[9] 'Suicide par tolérance', Gernet 1981: 255: a translation of a reprint of an article originally published in 1924, in response to Keramopoullos 1923 (for which cf. n. 12 below).

[10] Thus e.g. Gernet 1981 (1924): 256–7, against Keramopoullos (1923: e.g. 36). The text of Xen. *Hell.* 1. 7. 20 is less secure than Gernet implies (cf. n. 26 below), but the other passage which he cites (Pl. *Gorg.* 516d9–e2, discussed at n. 24 below) is more persuasive. (For a more sophisticated version of Keramopoullos's view, see Allen, forthcoming: ch. 6. 4.)

accepted that people were thrown alive into the *barathron*—that is, it was itself the means of execution and not simply the dumping-ground for the bodies of people executed in other ways—but there is, as we shall see in Act III of this chapter, no clear evidence for the use of this method after the mid-fifth century.

The third method of execution, though its existence is clearly attested in our sources, nevertheless created difficulties of interpretation particularly for earlier scholars, and deserves to be examined in detail. This is *apotumpanismos*, a term which was traditionally thought to derive from *tumpanon*, meaning a 'club' or a 'cudgel'; so that *apotumpanismos*, according to this view, involved the beating or cudgelling to death of the convicted offender.[11] In 1923, however, Keramopoullos published the results of an excavation in 1915 at Phaleron, which had discovered a group of seventeen skeletons in a mass grave, all with iron cramps round the neck, wrists, and ankles, and some with fragments of wood still adhering to the iron.[12] Keramopoullos noted that the word *tumpanon* could also denote a wooden 'board' or 'plank', and he suggested therefore that *apotumpanismos* involved the death of a victim fastened to such a board.

This interpretation has generally been accepted, not least because (as Keramopoullos himself pointed out) it enables us to make sense of an extended scene in Aristophanes' *Women at the Thesmophoria*, which had not previously been considered in discussions of the subject.[13] The play deals with the efforts of one of Euripides' in-laws, possibly named Mnesilochus, to gate-crash a religious festival restricted to women: after this man is finally unfrocked, he is fastened to a *sanis* ('plank', l. 940), apparently by the neck as well as by the limbs (he complains of 'throat-constricting agonies', l. 1054). This cannot, as Keramopoullos pointed out, be a reference to the stocks or the pillory (even though use of the former at least is attested in Athens), because it is in several places clearly implied that what is at issue is execution rather than temporary confinement.[14]

[11] For *apotumpanismos* as 'cudgelling', see e.g. Caillemer 1873: 327, and Lipsius 1905–15: 1. 77 n. 101.

[12] Keramopoullos 1923. The bodies were buried, though without grave goods. Keramopoullos dated the burial to the seventh century BC, on the basis of pottery found in surrounding graves, but his methodology was promptly criticized on this and other grounds by A. S. Arvanitopoulos, *Methodos pros ereunan tou Attikou poinikou dikaiou*, Volos, 1923 (cited by Bonner and Smith 1930–8: 2. 283, n. 1).

[13] Ar. *Thesm.* 929–1209.

[14] Note the words ἀποθανουμένῳ ('about to die', l. 938) and κόραξιν ἑστιῶν ('as food for

What is less clear is precisely how death was caused by this apparatus. Mnesilochus' neckband is apparently adjustable (ll. 1001–6), and can be tightened at will by the executioner after the manner of a garrotte, which causes death by strangulation. There is no trace of this refinement, however, in the neckbands of Keramopoullos's seventeen skeletons: their fate will have been more closely analogous to a bloodless crucifixion, with death resulting presumably from exposure. This degree of stylistic variation is at first sight disconcerting, but a parallel could be drawn with the case of hanging, in which the use of the trapdoor transforms strangulation into the dislocation of the vertebrae.[15]

No other methods of capital punishment are attested in formal juridical contexts at Athens. There is most notably no reference to beheading: indeed, with the possible exception of the *barathron*, and of an odd reference to 'the place where [the democratic counter-revolutionaries at Phyle in 404/3] slit the throats of any pirates or criminals they might happen to catch',[16] the penalties available are distinctively bloodless.[17] We do, admittedly, hear of a few cases of stoning at Athens, but the atmosphere is always that of a lynch-party; nobody, so far as we are aware, gets burned at the stake; and hanging in Greek literature is distinctively a means of (female) suicide rather than of execution.[18] There is no clear evidence that people could legally and deliberately be tortured to death under Athenian law. This refinement was apparently suggested at the trial of Phocion himself, as a way of livening up the assembly meeting,[19] but as a citizen Phocion was exempt from torture, which in the classical period could only be used against non-citizens.[20] According to Plutarch, the proposal to torture

the crows', l. 942), and the detailed parody of the tragic heroine Andromeda awaiting death (ll. 1009–1135 and esp. l. 1028).

[15] Successive changes in English methods of hanging (and their frequent mismanagement) are discussed in Gatrell 1994: 52–4.

[16] Lys. 13. 78 (but the context may be extra-constitutional). The Greek verb in this passage is ἀπέσφαττον, and the English 'criminals' here translates the Greek noun *kakourgos*, which may but need not have the technical meaning of 'an offender who is liable to summary arrest' (*apagoge*, for which see Act IV below).

[17] Contrast the use of crucifixion and the sword in Roman law.

[18] For stoning by lynch-mob, see e.g. Hdt. 9. 5. 2–3, more credible than the alternative account of the same events in Lycurgus 1. 122 (thus Rosivach 1987: 238–9). For hanging as female suicide, see Loraux 1987: 7–11.

[19] The significant phrase here is τὸν τροχὸν εἰσφέρειν, 'to bring *in* the instrument of torture' (Plut. *Phoc.* 35).

[20] In two cases a non-citizen is said to have been tortured and executed: a slave-girl who

Phocion was so unconstitutional that even the prosecutor repudiated it.

We are left, then, with three methods of execution, of which one indeed may have become obsolete at the start of the classical period. But the existence even of simple alternatives implies a question: how did the Athenians decide in which cases to offer hemlock and when to use *apotumpanismos*?

ACT III: SETTING THE SCENE

Our problem is that death (or at least in the case of executions the manner of death) is something about which the sources are rarely specific. References to the death-penalty itself are common, as indeed we should expect, because death was the penalty for a wide range of offences, and (what is not necessarily the same thing) the Athenians seem to have used it frequently.[21] But the bulk of these references come from the law-court speeches of the Attic orators, and here the terminology is surprisingly unimaginative: there is no slang, and rarely unnecessary detail.

The orators often say of a criminal that 'he died', or of the court that 'you killed him', or there may be a brief phrase such as 'punished with death'. But there is also a notable use of repeated euphemisms: the death-penalty is 'the greatest of punishments'; and the convicted offender is 'handed over to the Eleven' (the officials in charge of prisons and executions). 'Handing over to the Eleven', indeed, is even used to mean 'executing' in the official decree recording the death-sentence passed on the orator Antiphon.[22] There is an interesting coyness here, an unwillingness

was *τῷ . . . δημοκοίνῳ τροχισθεῖσα παρεδόθη* ('tortured on the wheel and handed over to the executioner', Antiph. 1. 20), and a man named Antiphon (neither the orator nor the sophist), whom the Athenians *στρεβλώσαντες . . . ἀπεκτείνατε* ('you racked and executed', Dem. 18. 133, cf. *ἐστρέβλωσαν . . . καὶ ἀπέκτειναν* 'they racked and executed' in Din. 1. 63). But even if these victims died while being tortured (rather than being tortured and then executed), it may simply mean that the torturer went too far.

[21] There is at Athens no trace of a patronage system in which the élite could exercise influence by obtaining pardon for those convicted (contrast the analysis of eighteenth-century England by Hay 1975). Where we hear of Athenians escaping the death-penalty, it is usually members of the élite who have withdrawn into exile in order not to stand trial.

[22] *ἀποθνῄσκω* ('to die', said of the victim): e.g. Lys. 19. 7; Dem. 19. 137. *ἀποκτείνω* ('to kill [him]', said of the court): e.g. Lys. 30. 25; Isae. 4. 28; Dem. 24. 138; Din. 1. 23. *θανάτῳ κολάζω* ('to punish with death'): e.g. Lys. 28. 3; Dem. 21. 176. *θανάτῳ ζημιόω* (same

verbally to go into too much detail in the face of death, and specifically perhaps the death of citizens: we may recall that even the executioner (at least as portrayed in Plato's *Phaedo*) consistently employs the euphemistic term *pharmakon* ('poison'? 'medicine'?) in place of the more brutal *koneion* ('hemlock').[23]

In how many cases can we be specific about the manner of execution? The nature and distribution of our evidence is important, and deserves for two reasons to be considered in some detail. In the first place, if we wish to draw substantive conclusions about how the death-penalty was organized, then it must be done on this basis. But secondly, it raises literary or perhaps procedural questions: how is the evidence presented in our sources, and what does this say about the death-penalty as a means of social organization in Athenian law and in Athenian public discourse?

There is no Athenian in our sources who is explicitly stated to have been executed by precipitation into the *barathron*. The only attested examples of such deaths occur when Persian envoys in the 490s, demanding earth and water as the traditional symbols of submission, were thrown at Athens into the *barathron*, as at Sparta down a well, where they could find not only earth but also water. No other reference to the *barathron* is more than hypothetical. There are two anecdotes told about early-fifth-century political leaders which seem to indicate that it could have been used against them but was not: Aristides is said to have remarked that 'if the Athenians had any sense, they would throw both him and Themistocles into it'; while at the trial of Miltiades, according to Plato, 'the Athenians voted to throw him in there' before having second thoughts.[24]

meaning): e.g. Lys. 12. 36; Dem. 19. 276; Din. 1. 23. ἡ μεγίστη δίκη ('the greatest of punishments'): e.g. Lys. 22. 16; 28. 17. Handing over to the Eleven: e.g. Antiph. 5. 69–70. Antiphon's death-sentence: [Plut.] *X Orat.* 834a.

[23] Euphemism in certain contexts to describe executions is not unusual. Gatrell (1994: 29) notes the tendency of eighteenth-century British Home Secretaries to write 'the law to take its course' on appeal dossiers, and of newspapers to speak of felons being 'launched into eternity'. But the phrasing of Antiphon's death-sentence implies the use of euphemism in a context where an early-modern judge would have been much more explicit: compare the detailed sentences quoted by Evans 1996: 32 (on a German bandit in 1654) and by Gatrell 1994: 316 (on an English traitor in 1803).

[24] The Persian envoys: Hdt. 7. 133. 1. Aristides and Themistocles: Plut. *Arist.* 3. Miltiades: Pl. *Gorg.* 516d9–e2. The Plato text is the strongest evidence that the *barathron* in the early fifth century was a means of execution, and not just a place where the Athenians disposed of the bodies of executed criminals (cf. n. 10 above): what Miltiades escaped was presumably death, rather than the subsequent disposal of his corpse.

The remaining references to the *barathron* are still further removed from reality: Aristophanes in a series of plays dating from the mid-420s to the early 380s repeatedly insists that various named individuals ought to be executed in that way, which indicates that the penalty was well known but not necessarily that it was still in use; while the fact that two late-fourth-century orators (one of whom may be quoting a fifth-century decree) describe the executioner as 'the man in charge of the *orugma*' may simply indicate that such a title has become traditional.[25]

The only text which even suggests the continuing availability of the *barathron* after the mid-fifth century is Xenophon's account of the trial of six Athenian generals after the battle of Arginusae in 406. He recounts that Euryptolemus, a relative of one of the defendants and a friend of another, proposed unsuccessfully that they should be tried under the provisions of the decree of Cannonus, which among other things specified that if convicted they should be thrown into the *barathron*. It is very difficult to interpret this proposal. For one thing, the text is disputed, and the precise role envisaged for the *barathron* is therefore uncertain.[26] Indeed, it is at least possible that the decree was obscure even to its proposer, because Euryptolemus seems to be dredging up out of the statute-book an obsolete but characteristically unrepealed procedure simply because it formally grants what was always the custom but was nowhere else explicitly stated, that each defendant had a right to an individual verdict.[27] But whatever we make of the details of this text, it indicates at most availability and not

[25] Aristophanes and the *barathron*: *Eq.* 1362–3; *Nub.* 1447–51; *Ran.* 574; *Plut.* 431. 'The man in charge of the *orugma*': Lycurgus 1. 121 (discussing and perhaps quoting a decree passed soon after 411); Din. 1. 62. For the tendency of our sources to speak of the *barathron* in fifth-century contexts, and of the *orugma* in fourth-century contexts, see Gernet 1981 (1924): 256 n. 28.

[26] The manuscript reading at Xen. *Hell.* 1. 7. 20 is 'be killed and thrown in' (ἀποθανόντα . . . ἐμβληθῆναι), but many editors accept the variant 'be thrown in and be killed' (ἀποθανεῖν . . . ἐμβληθέντα, which is attested in a scholion to Ar. *Eccl.* 1031): the latter reading envisages the *barathron* as a mode of execution, whereas the former sees it simply as a means of disposing of corpses (cf. n. 10 above).

[27] Thus Lavelle, who highlights the role of the decree in ensuring individual trials (1988: 20), and notes its possible archaic or archaizing features (Lavelle 1988: 21–2). Whitehorne, on the other hand, in a paper devoted primarily to the textual problem (see previous n.), argues for the amended text partly because he believes in the continued existence of death by precipitation at the end of the fifth century (Whitehorne 1989: 97), but his evidence for this belief is simply the Aristophanes passages cited in n. 25 above (and anyway, the continued use of the *barathron* would not itself prove the continued use of Cannonus' decree).

use: Euryptolemus' proposal was eventually rejected, and all six generals were convicted collectively on the basis of a single vote.[28]

As for hemlock, we can name precisely four cases in which it was used as a judicial penalty, along with two other passages in which its use in such contexts is mentioned without specifying the identity of the victim. Three of the four named instances are mentioned for anecdotal reasons, because the man being executed made a memorable remark or remarks when faced with death: Socrates, with his enigmatic instruction to Crito to sacrifice a cock to Asclepius; Phocion, with a series of such remarks attributed by Plutarch; and Theramenes, who played the aristocratic party-game of *kottabos* with his hemlock, flicking the dregs from his cup as an ironic dedication to Critias, his victorious enemy and fellow member of the Thirty Tyrants (the oligarchic junta of 404/3).[29]

The fourth named victim is at first sight more difficult to explain, because there is no memorable statement attributed to him: this is Polemarchus, brother of the orator Lysias, who, according to the latter, received from the Thirty Tyrants 'their accustomed order to drink hemlock, before he had even heard the charge against him'.[30] We cannot be sure why Lysias gives us this detail, but it is not quite unique: in another of Lysias' speeches, his client claims that numbers of his relatives 'drank hemlock under the Thirty',[31] an assertion which is applied generically to 'many Athenians' by Andocides.[32] It is tempting therefore to conclude that the Thirty had become associated in the public mind not simply with executions but specifically with hemlock-poisoning: perhaps (and here we can only speculate) they took what had previously been a private means of suicide and adapted it for judicial use.[33] Unlike the *barathron*, therefore, execution by hemlock is

[28] There is a reference to trial under the decree of Cannonus (though not to the *barathron*) in Ar. *Eccl.* 1089–90, dating to the late 390s. This may indicate that the procedure had remained notorious even from a trial fifteen years previously, but it may also be a literary joke, if (as is often suspected) the first two books of Xenophon's *Hellenica* were produced at some time in the 390s.

[29] Socrates: Pl. *Phd.* 118a7–8; Phocion: Plut. *Phoc.* 36 (see n. 3 above for the comparison with Plato's Socrates); Theramenes: Xen. *Hell.* 2. 3. 54–6.

[30] Lys. 12. 17.

[31] Lys. 18. 24–5.

[32] Andoc. 3. 10.

[33] Lipsius (1905–15: I. 77 n. 101) is one of several scholars to suggest that the Thirty may have invented the judicial use of hemlock, on the negative grounds that there is no earlier evidence for such use. Taken together, these three passages may provide some positive evidence to back him up; so may the proverbial reference (in a scholion to Ar. *Ran.* 541) to

clearly and positively attested, but only in certain very stereotyped literary contexts.

The pattern of references in our sources to *apotumpanismos*, on the other hand, is simultaneously more puzzling and also perhaps more illuminating. We have already considered (in Act II) the fictitious scene in Aristophanes' *Women at the Thesmophoria*. Apart from this, there is a rather weak joke in Aristophanes' *Knights*, that the slave Paphlagon, who represents the Athenian politician Cleon, ought to be secured in a 'wood with five holes';[34] this may be a reference to the five iron cramps in *apotumpanismos*, to parallel the list of individuals that Aristophanes would like to see thrown into the *barathron*.[35] There is also one anecdote: a certain Lysimachus (otherwise probably unknown) was so narrowly reprieved from execution that he acquired the nickname 'the man from the *tumpanon*';[36] the literary parallel here is with the memorable statements anecdotally attributed to Phocion, Theramenes, and Socrates.[37]

References like these are easy to explain on literary grounds, and we can for the moment ignore them.[38] We can also leave on one side a couple of passages in the orators which may refer to *apotumpanismos*, but which are so allusive that they retain no shock value. Aeschines for instance hints in the peroration to his *Embassy* speech that if he is convicted, his enemy Demosthenes will be able to watch him die; but the interpretation of this passage, as we shall see, is fraught with difficulty.[39] Similarly with Demosthenes' own attempt to arouse pity, when he describes Midias' unsuccessful

'the three things of Theramenes' (viz., the stocks, hemlock, and exile), if this refers to his activity as a member of the Thirty in punishing opponents of the regime (but it could refer to his membership of the Four Hundred in 411). Hemlock is attested as a means of suicide (but not necessarily of execution) in two independent passages in Aristophanes' *Frogs* (ll. 123–4 and 1051), produced in 405, shortly before the Thirty.

34 ἐν πεντεσυρίγγῳ ξύλῳ: Ar. *Eq.* 1049.

35 For Aristophanes and the *barathron*, see n. 25 above.

36 [Arist.] *Ath. Pol.* 45. 1.

37 For which see n. 29 above.

38 We may ignore cases of *apotumpanismos* under Athenian commanders abroad: certainly Agoratus' eldest brother (Lys. 13. 67, cf. below); probably Artayktes (Hdt. 7. 33 and 9. 120. 4); just possibly, assuming some confusion in the source, the Samian trierarchs (Plut. *Per.* 28). Also omitted here are two doubtful cases under foreign jurisdictions: the poet Antiphon at Syracuse (Arist. *Rhet.* 2. 6. 27 = 1385^a10–13, for which see n. 61 below, but the story sounds too good to be true); and the opponents of Euphraeus at Oreus (Dem. 9. 61, a hypothetical case, though possibly importing assumptions from Athenian law, cf. n. 45 below).

39 Aeschin. 2. 181–2 (discussed further in Act V).

attempt to have him implicated in the murder of Nicodemus, where the crucial phrase could be read as signifying either that 'I almost was executed in that way [i.e. that if convicted I would have been]' or that 'I almost would have been [i.e. I would not have been]'.[40]

We are left with five passages, all of them from the orators, which state explicitly that *apotumpanismos* either took place or ought to have taken place in a particular instance at Athens. What is striking about these passages is that they fall into two clearly defined groups. Two of them, indeed, come from the same speech, Lysias' *Against Agoratus*. Agoratus, the defendant in this speech, may have been born a slave, but he claims (plausibly, though Lysias of course denies this) to have been made a citizen by special decree. He admits that he caused the deaths of a number of citizens by his denunciations under the Thirty in 404/3. However, he insists (with some justice) that he is now protected by the amnesty of 403/2, and cannot therefore be charged with murdering them.

During his speech, Lysias discusses the case of one Menestratus, who like Agoratus had caused death by his denunciations under the Thirty, but who had himself been executed for homicide under the restored democracy. Presumably this is meant to serve as in some sense a substantive precedent for ignoring the amnesty in the present case. The parallel is not made explicit, perhaps because the precedent itself is weak: Lysias nowhere claims that the killings for which Menestratus was executed were those committed under the Thirty. What is, however, significant is that Menestratus is specifically stated to have suffered *apotumpanismos*,[41] and this (as we shall discover in Act IV) is probably the penalty which Agoratus himself is facing.

Menestratus, however, is not the only person in this speech to experience *apotumpanismos*. According at least to Lysias, Agoratus had had three brothers.[42] The middle one we may for our purposes ignore, because he had died in prison at Corinth. The youngest one, however, had been executed at Athens, again specifically by *apotumpanismos*; and the same penalty, incidentally, had befallen the eldest brother also, although in his case at the hands of the

[40] μόνον οὐ προσηλῶσθαι: Dem. 21. 105.

[41] Lys. 13. 55.

[42] Lys. 13. 67–8. There is uncertainty about the order of the text at sections 65–8, and some scholars reject sections 65–6, but sections 67–8 are generally accepted.

Athenian general Lamachus while on active service during the Sicilian Expedition. Here there can be no substantive precedent, and the amnesty is not in issue. But the thrust of the passage is obvious: a man coming from a family like that deserves no better fate. Nevertheless, Agoratus can hardly be the only Athenian litigant in the early fourth century facing *apotumpanismos*. What is it about him that makes it worth Lysias' while so to dwell on the point?

The references in the second group come from a number of speeches delivered by Demosthenes in the late 340s. In each case the context is hypothetical: death (specifically by *apotumpanismos*) is the penalty that the Athenians ought to impose on 'traitors' (i.e. the political opponents of Demosthenes). In the *Embassy* speech, for instance, 'if only Philip had heard that those men had immediately been executed by *apotumpanismos* . . .';[43] in the speech *On the Chersonese*, 'this is a struggle to the death, and you must hate and execute by *apotumpanismos* those who have sold themselves to Philip'—a passage which is repeated verbatim, save for the interesting variant 'publicly execute by *apotumpanismos*', in the probably spurious but quite possibly contemporary *Fourth Philippic*.[44] In the genuine *Third Philippic* there is a further case, admittedly outside Athenian jurisdiction but very possibly importing Athenian juridical assumptions: if only *apotumpanismos* had been the fate of Philip's supporters, the opponents of Euphraeus at Oreus.[45] Gernet (1981 [1924]: 260) quite correctly points out that none of these Demosthenic executions ever took place, and warns us against taking seriously the 'passion' of an Athenian orator. But why, once again, is such usage restricted to this orator, at this date, against these opponents?

ACT IV: LIFTING THE CURTAIN

What are we to make of this material? How do we explain why *apotumpanismos*, or conversely hemlock, is used in each of these particular cases and not in those ones? It is theoretically possible that the decision could have been made on an individual basis

[43] Dem. 19. 137.

[44] φανερῶς ('publicly', Dem. 10. 63) for μισεῖν καί ('hate and', Dem. 8. 61).

[45] Dem. 9. 61.

either by the court in passing sentence or by the public official responsible for carrying it out. Both of these possibilities, however, can in practice be discounted. Athenian law is notable for its refusal to grant significant discretion to its public officials; and although it is certainly true that penalties were regularly determined by the jury (in cases where there was no penalty fixed by statute) voting between two proposals, one by the prosecutor and the other by the defendant, nevertheless extant proposals for the death-penalty do not specify the means of death.[46] The tendency of scholars therefore has been to reject this type of *ad hoc* explanation, and to search instead for a single unifying rule to explain the pattern of use. Unfortunately, however, none of the four theories that have been proposed is above criticism.

Perrot (1873: 130) suggested that the deciding criterion was the offender's status, such that *apotumpanismos* was used against foreigners and slaves, whereas hemlock was a citizen's privilege. Menestratus, however, was a citizen, but suffered *apotumpanismos*; Polemarchus was a non-citizen, but was offered hemlock. Caillemer (1873: 327) proposed that *apotumpanismos* was used for certain offences, most notably crimes against the state, treason, and murder. But what connects these particular offences? And what of Theramenes and Phocion, both convicted of treason and yet allowed to drink hemlock? Barkan (1935: 81–2) believed that hemlock was introduced as a milder alternative to *apotumpanismos*, at just the time when the *barathron*, the most severe penalty, was finally abandoned. But this simply transfers the problem, because it is no easier to explain two pairs of overlapping penalties than one pair. Gernet (1981 (1924): 259–65) saw legal procedure as the determining criterion: *apotumpanismos*, he suggests, was used on those summarily arrested by *apagoge*. This was a form of action regularly applied against certain types of thief (like Agoratus' youngest brother), and against some homicides (like Agoratus himself, though in Menestratus' case we are left guessing); moreover, the procedure used against Mnesilochus for religious impiety was *ephegesis*, itself a variant form of *apagoge*.[47]

It is Gernet's theory that has achieved the status of orthodoxy.

[46] Most notably in Socrates' case (Pl. *Ap*. 36b, with Diog. Laert. 2. 40), but cf. also the decree proposing the death-sentence against Antiphon (cited at n. 22 above), which simply uses the euphemism 'hand over to the Eleven' without specifying how they are to carry out the sentence.

[47] For *apagoge* and related procedures, see now Hansen 1976.

But this is the type of orthodoxy that results less from conviction than from exhaustion. Gernet himself seems unhappy, for the purposes of his paper, with *apagoge* as it is attested in the fourth century, and devotes several pages to hypothesizing what must have been its scope in the archaic period. Moreover, his theory involves, as we have seen, the suppression of Demosthenes' traitors without any satisfactory explanation of their unique appearance; and worst of all, it fails to account for the hemlock offered to Polemarchus and to Theramenes, albeit under the Thirty, but both clearly arrested by *apagoge*. If the controversy has remained dormant since the 1930s, that is not because any of the theories proposed is satisfactory, but because the search for a clear rationale in these terms has proved inconclusive.[48]

Given the evidence available, there seems no point in trying to construct a single alternative theory to account for all of our cases. Methodologically, indeed, this may be a problem best approached not by deduction from the evidence to a (presumed) general rule, but rather inductively, starting with the general principles of Athenian law as we understand them, and seeking on that basis to make sense of the cases. The difficulty is, of course, that such principles are inevitably a matter for individual interpretation.

I have argued elsewhere that Athenian law seems to have been organized in terms of procedure and not of offence.[49] If that is correct, then Gernet's procedural emphasis would appear considerably more attractive than the substantive theory of Caillemer. Similarly, Barkan's theory of 'progressive niceness' is in my opinion fatally weakened by its evolutionary assumptions. On the other hand, although Perrot's explanation of *apotumpanismos* as a slave's death is obviously not a sufficient one, it does tie in nicely with what seems to be the continuing importance of status-distinctions in fourth-century Athens. It may also help to explain the sheer glee with which Lysias dwells on the fate of Agoratus' brothers. So far as I am aware, this is the only reference in the orators to the formal execution of an alleged slave; and since

[48] For the acceptance of Gernet's views (originally published in 1924), see e.g. Bonner and Smith 1930–8: 2. 285 n. 3, and more recently Cantarella 1991: 43. For Demosthenes' traitors, see nn. 43–5 above. For the hypothetical prehistory of *apagoge*, see Gernet 1981 (1924): 263–5.

[49] For the various principles suggested in this paragraph, see Todd 1993: 64–7 (on the role of procedure in Athenian law), 69–70 (on the absence of evolution), and 199–200 (on the continuing importance of status).

Agoratus himself claims citizenship not by descent but by decree, the suggestion that his brothers died such a death would be a legally irrelevant and typically Lysianic argument.

Here, however, we must confront the question, to what extent should we expect to find a single and consistent organizing principle behind the death-penalty? Athens had no penal code by which penalties were graded in relation to each other: indeed, the flexibility of Athenian law seems to be most clearly seen in the range (or one might say the disorganized overlap) of procedures and therefore of penalties available to a would-be prosecutor. How far then is the choice between hemlock and *apotumpanismos* merely the result of piecemeal legislation and the random phrasing of a particular decree?[50] Or how far, on the other hand, is there an underlying juristic subconsciousness: how far do the successive proposers of legislation share a sense that *apotumpanismos* ought to be used against certain types of offender, and that hemlock ought to be reserved for others? How far, in other words, is death and the means of death being used deliberately as a form of social engineering?

At this point we may return to Gernet's observation, that hemlock constitutes an invitation to commit suicide (cf. Act I above). We may note for instance the fact that Socrates' chains are removed on the morning of death, and that he has the right to die at the time of his choosing; family and friends are present, and the executioner has discreetly removed himself from the room; the body is at least under normal circumstances to be returned to the family for burial.[51] *Apotumpanismos* may by contrast represent a more conscious, deliberate, and humiliating expulsion from the community: of slaves, who have no standing; of traitors (or at least of some traitors), who have forfeited their standing; while *apagoge*, in which a defendant who confesses is executed without trial, would represent the denial of any such standing within the community.

50 For the choice of procedures and of penalties, see Osborne 1985. Piecemeal legislation, as we saw in Act III, may be the best way of reading the proposed use of the decree of Cannonus at the Arginusae trial.

51 Removal of chains: Pl. *Phd.* 59e6–7. Right to die at the time of his choosing: ibid. 116e1–6. Presence of family: ibid. 60a1–8 and 116a8–b5. Presence of friends: Pl. *Phd.* *passim*, and Plut. *Phoc.* 36. Absence of executioner: Pl. *Phd.* 116b6–d2 with 117a4–7. Return of body to family: explicitly at Lys. 12. 18 (evidently this applied even under the Thirty); implied at Pl. *Phd.* 115a7–8; and revoked only by special decree at Plut. *Phoc.* 37.

ACT V: LEAVING THE THEATRE

We turn finally to the literary or procedural questions about the distribution of our evidence which were raised at the start of Act III: why are gratuitous references to *apotumpanismos* confined to Lysias' *Agoratus* and to Demosthenes' 'traitors'? At first sight, this could be held to indicate a lack of public interest in the manner of their death; but that would not explain the existence of alternative methods of execution, and neither would it account for the presence and indeed the tone of these exceptional references.

There does seem at Athens to be an awareness that the manner of death could be used to humiliate the person being executed in a peculiarly final way.[52] *Apotumpanismos* was a nastier and more painful death, and it is possible (as has been suggested) that it was reserved for use against the outsider. Further refinements could be added: Mnesilochus, for instance, against his wishes and at the specific insistence of the boule which has summarily condemned him, is to be executed wearing as an added gesture of shame the woman's clothes in which he had attempted to gate-crash the festival.[53] The fate of the body after death could be used for further differentiation. Hemlock-victims, as we have seen, appear normally to have been returned to their families for burial. Some criminals on the other hand suffered *ataphia* (that is, they could not be buried within Attica).[54] This fate cannot simply be correlated with *apotumpanismos*, because Keramopoullos's seventeen skeletons were buried; but the burial of seventeen together, with no grave goods, presumably indicates that these bodies at least were not returned to their families.

This leads us to a final question, which needs to be asked even though it cannot conclusively be answered. Where did Athenian

[52] Not ultimately final, because you could always disinter a body in order to deny a burial that had taken place (for examples, see Thuc. 1. 126. 12 and Lycurgus 1. 115). It is harder to rehabilitate somebody once sentenced to death, at least if that sentence has been carried out (though Alcibiades, who had escaped execution by withdrawing into exile in 415 BC, was able to return to Athens in 407).

[53] Ar. *Thesm.* 939–46.

[54] Xen. *Hell.* 1. 7. 22 claims that this penalty applied in cases of treason and temple-robbery. According to Aeschin. 3. 244, inanimate objects found to have caused death were expelled from Attica, which may imply that the penalty applied also in other cases of homicide, but I can find no direct evidence for this.

executions take place: discreetly within the walls of the prison, or in public?[55] If executions (or at least some executions) did take place in public, then that would create an element of theatre, and Hunter has recently emphasized the role of public performance in the judicial treatment of slaves at Athens.[56] The theatrical aspects of execution have attracted considerable attention in recent scholarship on pre-industrial Europe: Hay, for instance, draws attention to the drama of trial and sentence in eighteenth-century England; and the elaborate staging of French and German executions in this period is discussed by Spierenburg and by Evans.[57] Of course the effect of such theatre depends on the audience's reactions (a point which has been emphasized by several pre-industrial historians),[58] and the reaction of the Athenian audience remains to be considered.

There are two texts which speak of executions taking place in the presence of the victorious prosecutor. Aeschines, charged at his *euthunai* (examination of accounts) with misconduct as ambassador—would this make him liable as a traitor to *apotumpanismos*?—insists that it is not so much death that is so terrible, but the shame of seeing, at the moment of death, the gloating face of your enemy.[59] Elsewhere, Demosthenes insists that under Athenian homicide law (form of execution disputed) the prosecutor must not take vengeance into his own hands: he is allowed to watch the culprit pay the penalty, but no further.[60]

One such passage could have been metaphorical, but hardly both, so we may safely infer the presence at least of the prosecutor at least at some executions. Hemlock, as we have seen, was drunk in the prison, and there is no sign in the *Phaedo* of the prosecutor Meletus. Is this simply a generous act in waiving his rights, or a

[55] The possibility that *apotumpanismos* took place in public is suggested in passing by Debrunner Hall 1996: 82–3.

[56] The standard judicial punishment for slave offences was whipping, and Hunter (1994: 155–8, and cf. ch. 1 of this volume) draws attention to several statutes which imply that this was to be done in public. She also argues that the judicial torture of slaves for evidence normally took place in public (Hunter 1994: 70–95): the conclusion is probably right, though some of her sources (e.g. Isoc. 17. 15 and Dem. 47. 12, cited on pp. 65, 70, and 92) may refer not to the activity of torture but to the handing over of the slave for torture.

[57] Hay 1975: 26–7; Spierenburg 1995: 55–8; Evans 1996: e.g. 77–108.

[58] The changing reaction over time of European audiences is discussed by Spierenburg 1995: 58–9; and there is a detailed analysis of the complexity of the response of English crowds in Gatrell 1994: 56–105.

[59] Lit. 'not death, but the *hubris* accompanying one's end', Aeschin. 2. 181–2.

[60] Dem. 23. 69.

Platonic cover-up, or was he formally excluded? Where did *apotumpanismos* occur? In prison, but with the prosecutor as a privileged viewer? Or on the public stage, where the prosecutor is only the most objectionable of spectators? We have no conclusive Athenian evidence. The *apotumpanismos* of Mnesilochus takes place in public, but that is a necessary function of Aristophanes' plot; and we should not perhaps lay too much weight on the use of the variant *phaneros*, 'publicly', in the probably spurious *Fourth Philippic* (cited at the end of Act III). There is, however, if it has any comparative value, the story of Antiphon the poet, executed at Syracuse, and the remark he is supposed to have made as they went out of the gates (of the prison? of the city?) to those about to suffer *apotumpanismos* with him: 'Why cover your faces? Are you afraid anybody will see you tomorrow?'[61]

At least in Antiphon's case (and at Athens also?), *apotumpanismos* has become a theatrical performance, and in a specifically public theatre. A dramatic and coded action, perhaps, which everyone can see and understand, but which, at least when the victim is a citizen, people are normally too reticent to put into words. After all, the person being executed is now marked out as an outsider, but if (s)he is also a citizen, this death is something which could happen to any one of the spectators. No such reticence of course is required on those rare occasions when the speaker thinks or pretends to think (and can get the audience to agree with him) that the victim(s) are so utterly outside the community that nobody is going to respond 'there, but for the grace of the gods, go I'. But such occasions are rare, requiring either a victim of a distinct status (such as a slave), whose fate serves explicitly to reinforce the distinction between opponent and audience, or else a readiness by the speaker to polarize political discourse to an unprecedented level.[62]

Under more normal circumstances, it is shameful and embarrassing to admit even to taking notice of executions. That at least is what is implied by Plato's story of Leontius, son of Aglaeon, who was walking from the Piraeus towards Athens along the outside of the North Long Wall, when he saw a sight that both revolted and

[61] Arist. *Rhet.* 2. 6. 27 = 1385^a10–13, but cf. n. 38 above.

[62] The role of public executions in eighteenth-century England in marking out 'social others' is discussed by Gatrell 1994: 280–97. What is striking about Athens is not so much the parallel but the contrast, in that private execution by hemlock is unlikely to have fulfilled such a role, and that extant literary sources are so silent about the apparent public significance of executions by *apotumpanismos*.

entranced him: literally perhaps 'bodies lying (i.e. horizontally) next to the executioner'.[63] It is often assumed that the executioner here was disposing of corpses, but it is tempting instead to read this as the final stage of *apotumpanismos*.[64] If that is correct, we have here a public theatre not just at Syracuse but at Athens also: death, in a public context but presumably by exposure (and thus not actually killed by the agents of the community), under guard but in another sense alone (we have in our sources for *apotumpanismos* no scenes around the foot of the cross), outside the city wall and symbolizing thereby the final expulsion of the outsider from the community.

EPILOGUE

This is not the type of paper that establishes firm conclusions. Instead, it has sought to re-examine a traditional problem (the basis on which different methods of capital punishment were applied in Athenian law), and to explore the significance of some points which have received less notice than they perhaps deserve. In particular, attention has been drawn to the likelihood that capital punishment by *apotumpanismos* was carried out in public, to the role of public punishments as a marker of status and a ritual of exclusion, to the theatrical function of such putatively public executions (hence the division of the paper into five Acts with somewhat melodramatic subtitles), and to the relationship between such public theatre and the euphemistic near-silence of our extant literary sources.

[63] *νεκροὺς παρὰ τῷ δημίῳ κειμένους*: Pl. *Resp*. 439e8–9.

[64] Disposal of corpses is the interpretation offered by Keramopoullos (1923: 36), and by Gernet (1981 [1924]: 255 with n. 25), but the Greek word *nekros*, though normally signifying a dead body, can also denote a body in its death throes (as at Antiph. 2. 4. 5). Elsewhere (1981 [1924]: 254 and n. 14), Gernet claims that in *apotumpanismos* the plank was normally positioned so that the victim was upright, but the evidence he cites is hardly conclusive.

References

ALLEN, D. (forthcoming). *Punishing and Politics in Ancient Athens: Anger, Desert, and Social Memory*. Princeton.

BARKAN, I. 1935. *Capital Punishment in Ancient Athens*. Chicago.

BONNER, R. J. and G. SMITH 1930–8. *The Administration of Justice from Homer to Aristotle*, 2 vols. Chicago.

CAILLEMER, E. 1873. s.v. 'Apotumpanismos', in Ch. Daremberg and E. Saglio (eds.), *Dictionnaire des antiquités grecques et romaines d'après les textes et les monuments*. Paris. I. 327.

CANTARELLA, E. 1991. *I supplizi capitali in Grecia e a Roma*. Milan.

DEBRUNNER HALL, M. 1996. 'Even Dogs Have Erinyes: Sanctions in Athenian Practice and Thinking', in L. Foxhall and A. D. E. Lewis (eds.), *Greek Law in Its Political Setting: Justifications Not Justice*. Oxford. 73–89.

EVANS, E. J. 1996. *Rituals of Retribution: Capital Punishment in Germany, 1600–1987*. Oxford and New York.

GATRELL, V. A. C. 1994. *The Hanging Tree: Execution and the English People, 1770–1868*. Oxford.

GERNET, L. 1981. 'Capital Punishment', in id., *The Anthropology of Ancient Greece*, tr. J. Hamilton and B. Nagy. Baltimore and London. 252–76 (originally published as 'Sur l'exécution capitale: à propos d'un ouvrage récent', *REG* 37 (1924): 261–93, and reprinted in L. Gernet, *Droit et institutions en Grèce antique*. Paris, 1968. 175–211).

GILL, C. 1973. 'The Death of Socrates', *CQ* 23: 25–8.

HANSEN, M. H. 1976. *'Apagoge', 'Endeixis' and 'Ephegesis' against 'Kakourgoi', 'Atimoi' and 'Pheugontes': A Study in the Athenian Administration of Justice in the Fourth Century* BC. Odense.

HARDING, R. 1997. *Private Prisons and Public Accountability*. Milton Keynes.

HAY, D. 1975. 'Property, Authority, and the Criminal Law', in D. Hay et al., *Albion's Fatal Tree: Crime and Society in Eighteenth-Century England*. Harmondsworth. 17–63.

HUNTER, V. J. 1994. *Policing Athens: Social Control in the Attic Lawsuits, 420–320* BC. Princeton.

KERAMOPOULLOS, A. D. 1923. *Ho Apotumpanismos*. Athens.

LAVELLE, B. M. 1988. '*Adikia*, the Decree of Kannonos, and the Trial of the Generals', *C&M* 39: 19–41.

LIPSIUS, J. H. 1905–15. *Das attische Recht und Rechtsverfahren*, 3 vols. in 4. Leipzig.

LORAUX, N. 1987. *Tragic Ways of Killing a Woman*. Cambridge, Mass.

MARKLE, M. M. 1985. 'Jury Pay and Assembly Pay at Athens', in P. A. Cartledge and F. D. Harvey (eds.), *Crux: Studies Presented to G. E. M. de Ste Croix on His 75th Birthday*. Exeter. 265–97.

OSBORNE, R. G. 1985. 'Law in Action in Classical Athens', *JHS* 105: 40–58.

PERROT, G. 1873. *L'éloquence politique et judiciaire à Athènes*. Paris.

PRIESTLY, P. 1985. *Victorian Prison Lives: English Prison Biography, 1830–1914*. London and New York.

ROSIVACH, V. J. 1987. 'Execution by Stoning at Athens', *Cl. Ant.* 6: 232–48.

SPIERENBURG, P. 1995. 'The Body and the State in Early Modern Europe', in N. Morris and D. J. Rothman (eds.), *The Oxford History of the Prison*. Oxford. 49–77.

TODD, S. C. 1993. *The Shape of Athenian Law*. Oxford.

WHITEHORNE, J. 1989. 'Punishment under the Decree of Cannonus', in G. Thür (ed.), *Symposion 1985: Vorträge zur griechischen und hellenistischen Rechtsgeschichte*. Cologne and Vienna. 89–97.

3
The Athenian Rationale for Torture

David C. Mirhady

αἰαῖ τὸ δοῦλον ὡς κακὸν πέφυκ' ἀεὶ
τολμᾷ θ' ἃ μὴ χρὴ τῇ βίᾳ νικώμενον

Oh, what an evil is slavery always; it submits
to what it must not, vanquished by violence
(Eur. *Hec.* 332–3)

In many speeches from the Athenian law courts, there is a report that one of the parties to the litigation challenged the other to have a slave tortured over some point in their dispute.[1] As distinct from 'judicial' torture, which was carried out by the Athenian polis in order to investigate some matter of public interest, what is primarily at issue here is what Gagarin calls 'evidentiary' torture, which was used by parties in a private dispute, by agreement and always on a slave, for the purpose of verifying a statement of one party or the other.[2] Recent studies of this matter, including my own,[3] have disputed the evidentiary role that this torture (*basanos*) played in the Athenian courts, whether or not it was always meant to decide the dispute with regard to which it was to be employed and whether or not it was actually employed much at all. Gagarin

As well as the editors and referees of this collection, my thanks are also due to Tom Figueira, Bill Fortenbaugh, Mark Golden, and the Dean of the Faculty of Humanities of the University of Calgary for help received during the preparation of this paper.

[1] Thür 1977: 59 n. 1 points out that there are twenty-three cases where such challenges are mentioned; Hunter 1994: 93–4 lists them in a convenient table. How often torture actually took place is a matter for debate and speculation. M. I. Finley (1980: 94) argued that 'there is in fact no ground for supposing anything one way or the other about the frequency of torture; there is only the free field of ideological play provided by the comic poets and orators'. His view is too sceptical.

[2] Gagarin 1996: 3. For instances of judicial torture, see Thuc. 8. 92; Lys. 13. 59; Dem. 18. 133; Aeschin. 3. 224; Din. 1. 63; and Plut. *Nic.* 30.

[3] e.g. Gagarin 1996; Thür 1996; Mirhady 1996. The most significant study is that of Thür 1977, whose conclusions have been followed by Gagarin 1990 and 1996 and Todd 1990.

sees evidentiary torture as a 'legal fiction', the challenge to which was used by a litigant to lend credibility to his report of what a slave might have said.[4] Thür sees the discussions of torture as a judicial relic used to embarrass the opponent.[5] I have simply concluded that evidentiary torture did sometimes take place and that it was decisive.[6] But no one has yet offered a sufficient explanation as to why the Athenians tortured their slaves in this context.[7] Whether the torture actually took place or was only a legal fiction or judicial relic, there has to have been a rationale for it in the minds of the Athenians, even if this rationale appears to us quite irrational. What will not suffice is simply to condemn the Athenian practice as 'an act of wanton and purposeless barbarity'.[8] Clearly, the Athenians believed it reliable when the correct procedures were followed.[9] Here I shall examine evidence from the Athenian law courts, from Aristotle, and from Athenian drama that reveal a consistent Athenian rationale for torture.

However, some points concerning its legal position need some brief comment. Gagarin, Thür, and I have taken differing positions on this issue. Together with Hunter, I have argued that a fulfilled *basanos*-challenge always decided the point in dispute. Gagarin (following Thür) has argued against this thesis, which was first put forward by Headlam over one hundred years ago.[10] There is likely no evidence that can decide the issue conclusively, and it is healthy

[4] Gagarin 1996: 1 *et passim*. By 'legal fiction' he states that he is employing the concept as it is used by Sir Henry Maine 1861: 21–2: 'an assumption which conceals, or attempts to conceal, the fact that a rule of law has undergone alteration, its letter remaining unchanged, its operation being modified'.

[5] Thür 1977 and 1996.

[6] Mirhady 1996.

[7] du Bois 1991 offers stimulating speculation about torture and its relationship to the Western philosophical tradition, but her approach hardly amounts to a sufficient historical explanation.

[8] MacDowell 1978: 246. For a collection of several similar judgements, see Gagarin 1996: 1.

[9] Thür 1977: 304 writes as follows: 'Der Grund . . . für die Beweiskraft einer Sklavenaussage war allein das *formrichtig durchgeführte Basanos-Verfahren*.' As Gagarin 1996: 7 writes, 'in their speeches they continually sing its praises and never once dispute the effectiveness of evidentiary basanos in general'. The author of Antiph. 2. 3. 4 argues that torture is only used where slaves have conspired with their owners, but most of the evidence contradicts this claim. Our own sensitivities are shaken by this fact, but it is also true that the Athenians were not the last to have believed in the reliability of torture when attempting to obtain or verify information. For a very accessible study of the forensic use of torture in Europe and England during the late Renaissance and early modern era, see Langbein 1977.

[10] Headlam 1893 and 1894. Thür 1977: 205–14 refers to it as 'Headlams Theorie'.

that the two views have been so fully expressed. Indeed, there is scarcely any disagreement on a vast number of points made by Gagarin and Thür, as well as by myself and Hunter, about the legal and rhetorical strategies employed by litigants in court. There is no doubt that the *basanos*-challenge was often used simply as a rhetorical tactic without any intention on the part of the challenger to have a *basanos* carried out. Litigants often refer to a *basanos* when in fact all that they can rightfully mean is a refused *basanos*-challenge. For example, in one speech Demosthenes refers to a challenge he made to support the testimony of his witnesses, 'so that there might be credibility for them from the *basanos*'.[11] He means, however, only the *basanos*-challenge.

Without reiterating what has already been said, I wish to make just a few points in response to the recent arguments of Gagarin and Thür. First, about Demosthenes 53. 25, where Apollodorus argues that if he had tortured the slaves privately 'everything would have been disputed' by his opponents.[12] If the evidence derived from the *basanos* had been disputed in court, the *basanos* would indeed have been indecisive. Contrary to what Gagarin has argued, however, Apollodorus does not actually envision such an indecisive *basanos*.[13] He is not denying the decisiveness of the *basanos*, but rather arguing that by even having accepted the challenge according to the terms set out by his opponents, he would have conceded his case, since he would have conceded his opponents' right to offer the slaves for private torture and thus their ownership of them, which is what he is disputing. Even if he had won through the *basanos*, the circumstances of the torture would have been invalid and the results, indeed everything about the procedure (*hapanta*), would easily have been contested. The opponents would have changed their position with regard to the correctness of the challenge and a new dispute would have resulted. Second, Gagarin's inference from Aristotle's discussion of arguments both for and against *basanos* in the *Rhetoric* (1. 15, 1376^{b}31–1377^{a}7), that the results of a *basanos* would be discussed in court by a litigant,[14] may likewise also be challenged. Earlier in the same chapter of the *Rhetoric* Aristotle offers arguments for use both for and against

[11] Dem. 29. 21: *ἵνα τὸ πιστὸν ἐκ τῆς βασάνου τούτοις ὑπάρχοι.*

[12] Dem. 53. 25: *ἀντελέγετ᾽ ἂν ἅπαντα ὑπὸ τούτων.*

[13] Gagarin 1996: 6.

[14] Ibid.

existing laws, but in fact none of the Attic orators even once has the temerity to criticize an existing law.[15] Aristotle's passion for symmetry (and reason) on such matters clearly gets the better of him; his comments about torture cannot be taken at face value as indications of actual Athenian practice in the *dikasterion*. Indeed, Aristotle makes no distinction between evidentiary, bilateral torture, and evidence derived from unilateral torture, such as that so thoroughly criticized in Antiphon 5. Third, the argument from silence, that if the *basanos* were automatically decisive 'we would still expect the orators to refer to previous instances of a completed *basanos*',[16] is likewise not compelling. In fact, we hear of no instance of evidentiary *basanos* that is indecisive either. I will argue below that its use did seem to depend on the disputants' willingness to seek a resolution short of going before the popular law court. That attitude could only have belonged to people who were unlikely to pursue an ongoing series of disputes.

The gap between the relative informality of procedures resulting from challenges, whether torture, oaths, or private arbitrations, and the formality of the *dikasterion* will always have required some fudging about the exact legal consequences of such attempts at out-of-court settlement. We know very little about the ways in which private settlements were regulated in the Athenian lawcode. We should not insist on seeing the language of dispute closure (*aphexis, appallage*) in order to infer that the parties agreed on the decisiveness of the *basanos*. Indeed, even today we may decide to settle a dispute by flipping a coin, but the irrationality of such a procedure does not diminish the possibility of its decisiveness, or legal validity. We should certainly avoid putting too much weight on the evidence of Pollux 8. 62 alone, although I have found him to be a very useful source.[17] Pollux describes a challenge (*proklesis*) as a resolution (*lusis*) of a dispute by various means, including the *basanos*, oath, private arbitration, and *marturia*. Thür cannot imagine an out-of-court settlement by means of *marturia*,[18] but what is meant by *marturia* here is not 'testimony in court', although that is the technical meaning of the word, but simply a statement (out of court, like the *diamarturia*) by someone qualified to give testimony in court, that is, a free adult male, without a requirement that he swear to his statement. Presumably he could be made

[15] Cf. Carey 1996.

[16] Gagarin 1996: 6.

[17] Mirhady 1996: 119 n. 7.

[18] Thür 1996: 134.

accountable for it by a suit for false testimony (*pseudomarturion*), like the witness in Isocrates 21. 11–12.

Whether or not we believe that the outcome of the evidentiary *basanos* was automatically decisive for a dispute, whether the challenge was simply always only a rhetorical trick or legal fiction, the challenges do presuppose that there is a rationale for using torture. If we relinquish what Peters calls the 'moral and sentimental outrage'[19] surrounding the word 'torture', which flows from our own abhorrence of the practice and prevents us from seeing a reasoning for it in any other culture or time, it may be possible for us to see what that rationale was for the Athenians. As I will show, the Athenian use of torture was based on several assumptions that we do not share. We reject slavery and the view that there are any people who are, or were, natural slaves. From our own experience we know that Aristotle, among other Greeks, was incorrect to believe that any race of people is naturally more or less intelligent than another. We also deny the efficacy (as well as the morality) of violence as a means of eliciting information from people. However, beyond these assumptions there are still attempts today to devise methods by which the veracity of statements can be guaranteed. In court an oath is administered to witnesses and legal penalties are applied to prevent perjury. In some situations, and without coercion, polygraph testing has achieved a very high degree of accuracy. Yet no method is foolproof and in many ways we find ourselves in a position similar to the Athenians when faced with a person, like an Athenian slave, who knows the truth about some critical point and yet has many reasons to lie. I hope to show that the Athenians, who clearly did not respect the 'human rights' of their slaves, applied what they thought to be an effective means of eliciting truth through violence.

The Athenian rationale for torture is not revealed simply by linguistic analysis. The word for torture, *basanos*, originally meant a touchstone used to test the purity of precious metals.[20] Since Bacchylides refers to *basanos* as the 'Lydian stone' (fr. 14), the word itself is probably of Eastern origin. The metaphorical usage of the word as a 'touchstone' for the quality of human character would suggest itself to us even if it did not appear in poets like Theognis

[19] Peters 1996: 3.

[20] See Thür 1977: 13–15, who cites Arist. *Hist. an.* 8. 12 597^{b}2–3; [*Col.*] 3. 7 793^b; Harpocration, s.v. *basanos*; and Pl. *Gorg.* 486d; and du Bois 1991: 9–34.

and Pindar.[21] Likewise, the appearance of the word in the semantic field of forceful interrogation should hardly be surprising. Even in metallurgy there is an aspect of roughing up the object of the test.

Four points must be recognized, I believe, in order to construct the Athenian rationale: first, slaves in Athens often knew things that were critical to legal disputes; second, the Athenians limited participation in judicial proceedings to free males, who alone had legal responsibility, while slaves, women, and children participated only through men, who were legally responsible for them, or indirectly, through extra-judicial procedures; third, the Athenians felt no compunction about using physical force against their slaves; and fourth, the Athenians believed that by torturing a slave correctly the truth could be achieved with reasonable certainty. Clearly, the last step is the most difficult, but the first three should not be left unexamined.

In her book *Policing Athens*, Hunter has catalogued a wide range of information to which slaves had access and which became at times critical in legal disputes. These included events in the lives of their owners, the family history of their household, business and financial matters.[22] Slaves had an almost ubiquitous presence in Athens, and it was recognized that they followed and understood what was going on. Of particular significance for our reconstruction of the Athenian rationale for torturing their slaves is the fact that an acknowledgement of a slave's actual knowledge of the specific points under dispute had to be claimed in order for a challenge to torture that slave to be plausible. The argument in Lysias 4. 15–16 underlines this point: the speaker claims that if his opponent's servants had been tortured, they would have gratified their owner and lied, but a slave that was commonly owned by both the opponent and the speaker not only knew more but would have spoken the truth. On a first reading, this passage might appear to tell against an Athenian belief in the universal efficacy of torture, since it appears to be acknowledged that some slaves, i.e. those wholly owned by the opponent, could lie under torture. But what the speaker is really arguing is that, unlike the jointly owned slave, his opponent's servants do not actually know the critical facts. We

[21] Theognis 1. 417, 450, 1105; Pindar *Pyth.* 10. 105. The word can often be translated as 'test' or 'interrogation', with no implication of violence; see n. 53, below.

[22] Hunter 1994: 74–5 and 94–5.

may infer that according to Athenian ideology slaves who knew the truth about a particular matter could be relied on to tell the truth under torture, but if slaves who did not know anything were tortured, they would make something up (cf. (Ant.) *Tetr.* 1. 2. 7). For this reason, to the Athenians it was crucial for the challenge and its acceptance that the two parties agree that the slaves to be tortured really did know the facts to be decided (cf. Dem. 29. 38). Any impression we might have had that the Athenians arbitrarily grabbed and tortured a slave who had no knowledge of the dispute in question should be discarded.

Like women and children in Athens, slaves lacked legal responsibility. They could neither bring a suit nor act as a witness, let alone serve as a judge. A slave who brought some serious matter to light, as a *menutes*, might expect to be rewarded with freedom (Lys. 5. 3; Antiph. 2. 3. 4). His statements might even be referred to as a *marturia* (see Ant. 1. 30, 5. 34), but this was a loose usage of the term. The information obtained in this way had to be pursued and corroborated by other evidence. Slaves could not be witnesses (*martures*) because they could not be held legally accountable for their testimony by being charged for false testimony (2. 4. 7). Neither could women or children.[23] The usual method of indicating a woman's knowledge of specific information was to make a challenge to have the woman swear an oath about what she knew,[24] but there must have been a tremendous social (and thus rhetorical) cost for a litigant to suggest bringing a free woman into the public sphere in this way. At any rate, we hear of it only seldom.

The third point in my reconstruction of the Athenian rationale, which involves the Athenian slave's vulnerability to violence, has also been thoroughly explored in the literature. The Athenians took violence inflicted upon citizens and other free people very seriously.[25] Moreover, no one could harm another man's slave. But a free person seems to have been free to do violence to his own slaves, short of murdering them.[26] The *basanos*-challenge and its

[23] Admittedly, the possibility of a child knowing anything relevant to a legal dispute in Athens does not arise in our sources. On the issue of children's rights, see Golden 1994.

[24] See Isae. 12. 9; Dem. 39. 3–4, 40. 10, 45. 27; Mirhady 1991; Gagarin 1997a.

[25] See Herman 1994, who, however, does not discuss violence against slaves, and D. Cohen 1995.

[26] See Golden 1984: 101–2. At the end of an article in which he catalogues a gruesome array of brutal punishments enacted by judges during the Roman principate, MacMullen

refusal may in many situations have implied a social, as well as legal challenge. As Lycurgus points out (1. 29), the *basanos* is both most just and most 'democratic', by which he means, I take it, that it is an institution that supports the societal norms of the Athenian democracy by confirming the status distinctions between Athenian citizens and their slaves.[27] The proposer of the challenge claims a superiority over his slaves both for himself and for the person he challenges. To reject the challenge was also to deny the opportunity to exercise this superiority. On the other hand, to accept the challenge was also to accept in the sharing of proprietary rights over the slave: it gave the opponent of the owner the right to inflict bodily pain on a slave whom he must normally have avoided striking. There is good evidence for the use of torture within households (e.g. Lys. 1. 16–19; Dem. 48. 16–18). By making the challenge to evidentiary *basanos*, the litigant also invited his opponent into the sphere of private settlement, almost as if the two men were deciding their dispute within the same household.[28] To this extent the *basanos*-challenge is even stronger than private arbitration. While avoiding a lengthier public process, private arbitration still relies on a third party, which the *basanos* does not (aside from the poor slave, who is of course normally a part of one of the two households). The *basanos*-challenge discussed in Antiphon 1, which involves a dispute between two brothers, takes place in a grey area between household and polis, which has led to complications in interpreting the potential legal force of the *basanos*.[29] The speaker seems both to have urged his brother to torture his slaves unilaterally and then also to have challenged him formally to do so (1. 6). Even then, he departed from usual practice by proposing that his brother, who owned the slaves, perform the torture, instead of demanding to torture them himself. As a brother and thus in an irregular status with regard to his opponent, he does not insist on actual participation in the torture, only on being present when it is performed and on the use of his questions, submitted in

(1986: 164) looks for an explanation for this behaviour in the social and political conditions of the empire, in which 'as men were distanced from each other, they might try to bend others to their will with ever greater ferocity; for they could not imagine themselves having to suffer what they inflicted on their inferiors'. The situation of the Athenians toward their slaves seems analogous.

[27] See Hunter 1992 and her chapter in this volume.

[28] On private arbitration, see Hunter 1994: 55–62.

[29] See Mirhady 1996: 125–6.

writing (1. 10). He was content to preserve the guise of a unilateral torture within a single household.

A case in which the speaker again disparages a challenge proffered by his opponent offers an interesting nuance. In Demosthenes 37. 41, the defendant, Nicoboulus, objects to a challenge that had been brought by his opponent, Pantaenetus, whom he describes as a sycophant. He objects on the grounds that it would have put him in the position of either losing two talents, which was the amount of Pantaenetus' claim, or, as he says, of having lost the 'body and life' of his slave, for which he would have been compensated only whatever the torturer had decided. He envisions having had to surrender his slave to the torturer, who would have followed Pantaenetus' directions to torture the slave to death, unless he got the response that Pantaenetus wanted. The implication is that Pantaenetus perverted the *basanos*-challenge by forcing Nicoboulus to decide between surrendering either the two talents or the life of a perfectly good slave. This is part and parcel of Nicoboulus' characterization of Pantaenetus as a sycophant: the emphasis is on the vexatiousness of Pantaenetus' suit and litigation strategy, not on concern for the slave. Indeed, in his own self-portrait, Nicoboulus says that he actually acceded finally to the challenge because he wished to get through the situation with, as he says, 'a preponderance of justice' on his side,[30] this being represented by the evidentiary-*basanos* procedure. Despite Pantaenctus' sycophancy, there was great pressure on Nicoboulus to seek this friendly, 'just', resolution.

Slaves in Athens possessed knowledge that was critical to many legal disputes and the Athenians felt little or no compunction about inflicting physical torments on them. But why did they think that inflicting such torments would get that knowledge with any reliability? We have no passage from an Athenian forensic oration in which an evidentiary *basanos* is fully carried out,[31] so we cannot examine how the process functioned in practice. However, in two speeches (5 and 6) the orator Antiphon reveals several points that, when combined with other passages, illuminate the issue significantly.

In Antiphon's fifth speech, Euxitheus has been accused of

[30] Dem. 37. 41.

[31] Ar. *Ran.* 615–70 details torture resulting from a challenge, but the rationale for the scene is comic and care must be taken in its interpretation. See below, pp. 70–1.

murdering Herodes. The family of Herodes has brought Euxitheus into court in Athens after having tortured two men, one of them a slave, the other free.[32] The family bought the slave from its former owners and conducted the torture unilaterally. It was thus not an evidentiary *basanos* at all, since it did not take place as a result of an agreement of both sides. In the course of the torture the slave finally implicated both Euxitheus and himself and as a result, after the torture was completed, the family executed the slave. On what grounds the free person was tortured is never stated, but, according to Euxitheus, the free man did not change his story throughout the torture and he continued to deny Euxitheus' involvement in Herodes' death.

In section 31 Euxitheus describes the torture of the slave: he argues that the slave was misled by a promise of freedom in exchange for a specific answer.[33] The implication for the Athenian rationale for torture is that the tortured person should not know what answer the torturer favours, as would be the case if a truly neutral party conducted the torture, or if it were conducted bilaterally by the disputing parties, which is the method most familiar to us from the other challenges. Aristotle (*Rhet.* 1. 15 1377^a3–5) and Anaximenes (*Rh. Al.* 16. 3) echo Antiphon almost exactly in giving as an argument against torture the fact that the slave gives whatever answer he thinks will end the torture most quickly. Anaximenes (*Rh. Al.* 13. 2) also mentions that 'it is necessary that those who are whipped agree to just what those who

[32] There is a detailed discussion of the torture (interrogation) of the two men by Gagarin 1988: 57–78. Cf. Thür 1977: 48–57.

[33] Antiph. 5. 31: 'Direct your attention to the torture itself, what sort of procedure was followed. Just as much as these men promised the slave his freedom and had it in their power to stop his suffering, so much was he persuaded by both these facts to lie against me—he hoped to gain freedom and wished immediately to be set free from the torture.' *προσέχετε δὲ τὸν νοῦν αὐτῇ τῇ βασάνῳ, οἵα γεγένηται. ὁ μὲν γὰρ δοῦλος, ᾧ ἴσως οὗτοι τοῦτο μὲν ἐλευθερίαν ὑπέσχοντο. τοῦτο δ' ἐπὶ τούτοις ἦν παύσασθαι κακούμενον αὐτόν, ἴσως ὑπ' ἀμφοῖν πεισθεὶς κατεψεύσατό μου, τὴν μὲν ἐλευθερίαν ἐλπίσας οἴσεσθαι, τῆς δὲ βασάνου εἰς τὸ παραχρῆμα βουλόμενος ἀπηλλάχθαι.* Gagarin 1988: 73 n. 40 follows many interpreters in understanding *ἴσως . . . ἴσως* as a qualification ('perhaps . . . perhaps') that 'seriously weakens Euxitheus' contention'. But it seems highly unlikely that Euxitheus would needlessly qualify his contention. Accordingly, I translate the words simply as correlative adverbs, although I can point to no other instance where this occurs. In his recent translation (Gagarin and MacDowell 1998: 58), Gagarin translates *ἴσως* as 'probably', but the syntax would still require this qualification to apply not only to his claim that they promised the slave his freedom but also to his statement that his opponents had the power to stop his suffering, which they *certainly* had, not *probably*.

are whipping [them] command'. These criticisms are clearly only appropriate against a *basanos* that is conducted unilaterally, not against the evidentiary *basanos*.[34]

Thür points out that in the surviving speeches, as a rule, the proposed torturer (*basanistes*) is not a third party, but the opponent of the slave's owner (see Antiph. 1. 10 for the exception that proves the rule). According to his view, the owner nevertheless maintains a *Kontrollerecht*: he may stop the torture if it is not carried out according to the agreement.[35] More recently Thür has emphasized that the control could not be exercised arbitrarily: once the torture was properly begun, there would be great pressure to see it through.[36] According to Thür's view, the incentive for the slave to tell the truth would result from a *Chancengleichheit*, a balance between the immediate power of the owner's opponent, who generally performed the torture, and the ongoing power of the owner, whose mere presence intimidated the slave.

Euxitheus explains that his friends were present when the slave was executed and that they protested the action, arguing that if Euxitheus had a chance to repeat the torture, he would get the opposite result. As it was, the slave recanted when faced with death. We can suspect that the slave saw that it was in his interest to encourage the party that was attempting to save his life by assuring them that if he lived, he would sing their tune. The procedure that was followed in the torture appears to have had two stages:[37] at first, after having been whipped but before being put on the wheel, the slave was asked whether Euxitheus had committed the murder and had denied it. Then he changed his story as a result of the extreme torture on the wheel. The way that Antiphon describes the opposition between 'using (or adhering to) the truth' on the one hand and 'using the compulsion' on the other indicates that if the torture had been performed properly, compulsion and truth would not have been in opposition. Rather, the slave would use the compulsion as a reason to reveal the truth. His owner could

[34] Antiph. 1. 10 and Dem. 37. 42 also illustrate the importance of who performs the torture.

[35] Thür 1977: 163–4 and 189.

[36] Thür 1996: 133.

[37] 5. 40: 'But look, at first, before being put on the wheel, the man used the truth (τῇ ἀληθείᾳ ἐχρῆτο) up to the last compulsion, and he acquitted me of the charge; but when he was put on the wheel, then he used the compulsion (τῇ ἀνάγκῃ χρώμενος) and lied against me because he wished to be released from the torture.'

not blame him if he were 'compelled' to tell the truth. In the *Rhetoric*, Aristotle says that compulsion (*ananke*) is the reason for the credibility of the *basanos*,[38] and there are several passages that identify acting under compulsion as a distinguishing mark of servile behaviour.[39]

The description of the torture of the free man comes in section 49.[40] The citizenship of the man, who remains nameless throughout, is nowhere given, which seems consistent with his being a freedman, or at best someone of very low status. The events transpired outside of Athens, so Athenian laws, which would have precluded the torture of a free man, were not necessarily observed. Euxitheus certainly makes no explicit point, however, that the torture of this man was illegal. He seems very likely to be the attendant of his who is mentioned in section 24. Because the family of Herodes suspected Euxitheus' guilt, they seized this attendant and tortured him. That he was brought into the court as a witness seems implied by Euxitheus' saying that the man has said nothing bad against him 'even up to now'. Euxitheus makes much of the inability of the prosecutors to offer the 'free' man his freedom.[41] But he is also said to have had a greater commitment to truth than the slave; he sticks to it, come what may. Antiphon presents this argument as if it is representative of a psychological difference between free and slave.

In his speech *On the Chorus Boy*, Antiphon takes a more positive attitude toward the *basanos*. The case does not depend on what anyone can say about what actually happened. It is agreed by both

[38] *Rhet.* 1. 15 1376^{b}32. It seems to me that the use of the word ἀνάγκη as a modal qualifier describing the 'necessity' of something being the case may also play a role here. Anaximenes *Rh. Al.* 16. 1 mentions that the *basanos* is elicited from someone who is 'unwilling'.

[39] e.g. Antiph. 1. 10; Arist. *Rhet.* 1. 11. 4 1370^{a}9–10, 1. 14. 7 1375^{a}16. See also the discussion of *Prometheus Bound*, below, p. 68.

[40] 5. 49–50: 'The free man has never said anything bad about me even up to now (οὐδέπω νῦν), even though he was tortured in the same way. It was not possible for them to offer him freedom the way they had persuaded the other. He wished to stick with the truth and run the risk of suffering whatever was necessary.' This passage has occasioned at least one interpreter to argue (wrongly) that it was legal to torture free non-citizens in Athens. See Bushala 1968 and (*contra*) Carey 1988. Aside from this speech there is possible evidence for the torturing of free non-citizens in only two other speeches. I join Thür 1977: 20–2 in rejecting both. The *pallake* in Antiph. 1 and the *meirakion* in Lys. 3 are both slaves. Hunter (1994: 174–6) provides a more nuanced account of the entire issue.

[41] I suspect that this 'free' man was actually Euxitheus' slave at the time of the torture and that he was subsequently freed by him for loyally sticking to his story, which was interpreted as indicative of his 'free' character. But Gagarin (1997b: 192) seems on surest ground in describing him as 'probably a Mytilenean of low standing'.

sides that a chorus boy died after being given a drug that was meant to improve his vocal performance. The question is whether the chorus-producer can be held responsible inasmuch as his agents administered the drug that led inadvertently to the misfortune. However, one part of his defence is devoted, reasonably enough, to confirming that the chorus-producer had no proximate involvement with the events that led to the boy's death. Before the main trial there was a series of preliminary hearings at one of which the producer made a challenge.[42] The passage again allows comparison of how interrogation of free and slave occurs. It is assumed that the free will tell the truth, as Antiphon writes, 'for their own sake and for the sake of justice', the implication being that there would be legal recourse (through a *dike pseudomarturion*) against those not telling the truth. With regard to the slaves, it appears possible that their statements would be accepted without torture, but the widest possible latitude is given to the opponent to conduct torture of any slave in any way he wishes. The chorus-producer knows that there was no one who could credibly say that he had personally administered the drug—and the case does not depend on this issue—so he is willing to appear extremely co-operative in his challenge. By the same token, the passage can serve as a model of how, according to Athenian ideology, the co-operative and just litigant was supposed to behave with regard to evidentiary *basanos*. The litigant allows his opponent access to any slave, so long as the slave is named in advance, and he allows interrogation initially without torture. If that interrogation is deemed inadequate by the opponent, they may proceed to whatever form of torture the opponent wishes, presumably so long as it is specified in advance.

What Antiphon writes for the chorus-producer about the parallel role of torture and the oath gives a particularly intriguing clue to the Athenian rationale for torture.[43] Here the oath and torture

[42] Antiph. 6. 23: 'I called on him to take as many witnesses as he liked to those people who had been present (at the poisoning and) said the name of each one. (I told him) to question and test the free in the manner that is necessary for free people, who would say for their own sake and for the sake of justice the truth of what occurred. (And I told him to question) the slaves, and if they appeared to him to be speaking the truth, (fine), if not, I said I was ready to hand over all my people for torture, and if he demanded some slaves of others, I agreed to persuade the master to hand them over to him to torture in whatever way he wished.'

[43] 6. 25: 'You know, gentlemen, that the compulsions (ἀνάγκαι) themselves are the strongest and greatest of those among human beings, and the tests (ἔλεγχοι) of them are the clearest and most credible concerning justice, when there are both free people who know

are explicitly compared as analogous methods of guaranteeing true statements from free people and slaves. What distinguishes them, to my mind, is their reversed sequences of time. A free person swears an oath with the expectation that if he (or she) commits perjury he or his descendants will suffer a grave punishment *in the future*. The slave, however, is made to suffer gravely *immediately*. If the torture is properly performed, he ought to be made to believe that as soon as he tells the truth, he will be released from the suffering.

Antiphon underlines this view with the statement that a slave under torture, in order to be free of his present suffering, will even say something that will lead to his own death later. A similar argument appears in Lysias 4. 35: the slave is unable fully to appreciate future consequences and is concerned only with his current bodily discomfort. Likewise, Aristotle says in the *Politics* that slaves are unable to appreciate future consequences in the way free people can.[44] While a free person valued his own future and that of his family, a slave could value only his body, and only for the moment.[45]

and slaves, and that it is possible to compel the free by means of oaths and pledges, which are very great and important for the free, and that it is possible to compel slaves by other compulsive measures under which, even though they may die after speaking, nevertheless they are compelled to speak the truth; for the present compulsion is stronger for each of them than the one which is going to be (ἡ γὰρ παροῦσα ἀνάγκη ἑκάστῳ ἰσχυροτέρα ἐστὶ τῆς μελλούσης ἔσεσθαι).' Dem. 29. 5–6 also juxtaposes challenges to torture and oath, the oath being the means for Demosthenes' mother to make a formal statement.

[44] Arist. *Pol.* 1. 2 1252ᵃ31–4: 'That which can foresee by means of understanding is by nature a leader and master, and that which can work with its body is led and is by nature a slave.' τὸ μὲν γὰρ δυνάμενον τῇ διανοίᾳ προορᾶν ἄρχον φύσει καὶ δεσπόζον φύσει, τὸ δὲ δυνάμενον τῷ σώματι πονεῖν ἀρχόμενον καὶ φύσει δοῦλον. Cf. 1. 5 1254ᵇ21–2 and Fortenbaugh 1977.

[45] For Aristotle and, apparently, in Athenian law, a free woman is distinguished from a slave in that, although both lack judicial rights, her deliberative faculty is recognized as equivalent to a man's, even if it lacks authority (*Pol.* 1. 13 1260ᵃ12–15). Accordingly, Athenian women could swear oaths that might result in the resolution of disputes because they could fully appreciate the consequences of perjury. See Mirhady 1991. It is interesting to note that according to [Plut.] *X Orat.* 842a, a law ascribed to Lycurgus prohibited Athenians and those resident at Athens from purchasing a captive who was of free birth. Problems of textual interpretation and authenticity preclude using the law as the basis of any firm conclusion, but since Lycurgus alone among the orators talks about the 'naturalness' of the efficacy of torture on slaves (1. 32) and his statements and legislation come close to the time when Aristotle was writing, we might infer that Macedonian domination was starting to challenge traditional notions of Greekness and slavery. The evidence smacks of attempts to rationalize a social and ethnic hierarchy that is under siege. Nevertheless, they may also be statements of views long embedded in Athenian social thought, even if not explicitly expressed before. Cf. Garnsey 1996: 3 n. 7.

It should not be overlooked that litigants also employ that most common of Greek rhetorical motifs with regard to *basanos*, the preference for action (*ergon*) over speech (*logos*) (see, e.g., Lyc. 1. 29). Issues of oral speech versus written text, speech versus action, and formalized speech (like oaths) versus informal speech were all prevalent in the classical period. The *basanos* created a formalized procedure that made speech into action in a way that went far beyond the requirements of Aristotelian *energeia*, which demands that words be 'brought before the eyes' (*Rhet.* 3. 11 $1411^{b}22$–$1412^{a}10$). Statements educed through torture do not just involve visual metaphor, for the slave's speech is not simply spoken. It *happens* in an extremely vivid way, with the crack of the whip and screams. As illogical and irrelevant as this may seem to us, for the Athenians I suspect it was crucial for the credibility of the procedure.

In view of this evidence, it does seem possible to draw some conclusions about what in general made the evidentiary *basanos* a rational and credible procedure for the Athenians. As long as a slave was under the control of his owner, he was likely to say whatever the owner wished,[46] unless he was given reason not to. Through the torture, therefore, the torturer attempted to create conditions under which the slave would believe that his best interest lay in telling the truth. Since the Athenians believed that slaves identified their best interests only with their immediate bodily welfare (Dem. 40. 41 and 49. 56), torture was applied to ensure that no considerations affected the slave's thoughts other than the directive to tell the truth.[47] The passages cited from Antiphon 5 detail the importance for the credibility of the torture that it be conducted bilaterally. This condition ensured that the slave would not attempt simply to please a single torturer.

[46] The likelihood that slaves lie for the sake of their owners is mentioned, for instance, in Lys. 4. 16; Lycurgus 1. 30; Isoc. 17. 55. Although his owner does not play any role in the dispute, the description of the behaviour of the slave Lampis in Dem. 34 is consistent with what is said here. Although a ship captain (*naukleros* 6), he was certainly a slave (*oiketes* 5, *pais* 10), who worked independently of his owner. He does not testify before a *dikasterion*—nor in Athens as a slave could he have testified before a *dikasterion*, let alone been a party to a suit (*pace* E. Cohen 1992: 97). The speaker's opponents appear to have requested private arbitration (18) in order to avoid the procedural rules of the *dikasterion*, which would have precluded a slave. Before the private arbitrator Lampis changed his story, testifying 'whatever he wanted' (18) and lamely claiming that he had been 'out of his mind' when he had agreed to support Chrysippus' position (20). An Athenian expected such fickleness from a slave.

[47] Isoc. 17. 15 suggests that in some cases the 'torture' might go no further than verbal questioning. Cf. Gagarin 1996: 2 n. 8.

Several passages from Athenian drama confirm these conclusions. They attest to the Athenians' familiarity with, and acceptance of, both judicial and evidentiary torture. One of the central tensions running through *Prometheus Bound*, for instance, is the pitting of Zeus' otherwise unchecked power against Prometheus' knowledge of Zeus' eventual fate. Zeus inflicts torments on Prometheus both as punishment for Prometheus' having championed the cause of humanity and in an attempt to learn Prometheus' secret (93, 100, 227, 256, 989). On his arrival, Hermes utters threats (952), to which Prometheus responds that he will not adopt Hermes' servility (*latreia* 966). Prometheus invites Zeus to use whatever torments he likes: Zeus has no device or torture by which to seize the information (989). Prometheus is able to withstand Zeus' torments because he is neither servile (cf. 966) nor womanish (1003),[48] and so the torments dishonour him (97; cf. 157), inasmuch as they reflect the treatment normally given to a slave. However, he asserts his status as a god (93, 157; cf. 927)—in a civic context we might expect him to assert his freeborn status[49]—so that although he admits to fear (126), the torture does not break him (173–4). In Athens Prometheus would be the Greek male, who ideally has a Promethean understanding of his lot (105, 248, 935) and is thus steadfast against torture, like the free man in Antiphon 5. The ideology thus declares that Athenian citizens are not tortured both because it would be uncivilized (*athetos* 150) and because they can successfully resist it.

In Sophocles' *Oedipus Tyrannus*, a Servant is brought in near the end of Oedipus' inquiry into the death of Laius, and it is his evidence that proves decisive. We should note that the issue over which the Servant is to give evidence, that is, whether Oedipus was the child whom the Servant had long ago given to the Messenger, is by no means the central question of the inquiry. But for the play it is nevertheless decisive because it finally makes sense out of so many of the other indications. The issue that was to be resolved through torture in Athens might often have appeared

[48] The status of a free woman with regard to torture seems to lie somewhere between that of a slave and a free male. According to the Aristotelian framework (see above, n. 44), she may be capable of swearing an oath because she can foresee the consequences of perjury, but she is also susceptible to torture because her deliberative faculty is not authoritative over her emotions, which would be affected by torture.

[49] In Athenian law it was normally forbidden to torture citizens: see Andoc. 1. 43; Isoc. 17. 14; Lys. 4. 14, 13. 27 and 59.

insignificant for the central point of inquiry in legal disputes also, so that despite Gagarin's concerns,[50] 'insignificance' seems no impediment to the decisiveness of a fulfilled *basanos*-challenge.

The situation in the *Oedipus* differs, however, from that imagined in most of the law-court orations since it is conducted unilaterally, in the manner of a judicial torture, rather than bilaterally, like the evidentiary torturing envisioned in the speeches. Nevertheless, Oedipus' motives for the torture are genuine—he wants the truth even though he will find it disagreeable—so the passage does offer sound evidence for the mentality and the methods that were actually employed during forceful interrogations in Athens. The speeches from the law courts cannot supply this evidence because no properly performed evidentiary *basanos* is ever fully described in them. However, the most widely used rhetorical argument concerning *basanos*, 'that concerning both private and public matters nothing is more credible or truer',[51] indicates clearly that a consistent mentality was at play regarding both evidentiary torture, where private matters were at stake, and judicial torture, where public inquiries were pursued.

It is pointed out that the Servant was born into Laius' house (1123)—he knows its history—and he has already been described as trustworthy (*pistos*) by the standards appropriate to a herdsman (1118). Oedipus initially asks the Servant whether he has ever had dealings with the Messenger from Corinth. At first the Servant attempts to plead a poor memory (1131), but with some gentle prompting from the Messenger he recalls their association (1141). However, to the Messenger's claim that Oedipus is the baby they once exchanged, the immediate point at issue, the Servant insists on silence (1146). At Oedipus' first threat of punishment the Servant asks whether he has done wrong (1149) and claims that the Messenger is ignorant (1151). So Oedipus insists that if the Servant will not speak to gratify him (*pros charin*), he will speak in cries (*klaion*), whereupon the slave pleads, as an old man, not to be tortured. The torture is then applied, however, by twisting back the Servant's hands (1154),[52] and he immediately surrenders

[50] Gagarin 1996: 6; cf. Mirhady 1996: 121.

[51] Isoc. 17. 54; Anax. *Rh. Al.* 16. 1; Isae. 8. 12; Dem. 30. 37.

[52] It seems to be at the discretion of the play's director whether or not the hands are actually bent back—I think they are. At any rate, it is either actual torture or the immediate threat of it that breaks the Servant's will. In the hypothesis of a play that appears to have had

the information. To Oedipus' insistence on the whole story, the Servant claims that the more he tells, the more his destruction will result. Nevertheless, as a result of the torture the full truth is revealed. Oedipus, who is elsewhere described as a benevolent master, is here portrayed using torture on a slave as a matter of course.

The slave's evidence is accepted as decisive, but details are also sought in order to confirm its accuracy. This point deserves to be underlined, since it seems likely that it played a role in evidentiary *basanos* for private disputes as well. Although with evidentiary *basanos* only one of two possible answers was sought—favouring either the one party or the other—once the truth started to come out, it seems likely that the slave would be questioned further in order to reveal details that would confirm the story to everyone's satisfaction, bystanders as well as the two parties. This questioning is different from the investigation that followed the revelation of an informer (*menutes*), which relied on other sources as well. It might even reveal that the slave's evidence was equivocal, that the decisiveness of the *basanos* would have to be abandoned. But I assume that once that moment was achieved in which it appeared that the slave's will to resist telling the truth was broken, then everyone present would assume that the truth was now all coming out. The details would serve only to confirm the central point.

In Aristophanes' *Frogs*, torture is also employed at a crucial moment. Dionysus has so humbled himself that he has donned the clothing of his slave, Xanthias. At the gate to Hades, he and Xanthias encounter a Gatekeeper who accuses Xanthias, who is dressed like Heracles, of having stolen Cerberus. Xanthias attempts to avoid the Gatekeeper's prosecution by swearing in an improvised oath-challenge that he never stole anything from the Gatekeeper (612–13), but he anticipates that his oath will not be accepted and goes on to make an offer of his slave on the point at issue (615–18).[53] The offer is called just, and they agree on the method of torture, which turns out to be whipping. The Gatekeeper even agrees to pay damages, to Xanthias, for damage to

several thematic parallels with the *Oedipus Tyrannus*, Euripides' *Alexandros*, a herdsman is also 'compelled to tell the truth' about Alexander's provenance.

[53] *Pace* Gagarin 1996: 15 n. 53, I think that this passage does fit the model of an evidentiary *basanos* very well, that is, until it turns out that both 'owner' and 'slave' will be whipped. On some of the ideological ramifications of the passage, see Konstan 1995: 67–8.

his 'slave'. Although the events that follow break down into farce, they also demonstrate the fecklessness of Dionysus, who allows himself to be treated like a slave. In fact, they demonstrate this fecklessness to the god also. He therefore reasserts his divine identity (631) and goes on to take on a determinant role in the second half of the play.

The comedy of this scene depends on its familiarity to the Athenians. The evidentiary *basanos* does not appear as an archaic relic but as a ready-to-hand solution for the dispute, and it decisively turns the play around, even though both the challenge and the torture are based on comic premises. After the parabasis we learn that Xanthias has returned to his servile role, and his owner is complimented by Xanthias' fellow slave for not beating him (738–9). Indeed, the slaves even find solidarity in sharing the status of being whipped (756). Despite its failure to achieve an unequivocal result, the torture scene seems to re-establish a correct social hierarchy.[54]

Passages from Athenian drama are certainly problematic evidence to use in regard to social and legal practices of Athens, but they do afford a glimpse of the mentality of the Athenians, which saw the torture of slaves both as an entirely appropriate way of eliciting the truth and as a means for confirming their own social hierarchy and cohesion. It is difficult for us properly to imagine the social constructs that gave rise to their rationale for torture, but clearly the best reason for the Athenians to have used torture was that it worked. The Athenians lived with, worked with, and dealt with their slaves in almost every aspect of their lives, and the evidence indicates that they used torture and the threat of torture with some regularity both within their own homes and as part of judicial inquiries. We must assume that they did so with some confidence. The evidence from the Athenian courts, from Aristotle, and from the Athenian stage points consistently in this direction.

The requirements that were placed on the evidentiary *basanos*,

[54] At Ar. *Ach.* 110, Dicaeopolis also uses the language of the *basanos* and threatens the 'Persian' Pseudartabas in his interrogation. Such treatment of the 'barbarian' like a slave conforms to Aristotle's views of barbarians as slaves by nature (cf. *Pol.* $1252^{a}24$–$1255^{b}40$ and $1284^{b}35$–$1285^{b}33$). Except for the central torture scene in the *Frogs*, the other fifteen instances of βάσανος/βασανίζω in Aristophanes (*Ach.* 647; *Eq.* 513, 1212; *Vesp.* 547; *Lys.* 478; *Thesm.* 626, 800–1; *Ran.* 802, 826, 1121, 1123, 1367; *Ecc.* 523, 748) do not relate to torture. They refer simply to a test or questioning.

which involved the agreement of both disputants to the terms and conditions of the torture, did not adversely restrict its ability to achieve the full truth.[55] There must have been many disputes (not reported) in which this procedure became a very attractive alternative to the costs and uncertainties of a full process before a popular court (the source of our evidence). Not all disputes would have been entered into with an attitude of winning at any cost. Some will have involved wrongs done by the slaves themselves; these in particular would have recommended the *basanos* as a resolution. But many disputes will also not have had so much at stake that anyone would have sought a resolution other than one like the *basanos* (or an oath or a private arbitration) that served to preserve the social fabric. Even the threat of only minor pain, when mutually exercised on a slave by the disputing parties, probably elicited the truth to their satisfaction in many situations. There is no need to imagine, as does Thür,[56] that the evidentiary *basanos* was a relic from a time in which one of the parties was forced to deliver a slave for torture. Thür is right, however, that, concerning very important matters, litigants were likely loath to depend on the answer of a slave.[57] In many such disputes, like those that are reported to us in the speeches, the evidentiary *basanos* is fictive, a rhetorical trick, but for its rhetorical effectiveness it had to rely on a reality in which violence and torture against slaves was common practice. Otherwise, the fiction would have been utterly transparent.

References

Bushala, E. W. 1968. 'Torture of Non-Citizens in Homicide Investigations', *GRBS* 9: 61–8.

Carey, C. 1988. 'A Note on Torture in Athenian Homicide Cases', *Historia* 37: 241–5.

—— 1996. '*Nomos* in Attic Rhetoric and Oratory', *JHS* 116: 33–46.

Cohen, D. 1995. *Law, Violence and Community in Classical Athens*. Cambridge.

[55] *Pace* Gagarin 1996: 16.
[56] Thür 1996: 134.
[57] Ibid.

COHEN, E. E. 1992. *Athenian Economy and Society: A Banking Perspective*. Princeton.

DU BOIS, P. 1991. *Torture and Truth*. New York.

FINLEY, M. I. 1980. *Ancient Slavery and Modern Ideology*. New York.

FORTENBAUGH, W. W. 1977. 'Aristotle on Slaves and Women', in J. Barnes et al. (eds.), *Articles on Aristotle*, ii: *Ethics and Politics*. London. 135–9.

GAGARIN, M. 1988. *The Murder of Herodes: A Study of Antiphon 5*. Frankfurt.

—— 1990. 'The Nature of Proofs in Antiphon', *CP* 85: 22–32.

—— 1996. 'The Torture of Slaves in Athenian Law', *CP* 91: 1–18.

—— 1997a. 'Oaths and Oath-Challenges in Greek law', in G. Thür and J. Vélissaropoulos-Karakostas (eds.), *Symposion 1995*. Cologne. 125–34.

—— (ed.) 1997b. *Antiphon: The Speeches*. Cambridge.

GAGARIN, M. and D. M. MACDOWELL (tr.) 1998. *Antiphon and Andocides*. Austin.

GARNSEY, P. 1996. *Ideas of Slavery from Aristotle to Augustine*. Cambridge.

GOLDEN, M. 1984. '*Pais*, "Child" and "Slave"', *Ant. Cl.* 54: 91–104.

—— 1994. 'Children's Rights, Children's Speech and *Agamemnon*', in R. G. Osborne and S. Hornblower (eds.), *Ritual, Finance, Politics: Athenian Democratic Accounts Presented to David Lewis*. Oxford. 371–83.

HEADLAM, J. W. 1893. 'On the *πρόκλησις εἰς βάσανον* in Attic Law', *CR* 7: 1–5.

—— 1894. 'Slave Torture in Athens', *CR* 8: 136–7.

HERMAN, G. 1994. 'How Violent was Athenian Society?', in R. G. Osborne and S. Hornblower (eds.), *Ritual, Finance, Politics: Athenian Democratic Accounts Presented to David Lewis*. Oxford. 99–118.

HUNTER, V. J. 1992. 'Constructing the Body of the Citizen: Corporal Punishment in Classical Athens', *EMC/CV* 36: 271–91.

—— 1994. *Policing Athens: Social Control in the Attic Lawsuits, 420–320 BC*. Princeton.

KONSTAN, D. 1995. *Greek Comedy and Ideology*. New York and Oxford.

LANGBEIN, J. H. 1977. *Torture and the Law of Proof*. Chicago.

MACDOWELL, D. M. 1978. *The Law in Classical Athens*. London.

MACMULLEN, R. 1986. 'Judicial Savagery in the Roman Empire', *Chiron* 16: 147–66.

MAINE, H. 1861. *Ancient Law*. London.

MIRHADY, D. C. 1991. 'The Oath-Challenge in Athens', *CQ* 41: 78–83.

—— 1996. 'Torture and Rhetoric in Athens', *JHS* 116: 119–31.

PETERS, E. 1996 (1985). *Torture*. Philadelphia (expanded edn.; original edn., Oxford 1985).

THÜR, G. 1977. *Beweisführung vor den Schwurgerichtshöfen Athens. Die Proklesis zur Basanos*. Vienna.

—— 1996. 'Reply to D. C. Mirhady: Torture and Rhetoric in Athens', *JHS* 116: 132–4.

Todd, S. C. 1990. 'The Purpose of Evidence in Athenian Courts', in P. Cartledge, P. Millett, and S. C. Todd (eds.), *Nomos: Essays in Athenian Law, Politics and Society*. Cambridge. 19–40.

4

Religion, Imperial Politics, and the Offering of Freedom to Slaves

Robin Osborne

The Athenians ran their judicial system without a paid body of investigators and without a paid judiciary. This created various problems for them, particularly how to ensure that breaches of the law were punished and that legal procedures were followed. In this chapter I am concerned with the first of these questions, and particularly with the secondary effects of measures that are adopted to ensure that wrongdoing is prosecuted. I want to suggest that a proper understanding of what Athenians were, and were not, normally prepared to do in order to encourage prosecution sheds important light both upon Athenian social relations and upon the nature of Athenian relations with the allied cities of Ceos in particular, and perhaps the allies of the Second Athenian Confederacy more generally.

Athenian fears about the consequences of leaving prosecution in private hands seem to me well revealed in the construction of the sycophant. Prosecutors of certain offences were regularly given monetary rewards at Athens. The offences that qualified for such rewards seem to have been those where the only party directly injured was the state: rewards encourage denunciation of public debtors, the prosecution of those who have breached commercial regulations or regulations covering other state-controlled activities, and the prosecution of those who breach citizenship regulations by marriage to a non-Athenian.[1] Although surviving evidence does

The seed for this paper was sowed by a question Oliver Russ asked me in a tutorial; it grew at the request of Virginia Hunter and Jonathan Edmondson, and has been cultivated by the comments and criticisms of those at the Toronto conference, of the readers for Oxford University Press, and of Peter Rhodes. I am very grateful to all for the ways in which they have winnowed my thoughts.

[1] See Osborne 1985: 44–8, and, on *phasis*, MacDowell 1992.

not suggest that any of these prosecutions was undertaken with abusive frequency by those out for the reward, the man who prosecuted to enrich himself became the bogey of the Athenian courtroom.[2] It is true that sycophants are presented in some cases as enriching themselves through illegal as well as legal means, but the construct nevertheless well reveals Athenian anxiety about the consequences of rewarding prosecution. As the famous scene in Aristophanes' *Wealth* (850–950) makes clear, the Athenians were well aware that sycophancy went hand in hand with volunteer prosecution: *ho boulomenos* was the sycophant under another name.

But what exactly was wrong with voluntarily prosecuting in order to gain the reward for doing so? For us any moral objections are likely to be to individuals who enrich themselves by prosecuting others who have done them no harm, but that can hardly be the Athenian concern, since the whole system of rewarding prosecution is set up to encourage such behaviour. More in line, perhaps, with Athenian concerns, would be the professionalism often imputed to the sycophant. In a system which did not permit professional advocacy, the more a man became the regular watch-dog for the public interest, the greater the conflict with the whole ethos of the system. But if Sally Humphreys and I, followed by David Cohen, have been right to put stress on the courts as places in which social standing is contested, there may be another aspect also to take into account.[3]

Prosecuting on behalf of the state was anomalous in a system of personal prosecution. In a *dike*, where the injured party attempted to restore his position *vis-à-vis* the man who had done him the injury, the courts can be seen to be a publicly visible, non-violent, mechanism for determining the social position of the parties within the community. In a *graphe*, open to third-party prosecutors, the possibility arises of an individual not already involved in a dispute using the courts to score against the man prosecuted, that is, of the courts being used to open rather than to continue or close a dispute and to settle scores not related to the subject of the charge. That

[2] On prosecution for reward, its motives, and frequency, see the debate between Osborne 1990 and Harvey 1990. If the extent to which the category 'sycophant' was merely an abusive construct can still be debated, that it was in part an abusive construct is, I think, beyond dispute. See further Christ 1992 on the links between sycophancy and the deception of the people, and on the use of the charge by the Thirty.

[3] Humphreys 1985 and 1986; Osborne 1985; and Cohen 1995. See now also Foxhall 1996.

this might indeed be a concern is suggested by Apollodorus' insistence that he brings an *apographe* against Nicostratus only because he had indeed been previously wronged by him ([Dem.] 53. 1). Breaches of mining regulations, or marrying non-Athenian women, did not systematically damage the interests of specific individual Athenian citizens, for had they done so it would not have been necessary to institute rewards to ensure their prosecution, but citizens with other grievances against such individuals will have leapt at the opportunity to prosecute them for these offences. The successful prosecutor in these actions stood to gain not only money but the chance to reposition himself with regard to the party prosecuted. In coming to the aid of the state, the prosecutor in these actions laid claim for himself to the social superiority stemming from successful action which in a sense rightly belonged to the state. That 'social superiority' might of course bring its dangers as well as its advantages—a man convicted of mining offences might well be on the lookout for opportunities to return charges against his prosecutor—but that only serves to stress the real changes in personal standing which such prosecutions entailed.

But why should it provoke general animosity that the successful prosecutor in prosecutions that were rewarded stood not only to gain money but also to enhance his own position in relationship to the convicted party? Although our data are not rich enough to enable proof, I suggest that in general court actions at Athens were, and were expected to be, struggles between parties who were effectively social equals. There obviously were thefts from the rich by the poor, and thefts by and from individuals unknown to each other, but theft is precisely an offence which state officers can be brought in to help clear up. The majority of the offences represented in the orators are offences committed by and on individuals known to each other: Midias' attack on Demosthenes (Dem. 21), or Conon's on Ariston (Dem. 54), or his guardians' offence against Demosthenes (Dem. 27–8), are my model cases in this regard. Whoever wins the prosecution in such cases repositions himself within a small social group, within his own sector of society. But if a man prosecutes in a case where the offence did not affect him and where the person prosecuted is not known to him, the social repositioning which successful prosecution entails could involve very much more than a small social group. The penalty to which prosecutors of *graphai* were liable presumably often served to scare prosecutors from different social circles away from such actions. But prosecutions that are rewarded represent a particularly severe case of third-party prosecutions in which both the size of the potential monetary rewards, and the possible gap between the social position of the prosecutor and the prosecuted, threatened to make successful prosecution seriously socially disruptive.

The threat of seriously redrawing the social boundaries arguably links taking up prosecution on behalf of the state with being prepared to buy off prosecution. As I have argued on a previous occasion (Osborne 1990), to understand blackmail we need to look into the reasons why men buy off prosecutions as well as the motives of those who allow themselves to be bought off. The calculation made by the man who buys out his potential prosecutor is presumably that the risks and costs of conviction outweigh the costs of buying the prosecution out. Among the costs we should take account of social as well as monetary costs: for a wealthy man to lose a case to one who was socially inferior involved not just loss of money but loss of honour. Crito's famous adoption of Archedemus as a friend who by his own litigious activity kept off potential prosecutors (Xen. *Mem.* 2. 9) saved him both from the risk of losing a case to an inferior opponent and from demeaning himself by the implication of equality with his opponents that would be involved if he himself prosecuted those who threatened him with actions. The cost was that he ended up treating the poor man Archedemus as his equal.

I have revisited the sycophant at some length here, trying to draw out more from the evidence than I have previously done, because I have come to think that Athenian embarrassment over the sycophant, whom they could neither live with nor live without, is but one aspect of a more fundamental conflict between law enforcement and the maintenance of existing social relations. It is hard to see that it is in the interests of law enforcement that, for example, in at least some *graphai* the rights of metics to prosecute should apparently have been restricted,[4] and for that reason this restriction has puzzled scholars. But it is easy to see that, as far as the established social order was concerned, the possibility of metics taking on such third-party prosecutions was even more

[4] Todd 1993: 196, quoting Dem. 21. 47 (on *hubris*), and [Dem.] 59. 64–6 (on *xenias*); MacDowell 1990: 265. See also Patterson, this volume.

threatening than letting Athenians from different social groups employ such actions against one another. Aspects of the politics of Athenian controls on metic prosecutions have recently been clarified by Matthew Christ;[5] in this chapter I want to turn my attention still further down the social scale, and from prosecution to witnesses.

The ability successfully to prosecute wrongdoing depends not simply on there being men able and willing to prosecute, but upon there being people able and willing to give evidence. Just as not everyone was able, in the sense of permitted, to bring a prosecution, so not everyone was able, permitted, to be a witness. 'Athenian law, like English law, had clearly defined exclusionary rules of evidence; but whereas our rules are concerned with categories either of evidence or of information, the Athenian rules were concerned with categories of people: slaves, women and children could not be witnesses.'[6] Stephen Todd, whose words these are, draws attention to the way modern scholars have found the Athenian rules 'remarkable', and suggests that the way to understand them is to see that witnesses in Athenian courts play a different function from witnesses in English courts. In particular he lays stress on the role of the witness as supporter and on (false) witnessing for one party being an offence against the other party. For Todd women, children, and slaves cannot witness because they cannot be sued for false witness: if a person cannot be sued for false witness no risk attaches to their witnessing, but if no risk attaches to the witnessing the witness cannot be seen to be giving support. Another way of putting this is that the real issue does not concern witnessing at all; it concerns legal capacity in general. What needs explaining is not why slaves, women, and children cannot be witnesses, but why they cannot be sued on a charge of false witness (*dike pseudomarturion*).

As Simon Goldhill has recently pointed out, the exclusion of women from the law courts was even more radical than legal scholars have in the past maintained: not only could they not sue, no citizen woman appears in court even when being sued, and women were not even produced to cry.[7] Goldhill goes too far

[5] Christ 1992: 341–6.

[6] Todd 1990: 25–6.

[7] Goldhill 1994: 357–60: as far as the prosecutor was concerned, Neaera, who is pointed to in court ([Dem.] 59. 14, 17), was not an *aste*. Crying children are a different matter, see e.g. Ar. *Vesp*. 568–73 and 976–8.

when he says that 'The lawcourt remained fundamentally a citizen audience judging the contests of citizens', for the Athenians' courts were available to metics even if their interventions as prosecutors were resented.[8] But Goldhill's inclinations are surely in the right direction: we should think of the law courts as an arena for a competition for a self-selecting élite, not as a tribunal before which all have the right to appear. The trying of military offences before a court of soldiers is but an extension of the way in which courts ideally operate within a closed group. Court cases are about the redistribution of honour: to be allowed to compete there is to be allowed to acquire honour, indeed to acquire differential honour. All who play in this arena stand to win or lose, remove or bestow, honour; it is not only those who prosecute who compete. Witnesses as supporters of speakers in court play a part in the gaining of honour by the successful party, and share the loss of honour by the losing party. To allow children, women, or slaves into court as witnesses would be to allow them shares of honour, setting up differential honours in the juvenile, servile, or female community, and to allow them a part in sharing out honour to men.

If I am right to suggest that in the differentiated world of male honour, there is considerable embarrassment about procedures that allow, let alone encourage, groups who stand at very different points of the honorific scale to come into conflict, then it is not difficult to understand the impossibility of allowing parties quite outside that world to bestow or remove male honour. How could the honour of the male citizen be made to depend upon the supporting action and word of a woman or of a slave who was treated just like a free man (i.e. voluntarily given and not tortured)?[9] What is important here is the notion of supporting action: women could not be witnesses, but their oaths could be used as evidence. Slaves could not be witnesses, but their word under torture could be used as evidence or perhaps even settle a case.[10] What the oath and the torture did was to turn the slave's or woman's words into something that had the same status as the laws which speeches might

[8] See further Patterson, this volume.

[9] Compare Lys. 4. 19, cited by Thür 1996: 134.

[10] On the question of the precise value of evidence elicited by torture, see the debate between Mirhady 1996 and Thür 1996; in the absence of any known case in which the challenge to torture was accepted, the point at issue seems to me impossible finally to resolve. For further discussion of the rationale for torture, see Mirhady's chapter in this volume.

also quote: they ceased to be statements of support and became evidence to be cited. The words were separated from the person; neither the free woman nor the slave appeared in court to give personal backing to their statement: it was not the individuals who had uttered the statement, but the gods who presided over the oath, in the case of free women, and the violence done to their bodies, in the case of slaves, that served to guarantee the woman's or slave's words. It is not, I think, accidental that arguments for and against believing the evidence of slaves are always generalized: the person of the slave could not be allowed to be accorded importance.[11]

Yet there were indeed formal circumstances in which slaves could not only give testimony, voluntarily and without submitting to torture, but could even effectively initiate the prosecution of citizens.[12] What the circumstances were in which denunciation (*menusis*) by slaves was allowed is not easy to recover from the limited evidence, though modern handbooks write confidently enough about 'certain cases with serious religious and/or political consequences' or 'cases of treason, sacrilege, or theft of public money'.[13]

The circumstance in which we are best informed about *menusis* is the affair of the Herms and the Mysteries. Thucydides (6. 27. 2) says of the mutilation of the Herms: 'No one knew who had done it, but the offenders were publicly sought out by means of great rewards for informing, and it was also decreed that if anyone knew of any other impiety that had been committed, any citizen or stranger or slave that wished to should give information with impunity.' Andocides (1. 20) expects his audience in 399 BC to believe that the conditions under which information was given in 415 were that: 'if someone gave true information, they had impunity; if false, they were executed'. He also (1. 27–8, cf. 40) records that the rewards for informing were set at 1,000 drachmas by a decree of Cleonymus, and at 10,000 drachmas by a decree of Pisander, and he lays out in detail the content of four acts of informing about the Mysteries (1. 13–18) and two acts of informing about the Herms. The information is given by slaves in two cases

[11] For examples of both arguments, see Antiph. 5. 31–3 and 6. 25–7.

[12] Whether these circumstances included homicide trials is disputed: for recent discussion, see Todd 1990: 26 n. 12; Carey 1988: 241 n. 1.

[13] Quotations from Todd 1993: 187 and Harrison 1968: 171 respectively.

(Andromachus and Lydus), a metic (Teucrus) in one case, a woman (Agariste, of Alcmaeonid family (Davies *APF* 382–3)) in one case, and a citizen (Dioclides) in one case. Agariste, it is of some interest to note, informs on an event held in a house not her own (Charmides') in which the participants do not, on Andocides' record at least, include her husband. But both the slaves give information against their owners, in one case of events at the master's house, in the other of events in which the master took part.

From the point of view of slaves and informing, four points are to be noted. First, it is specifically about impiety that information is sought. Second, two separate rewards have to be offered. This may mark impatience on the part of the Athenians in general, or it may mark a desire by Pisander to cap the enthusiasm shown by Cleonymus for nailing down the culprits, but it would certainly seem to indicate that neither the offer of freedom and impunity alone, nor even the possibility of a 1,000 drachmas reward, was enough to elicit information from slaves. Third, it seems extremely unlikely that Andromachus and Lydus were the only slaves in the know, yet they alone came forward. The fourth point is that although slaves have considerably more incentive to inform, it is a metic, Teucrus, who gives information for reasons that seem most likely to be wholly personal (partly mercenary and partly desire to secure continued residence in Athens (though we cannot entirely exclude that both Teucrus and Agariste had religious motives for informing)), and it is a citizen, Dioclides, who is convicted of giving false information.

The other Athenian literary evidence about *menusis* by slaves comes from Lysias. In the speech about the sacred olive (7. 16) the speaker states that the silence of his slaves is strong evidence in his favour, since they could have their freedom by giving information against him. In the fragment of the speech defending Callias on the charge of *hierosulia* (5. 5) the speaker claims that if Callias is convicted (on the information given by his slaves), then all slaves will in future look to gain their freedom not by serving their masters well but by laying false information against them. He claims that the slaves will, if Callias is acquitted, simply stay in their current position, while if he is convicted they will enjoy freedom, and he uses the fact that they stand to gain from the conviction as a *prima facie* reason for doubting their evidence (5. 4). Both these cases once more concern religious offences.

All this evidence, therefore, concerns religious offences. While it may be the political implications that ensure that rewards for informing are offered in 415 BC, there is no reason to think that anything more than an act of impiety was needed to make freedom available to the slave giving information. But is this concentration on religious offences simply a matter of the chance that these alone are mentioned in our sources? One good reason for thinking not, is that the argument used in Lysias 7 is one that might readily be wheeled out by a defendant on any charge for which the procedure of *menusis* was available. Of the particular suggestions made, and much repeated, by recent scholars, that *menusis* was available against political subversives seems ruled out by its not appearing either in the decree of Demophantus (Andoc. 1. 96–8) or in the tyranny law of 337 BC (*SEG* XII. 87);[14] that it may have been available against treason is rendered attractive only by the way in which Xenophon (*Hell.* 1. 7. 22) has Euryptolemus imply that a single law covered *prodosia* and *hierosulia*; there is no positive evidence.[15]

The absence of provision for slave informers in the tyranny and subversion laws looks particularly significant in the light of practice elsewhere. At almost the same moment as the Athenians passed the decree of Demophantus, the Thasians passed a law rewarding those that inform about plots for constitutional revolution (ML 83). Both the provision regarding Thasos itself and that regarding its settlements abroad allow for slave informers—who are to be granted freedom and the same monetary reward as that offered to free persons: 1,000 staters on Thasos, 200 at settlements abroad. In the

[14] *SEG* XII. 87 is not the complete law about conspiracy to overthrow democracy, and we cannot exclude the possibility that if we had the complete law we would find a *menusis* clause.

[15] I have restricted my discussion here to *menusis* in the sense of bringing information for reward (of money or freedom). *Menusis* and its verbal cognates are used by the orators also to cover instances of informing which are not necessarily in an Athenian legal context at all (e.g. Lys. 2. 54 or 14. 37—which also casts its shadow over 14. 35) or where reward is probably or certainly not at issue (Lys. 3. 33 uses *menusis* to cover all slave testimony under torture; Lys. 29. 6 uses *menusis* of revealing a breach in a private contract). Antiphon 5. 34 plays on the possibility of slipping from *menusis* as the giving of information to *menusis* as the giving of information for reward. The repeated description of the activities of Agoratus in Lysias 13 as *menusis* (Lys. 13. 2, 18, 19, 21, 22, 32, 48, 51, 56) when official monetary reward for his laying of information is apparently never at issue (it is hard to believe that Lysias would have deliberately passed over such rewards, which would offer the opportunity further to denigrate Agoratus' character) may suggest that even the general use of the word had come to be associated particularly with slaves (as Agoratus is claimed to be).

early third century when Ilion offers rewards to those who slay tyrants, slaves are offered citizenship, 30 minas (half what citizens are to get), and a pension (perhaps at 1 drachma a day, half the citizen rate)—citizens also get a statue, free food in the *prytaneion*, and *proedria* (*OGIS* 218 = *Inscriptions Juridiques Grecques*, ii. 22). There is a lot of debate about the circumstances in which the Thasian law was passed. Pouilloux argued that it was passed by the oligarchy which installed itself in 411, but the grounds for this belief are not strong.[16] It would be easier to see that democrats would be keen to encourage the slaves of oligarchs to inform than that oligarchs would think it worth risking the results of encouraging slaves to tell tales, although the Roman oligarchy was prepared to reward slaves who revealed conspiracy.[17] But if this is a democratic law on Thasos, that only makes the contrast with Athens the more striking.

Further indirect evidence for the scope of *menusis* at Athens is provided by Plato *Laws*. Plato provides for freedom for informing slaves in two cases. First, in the case of children not taking care of their parents (932d): 'If the informant is a slave, he should be given his freedom; if he belongs to the criminal or his victim, he must be released by the authorities; and if he belongs to some other citizen, the public treasury is to see that the owner is reimbursed. Official action must be taken to stop anyone injuring him in revenge for giving information.' Second, in the case of a man finding treasure trove and not declaring it (914a): 'If the informant is a slave, then as a reward he will deservedly be presented with freedom by the state, which will give his master what he is worth, but if a slave fails to inform, he must be punished by death.' Neither of these two provisions is straightforwardly a religious matter, but both do have religious connections: Plato has his Athenian order that when treasure trove is found, 'On receiving the information the state should send to Delphi and in submission to the oracles of the god do whatever he ordains about the objects and the person who removed them', and he prefaces his law about respect for parents in the following way (930e–931a): 'Time-honoured cult observances all over the world fall into two categories. Man exalts some of the gods because he can see them with his own eyes, others he represents, by setting up statues of them, and believes that his worship of

[16] Pouilloux 1954: 139–62 and, for reservations, see commentary on ML 83.
[17] Livy 32. 26. 14 with Nippel 1995: 28.

these inanimate "gods" ensures him the abundant gratitude and benevolence of their real and living counterparts. This means that no one who has living in his house his father or mother, or their mothers and fathers, treasures old and frail, must ever forget that so long as he possesses such a "shrine" at his hearth and looks after it properly, no other objects of worship will ever do him as much good.' Even for those inclined to believe that Athenian procedure lurks behind the provisions in Plato's ideal city, these passages of *Laws* give no reason to suggest that the scope of *menusis* extended beyond matters in which the gods have an intimate concern.

That *menusis* should be restricted to patrolling the interests of the gods makes good sense in the light of my earlier discussion of courts and the redistribution of honour. This is best understood, I think, by thinking of actions where *menusis* is allowable as a subset of actions for which third-party prosecution was available. Third-party prosecution deals with cases where the nature either of the crime or of the victim more or less certainly excludes prosecution by the injured party, and it thus covers *hubris* and being wrongly shut up as an adulterer on the one hand and desertion, where it is the state that is hurt, and crimes against the gods on the other. What marks out crimes against the gods is that, unlike the state whose interests are embodied in individual citizens, their interests are not necessarily the interests of any particular individuals. Rewarding those who make it possible to convict offenders against the gods is a way of further suggesting that the punishment of the offender is not the informer's reward. Moreover, while if individuals do not act on behalf of the state, no action at all will be taken in response to the offence, if individuals do not act on behalf of the gods, the gods might themselves respond in extra-legal fashion. Arguably the state cannot afford *not* to take every possible measure to demonstrate its concern that the gods be not dishonoured. Arguably also, however, the gods live off the scale, in terms of human honour, and granting a role to slaves (and women) in redistributing honour to the gods is actually markedly less subversive than granting them a role in redistributing honour among male citizens.

Menusis at Athens can be seen, therefore, to be yet another feature of Athenian law which set Athenian citizens apart from other groups. So determined a separation is itself evidence for the concern of law being primarily the regulation of relations between citizens, rather than the control of human conduct.[18] The similarities between the exclusion of slaves and the exclusion of women suggest that, despite the formulation at the end of Lysias 5, we should emphasize not the class interests of citizens as slave-owners, and the reluctance of a slave-owning class to allow themselves to be threatened, individually or as a group, by their slaves, but the political exclusiveness of the enfranchised: it is the restriction of citizenship to males over the age of eighteen, not the exclusion of slaves and women from owning the means of production, that is directly threatened if citizens may be condemned on the evidence of women and slaves. In what I would see as an implicit debate between Virginia Hunter and Stephen Todd, I think that *menusis* weighs in for Todd: it is more important that the challenge to hand over a slave to be tortured is always refused than that the theoretical possibility of slaves giving evidence under torture exists.[19]

The story of *menusis* at Athens ought to end there. But it does not, for there is one more piece of evidence, and it is discordant. Sometime in the second quarter of the fourth century most probably, the Athenians set up on the Acropolis a long inscription of which only the bottom forty lines survive (*IG* II^2 1128; Tod *GHI* 162). They record the adoption by the cities of Carthaea, Coressus, and Iulis of regulations dictated by the Athenians which gave the Athenians a monopoly of Cean ruddle. Only the very end of the Carthaea decree is preserved, but most of the regulations adopted by the other two cities can be restored with some confidence. There is very interesting material here in terms of the different reactions of the two cities to Athens' instructions, and the degree of variation which Athens allows: Coressus inserts a fee that those who exploit and export the ruddle must pay to the shipowners, and specifies the magistrates to whom information about breaches of the law is to be given, but Iulis does neither.[20] But my interest here is in a feature common to both regulations, which is surely part of the instructions from Athens: the person bringing a prose-

[18] Compare Carey 1998 on what sorts of Athenian laws have a procedural and what sorts a substantive bias.

[19] Todd 1990: 33–5; Hunter 1994: ch. 3.

[20] We cannot be entirely certain whether what one city has and another lacks is the result of addition by the one or omission by the other. I discuss such 'editorial' questions with regard to Athenian decrees in Osborne 1999. In this case the fact that we have measures imposed by Athens may suggest that omission is the less likely possibility.

cution under these laws, whether by *phasis* or by *endeixis*, is to be rewarded, probably with half the value of the cargo involved. If the informer is a slave, he is to be freed as well as given a monetary reward. There is a difference between the regulations at Coressus and those at Iulis, in that Coressus alone differentiates between the case in which the slave belongs to the illegal exporter and the case in which he does not, but that difference does not affect the principle of the matter.

Harrison includes this inscription in the footnote with which he supports his claim that 'a slave might earn manumission . . . as informer against certain wrongdoers', and notes that 'the rule is Cean but seems to have been enforceable at Athens'.[21] Strictly this is correct, but given that the Athenian monopoly on their ruddle can hardly have been in the interests of the people of Coressus and Iulis, we can have no serious doubt that the clause about slave informers does not stem from local practice but from the Athenian demand. Athens was requiring the cities of Ceos to impose upon their citizens a mechanism for the enforcing of a non-religious law that, to judge by the evidence surveyed above, she did not impose on her own citizens. Athenian citizens were encouraged by the procedure of *phasis* to inform on other citizens who broke trading regulations, but we have no evidence that the rewards offered to prosecutors in cases brought by that procedure included the offer of freedom to slaves. When *phasis* is made the procedure for pursuing those who fail to accept silver coin which the public Certifier (*dokimastes*) has approved, the law recognizes that the *offender* may be a slave, but makes no provision for a slave bringing the *phasis* (Stroud 1974 = *SEG XXVI.* 72 ll. 28–32). Similarly, no provision is made for slaves bringing *phaseis* over Athenian property acquired in the territories of the allies of the Second Athenian Confederacy (Tod *GHI* 123. 44–6). The charter of the Second Athenian Confederacy suggests that Athens was keen to be seen by her new allies to be doing all that was reasonable to keep her nose clean; encouraging slaves to inform on rule-breaking Athenian masters would seem to be evidently beyond what is reasonable. Yet Cean slaves were to be encouraged, as Athenian slaves were not, to inform on their masters who broke an Athenian-imposed trading regulation.

The provisions for slave informers in the Cean ruddle decree,

[21] Harrison 1968: 182 n. 1.

and the contrast with the provisions which Athenians include in laws for home consumption, throw into relief both Athenian domestic practice and Athenian attitudes towards the allies of the Second Athenian Confederacy. The importance for Athenian domestic practice lies in the way that the Cean decrees show that it was perfectly conceivable to the Athenians that one might encourage slaves to inform in order to police laws. The Athens of Virginia Hunter, in which slaves denounce their masters 'as a form of social control, making the eyes and ears of the slaves in the household a potential danger to its free members', was an Athens which fourth-century Athenians could imagine.[22] The strict limitation in Athens of encouragement to slaves to inform in cases with religious implications was not a limitation that was unthinkingly inherited from the past, but one consciously reaffirmed every time the Athenians legislated anew and made no provision for slave information. Virginia Hunter's policing mechanism was rejected as repeatedly by the *nomothetai* as the challenge to torture slaves was rejected by prosecutors and defendants alike in the courts.

The importance for understanding Athens' relations to her Second Athenian Confederacy allies lies in Athens' willingness to impose upon them a procedure which she would not impose upon herself. We do not know why Athens wanted ruddle, indeed we do not know whether she wanted it at all.[23] Attempts by those of a Hasebroekian persuasion to prove that ruddle was a military necessity to Athens fall for lack of other evidence.[24] Whether we go for an economic explanation, which has no more evidence to back it up, or see it as a gratuitous obligation imposed for purely political reasons, parallel perhaps to the fifth-century weights and measures decree (ML 45),[25] there can be no doubt that the encouragement of slave informers here falls well outside the area in which slave informers were employed at Athens. Those who deny imperial ambitions to Athens do well to keep this inscription out of sight.[26] Those who consider the Second Athenian Confederacy to be a Free Alliance need either to find a way of mentioning this

[22] Hunter 1994: 70.

[23] On Cean ruddle, see now Photos-Jones et al. 1997.

[24] Hasebroek 1933: 140–1.

[25] See, briefly, Osborne 2000: no. 198.

[26] Cf. e.g. Harding 1995 for the denial of imperial ambitions. Harding omits the Cean ruddle inscription from his collection of fourth-century inscriptions: Harding 1985; contrast Brodersen, Günther, and Schmitt 1996.

decree without discussing it, or to date it down into the Social War or beyond, when even they allow that under provocation Athens was not as nice to her allies as she might have been.[27] Even F. H. Marshall seems to miss the full implications when he writes: 'Here is another piece of evidence to show that Athens was very ready to seize any opportunity of lessening the rights of the members of the Confederacy to her own advantage.'[28] For in respect of slave informers Athens lessens the rights of citizens of Ceos by comparison to those of citizens of Athens without any significant material or strategic advantage accruing to herself at all.

I want to argue that the Cean ruddle decree cuts both ways. That it is the only certain case of the Athenians inviting slaves to inform, except where the wrath of the gods is the alternative, suggests that the solidarity of the citizen population in the face of slaves was very strong. That it is in this particular case that the Athenians, exceptionally, invited slave informers seems to me to indicate the extent of Athenian imperialism. Past scholarship, in suggesting that there might be circumstances other than religious crimes in which slave informers might be sought, has underestimated the importance to Athenians of keeping slaves out of the courts and of not making citizen standing depend upon slave testimony; in doing so it has missed a way in which Athens was actually more restrictive about slaves than other places—for reasons I think not hard to understand.[29] At the same time, in focusing solely on the economic side of the ruddle inscription, past scholarship has missed an indicator of Athenian imperialism that swings the balance of overall interpretation of the Second Athenian Confederacy away from Free Alliance and towards empire. It is time this particular 'informer' received its reward.

Democracy and liberalism have become so intertwined in modern Western thought, and Athens has become so much the paradigmatic example of a Greek democratic regime, that it is a constant temptation to assume that Athens was a liberal state. That Athens was unusually restrictive in the rights it gave to women and unusually reluctant to extend citizenship to any born to non-Athenian parents has been increasingly stressed by recent work.[30]

[27] Cargill 1981: 138 manages to mention the decree without discussion.

[28] Marshall 1905: 50.

[29] Cf. Osborne 1995.

[30] For the former, see Schaps 1979. I have myself recently discussed the latter: Osborne 1997.

In this chapter I have drawn attention to the Athenian legal treatment of slaves, and in particular to the very restricted circumstances in which Athenians were prepared to offer their own slaves freedom in return for informing on illegal activities within the state, and have suggested that this should be seen as yet another area in which Athenian law defended the *status quo*, and in particular protected existing status boundaries. At the same time, I have drawn attention to a case in which the Athenians seem to have obliged another state to impose upon itself laws which the Athenians were not prepared to impose upon themselves, and I have argued that the Athenians did so aware that those laws were likely to be socially subversive.

For all that it restricted the vote to men over eighteen of free birth and Athenian parentage, classical Athens did involve a higher proportion of its population in its routine political decision-making than any democracy today can boast. But mass involvement in politics was not then, and is not now, a defence against prejudice or against the imposing upon others of restrictions and demands to which the imposers themselves do not submit. Double standards and the flexing of imperial muscles are unattractive, but we do well to be aware that the social structures upon which the institutions that we do admire were based were themselves dependent upon allowing different legal privileges to different social statuses.

References

BRODERSEN, K., W. GÜNTHER, and H. SCHMITT 1996. *Historische Griechische Inschriften in Übersetzung. Band II. Spätklassik und früher Hellenismus*. Darmstadt.

CAREY, C. 1988. 'A Note on Torture in Athenian Homicide Cases', *Historia* 37: 241–5.

—— 1998. 'The Shapes of Athenian Laws', *CQ* 48: 93–109.

CARGILL, J. 1981. *The Second Athenian League*. Berkeley.

CARTLEDGE, P., P. MILLETT, and S. C. TODD (eds.) 1990. *Nomos: Essays in Athenian Law, Politics and Society*. Cambridge.

CHRIST, M. 1992. 'Ostracism, Sycophancy, and the Deception of the Demos', *CQ* 42: 336–46.

COHEN, D. 1995. *Law, Violence and Community in Classical Athens.* Cambridge.

FOXHALL, L. 1996. 'The Law and the Lady: Women and Legal Proceedings in Classical Athens', in L. Foxhall and A. D. E. Lewis (eds.), *Greek Law in its Political Setting.* Oxford. 133–52.

GOLDHILL, S. 1994. 'Representing Democracy: Women at the Great Dionysia', in R. Osborne and S. Hornblower (eds.), *Ritual, Finance, Politics: Athenian Democratic Accounts Presented to David Lewis.* Oxford. 347–70.

HARDING, P. 1985. *From the End of the Peloponnesian War to the Battle of Ipsus: Translated Documents of Greece and Rome*, ii. Cambridge.

—— 1995. 'Athenian Foreign Policy in the Fourth Century', *Klio* 77: 105–25.

HARRISON, A. R. W. 1968. *The Law of Athens*, i: *The Family and Property.* Oxford.

HARVEY, F. D. 1990. 'The Sykophant and Sykophancy: Vexatious Redefinition?', in P. Cartledge, P. Millett, and S. Todd (eds.), *Nomos: Essays in Athenian Law, Politics and Society.* Cambridge. 103–22.

HASEBROEK, J. 1933. *Trade and Politics in Ancient Greece.* London.

HUMPHREYS, S. C. 1985. 'Social Relations on Stage: Witnesses in Classical Athens', in S. C. Humphreys (ed.), *The Discourse of Law: History and Anthropology.* London. i. 2: 313–69.

—— 1986. 'Kinship Patterns in the Athenian Courts', *GRBS* 27: 57–91.

HUNTER, V. J. 1994. *Policing Athens: Social Control in the Attic Lawsuits, 420–320 BC.* Princeton.

MACDOWELL, D. M. (ed.) 1990. *Demosthenes, Against Meidias (Oration 21).* Oxford.

—— 1992. 'The Athenian Procedure of *Phasis*', in M. Gagarin (ed.), *Symposion 1990: Vorträge zur griechischen und hellenistischen Rechtsgeschichte.* Cologne, Weimar, and Vienna. 187–98.

MARSHALL, F. H. 1905. *The Second Athenian Confederacy.* Cambridge.

MIRHADY, D. C. 1996. 'Torture and Rhetoric in Athens', *JHS* 116: 119–31.

NIPPEL, W. 1995. *Public Order in Ancient Rome.* Cambridge.

OSBORNE, R. G. 1985. 'Law in Action in Classical Athens', *JHS* 105: 40–58.

—— 1990. 'Vexatious Litigation in Classical Athens: Sykophancy and the Sykophant', in P. Cartledge, P. Millett, and S. C. Todd (eds.), *Nomos: Essays in Athenian Law, Politics and Society.* Cambridge. 83–102.

—— 1995. 'The Economics and Politics of Slavery at Athens', in A. Powell (ed.), *The Greek World.* London. 27–43.

—— 1997. 'Law, the Democratic Citizen and the Representation of Women in Classical Athens', *Past and Present* 155: 3–33.

—— 1999. 'Inscribing Performance', in S. Goldhill and R. G. Osborne (eds.), *Performance Culture and Athenian Democracy*. Cambridge.

—— 2000. *The Athenian Empire*. LACTOR 1, 4th edn. London.

Photos-Jones, E. S., A. Cottier, A. J. Hall, and L. G. Mendoni, 1997. 'Kean Miltos: The Well-Known Iron-Oxides of Antiquity', *ABSA* 92: 359–72.

Pouilloux, J. 1954. *Recherches sur l'histoire et les cultes de Thasos*, vol. i. Paris.

Schaps, D. M. 1979. *Economic Rights of Women in Ancient Greece*. Edinburgh.

Stroud, R. S. 1974. 'An Athenian Law on Silver Coinage', *Hesperia* 43: 157–88.

Thür, G. 1996. 'Reply to D. C. Mirhady: Torture and Rhetoric in Athens', *JHS* 116: 132–4.

Todd, S. C. 1990. 'The Purpose of Evidence in Athenian Courts', in P. Cartledge, P. Millett, and S. C. Todd (eds.), *Nomos: Essays in Athenian Law, Politics and Society*. Cambridge. 19–39.

—— 1993. *The Shape of Athenian Law*. Oxford.

5
The Hospitality of Athenian Justice: The Metic in Court

Cynthia Patterson

By common judgement, ancient and modern, the popular courts were the emblem of classical Athenian democracy. For better or worse, the Athenians themselves viewed the institution of popular justice delivered by large juries who were paid for their services as their own distinctive democratic invention.[1] Modern commentators have not failed to appreciate both the practical and ideological importance of the Athenian jury to the character and stability of Athenian democracy; in recent years careful (and sociologically informed) reading of the rhetoric of the Athenian courtroom has illuminated the courts as the focal point of the expression of democratic civic ideology and as a forum for élite display and mass validation of public status and prestige within the citizen community.[2] In the courts, Athenian litigants articulated for Athenian juries the meaning of their common citizenship in a democratic city. But the Athenians did not reserve their justice, nor their expression of civic ideology, for themselves. Another distinctive feature of Athenian democracy and Athenian justice—one also prized by the Athenians themselves—is what I have called in my title its hospitality (or *xenia*), the provision of judicial process and judgement to foreigners (*xenoi*). In this chapter, therefore, I add the

[1] Plato's negative judgement is well known: 'For I am told that Pericles made the Athenians idle and cowardly and talkative and covetous, because he was the first to establish pay for [jury] service among them' (Pl. *Gorg.* 515e, tr. Woodhead). On the democratic character of the courts, see e.g. Aristotle's comment on the importance of the popular courts for the development of Athenian democracy (*Ath. Pol.* 9); and for their distinctiveness to Athens, old Strepsiades' protest in the *Clouds*: '*That* Athens? Don't be ridiculous. Why, I can't see even a single lawcourt in session' (206–8, tr. Arrowsmith). For discussion of the Athenian reputation for litigiousness, see Todd 1993: 147–51.

[2] See Ober 1989; D. Cohen 1991; 1995; Hunter 1994; Foxhall and Lewis 1996; and Osborne in this volume.

theme of judicial *xenia* into the ideological mix of democratic legal rhetoric, with a view toward understanding both the character of Athens' judicial relations with its resident guests and also the way in which the presence of those outsiders in Athenian courts illuminates the élite insider position of all Athenians as shareholders in the Athenian state, its land, and its families.

The evaluation of Athenian justice for non-Athenians, like the evaluation of the Athenian courts themselves, was and is mixed. Thucydides presents the Athenians as proudly claiming that allies are judged according to the same laws as are Athenians and that their allies 'are used to being treated as equals' and so 'cease to feel grateful' for the legal access given them when they do not happen to be successful in court (1. 77). More cynically, the so-called Old Oligarch comments that the Athenian demos benefits greatly from this system of justice since 'each individual ally is compelled to flatter the common people of Athens, realizing that having come to Athens, the penalty or satisfaction that he receives at law depends solely upon the common people' (I. 18).[3] Clearly, there is room for debate on the topic of Athenian imperial justice. For the purposes of this short chapter, however, I focus more specifically on the figure of the *resident* foreigner, the 'metic', and on his and her legal status and rhetorical representation within the Athenian system of popular justice in the fourth century. In brief, I argue that whatever might have been his or her experience in prior formal or informal procedures of arbitration, the metic in court, facing the assembled *andres Athenaioi*, was a peculiarly isolated and thus vulnerable figure. Not a surprising thesis perhaps, but what I find interesting is the way in which, within a legal system that may indeed have given some degree of 'equal' or 'symmetrical' treatment to the resident alien, the metic was nonetheless isolated as an independent legal persona, without connection to the Athenian land or to Athenian household and kinship structures so important in Athenian litigation.[4] This isolation, I suggest, jeopardized the exercise of legal privilege and fostered the creation of the *topos* of the rootless metic whose loyalty and services might be held up to rebuke the wayward citizen, but whose crimes clearly revealed the dangers of the '*xenos* within'. For the resident alien in Athens,

[3] Tr. Moore.

[4] See, for example, the discussions of Humphreys 1985; 1986; Osborne 1985; and D. Cohen 1995: 163–80.

the *xenos metoikos*, legal rules alone could not provide status or security when he or she stood outside the protective net of Athenian kin and household relationships.

Before looking at the cast of metics in court, a few words of historical and legal background may be useful. Here, David Whitehead's *The Ideology of the Athenian Metic* (1977) remains an invaluable guide, providing a careful and clear-eyed discussion of both the historical institution of metic status and the social meaning of that status.[5] Whitehead argues that the formal registration and regulation in Athens of the resident alien, the '*xenos metoikos*' or simply '*metoikos*' (metic), began with Cleisthenes' restructuring of the tribal order in 508/7 and continued to develop as Athens grew into a major commercial and economic centre in the fifth and fourth centuries. By the end of the fifth century, it seems that any alien permanently residing in Athens was required to register as 'living in' a particular deme and to pay a tax (*metoikion*) of 12 drachmas per year for a man and 6 for a woman. As Whitehead (1977: 75–6) comments, this was a unique tax for Athens in that it was 'levied on the person rather than his (or her) property or activities'. In this way, the system gave legal recognition to the individual alien as such, male or female. That may sound like a good thing—and for a woman a better situation than the dependent legal status of Athenian women; but, as will be seen, to be an independent party was not in itself a secure position in the Athenian courts. The other side of independence could be isolation and vulnerability.

At the time of enrolment, the metic established a relationship with an Athenian citizen who became his or her representative (*prostates*); the extent of the role, legal or otherwise, played by the *prostates*, however, is unclear and so much debated.[6] Also, in addition to the basic *metoikion*, wealthy metics could be asked to pay further taxes and perform liturgies such as the *choregia*.[7] Finally, to

[5] Whitehead (1977: 1–5) discusses the character and substance of earlier discussion, including Clerc 1893, who articulated in a 'more reasoned and ample context' the thesis of Wilamowitz (1887) that metic status was a kind of 'quasi-citizenship'. For the present topic, Gauthier 1972 is most directly relevant. For post-Whitehead views of the metic, see Hansen 1991: 116–20 and Todd 1993: 194–9.

[6] Whitehead 1977: 90–1. Although Aristotle asserts in the *Politics* that the metic needed a *prostates* to prosecute or defend himself in court (*Pol.* 1275^{a}7–14), such figures are for the most part not found in surviving cases involving metics. (See also earlier discussion of Harrison 1968: 189–93; Gauthier 1972: 126–36; and, since Whitehead, Todd 1993: 198–9.)

[7] Whitehead 1977: 80–2. It is unclear whether or not female metics, if wealthy enough,

conclude this catalogue of metic responsibilities, male metics were expected to fight for the city in special metic regiments of the army (Thuc. 2. 13, 31).

What did the metic get in return? In addition to the opportunities for adventure, entertainment, and profit within an emerging urban centre, what protection did the Athenian polis give its enrolled metic? In answering these questions we enter more directly into the topic at hand, the legal status of the Athenian metic, and also into the contested area of the moral evaluation of this Athenian institution. As Whitehead observed (1977: 1–2), modern portrayal of Athenian metics has moved from viewing them as abused victims of a 'narrow-minded, vindictive citizenry' to privileged and highly valued 'quasi-citizens'. Without question, the institution reflects on the character of Athenian democracy, and evaluations of the institution are difficult to separate from the evaluator's view of that democracy. Whitehead is unimpressed by the logic and argument of both extreme views and aims instead at a 'morally neutral' analysis—perhaps even 'the first sensible investigation' (1977: 2). In fact, the greater burden of his analysis is to dispute the then orthodox view of the metic as 'privileged' alien; instead Whitehead emphasizes the restrictions and limitations of metic status as essentially an *alien* status constructed by the citizen demos in its own interest. Whitehead demonstrates (1977: 38) that identification as a metic was never a focus of pride for the aliens/metics themselves and supports his argument with a careful catalogue of epigraphic and literary references: the epitaphs of metics record their citizen or ethnic identity, not their metic status in Athens; and in drama the metic identity is for the most part 'something unattractive, precarious . . . and pathetic'. One remarkable example of this pathos is the figure of Sophocles' Antigone, who three times refers to herself as a metic, including her lament at lines 867–8: 'I go accursed, unwed, a metic.'[8] Using this metaphor she vividly articulates her isolation from both her city and her family. Divorced in sentiment and in physical presence

were so 'taxed'—I have found no evidence or discussion one way or the other. From Lysias' reference to his family's *choregia* (12. 20), it is clear that metic liturgies could be a source of public honour. However, the *trierarchia* was a service that was not apparently open to the metic, a clear indication of the essential political divide between citizen and foreigner (see Whitehead 1977: 80–2).

[8] See also *Antigone* 852 and 890.

from the members of her own family, she is indeed the quintessential metic.[9]

Thus, a euphemistic reading of metic status as privileged or honourable has little to recommend it. There remains, however, the significant question of the formal legal status and the formal protection and/or opportunities afforded the metic by the Athenian judicial system. Here Aristotle in the *Constitution of the Athenians* offers a straightforward account of fourth-century rules and procedures, which can serve as the basis for discussion. Although we should not assume that the system Aristotle described at the end of the fourth century was necessarily in place at the end of the fifth, his account can for present purposes be taken to reveal some essential principles and peculiarities of metic status in the eyes of Athenian law. When detailing the responsibilities of the polemarch in chapter 58, Aristotle says:

> He hears only private suits which involve metics, tax-exempt metics (*isoteleis*) and *proxenoi*; it is his duty to take them and divide them into ten groups, and to assign by lot one group to each of the ten tribes, and the jurors of the tribe must then bring them before the Arbitrators. The Polemarch himself introduces cases where a man is accused of disregarding his patron or not having one, and also cases involving inheritance and *epikleroi* of the metics; in other respects, the Polemarch performs for the metics the same duties as the Archon performs for citizens.[10]

Many things could be said about this passage—beginning with the clear significance of the jurisdiction of the polemarch (the 'war' archon) over metic affairs. The metic is a *xenos*, and, despite the conventions of *xenia*, relations with *xenoi* are always potentially hostile.[11] If a metic alien does not follow the rules and has no *prostates*, then it is up to the polemarch to pursue him and enforce

[9] Another group of well-known literary metics are the Eumenides of Aeschylus' *Oresteia*. Note that although they receive *timai* and a definite place within the Athenian polis, they are barren, unwed virgins, who protect Athenian families but have no families themselves. And while Athena prefers to use persuasion to convince them to stay and bless her city, she keeps her thunderbolt in reserve.

[10] *Ath. Pol.* 58, tr. J. M. Moore. Himself a metic, Aristotle may have been motivated to emphasize the legal status of metics as parallel if inferior to that of citizens; note also his comments in Book 3 of the *Politics* on the metic as a sort of 'qualified' citizen (1275^{a}16).

[11] Cf. Todd's comment: 'every *xenos* is logically an enemy', followed immediately by 'nevertheless, even in Homer, the word *xenos* has another and more positive meaning' (1993: 194).

the penalty for such behaviour, that is, slavery.[12] Abandoning (or abandoned by) his host the *prostates*, the metic is revealed and treated as an enemy: he is sold into slavery.

It is also worth noting that the polemarch assigns the cases for arbitration to the tribes *by lot*; since the metic has no tribe, his case cannot be assigned according to the defendant's tribe, as Aristotle had outlined for citizen arbitration procedures in an earlier chapter (*Ath. Pol.* 53). The metic is registered as 'living in' one deme or another, but he cannot own land in Attica and cannot be a part of, or have a share in, either deme or tribe. He stands apart—and on his own. Unlike the Athenian who comes to settle his cases before fellow tribesmen, the metic goes into public arbitration as a clear outsider, a *xenos* among *astoi*.[13]

The last section of chapter 58 seems more broadly protective of the metics' well-being and at first sight suggests a certain symmetry: the polemarch performs for the metics the same duties as the archon performs for citizens (including such things as presiding over disputes involving inheritance and *epikleroi* mentioned by Aristotle earlier in chapter 56). But when we consider and compare just how such cases arose and were handled among citizens, the symmetry seems to be illusory. How often did a metic have a substantial family resident in Athens with household resources and a kinship network essential for success in litigating such cases in court? How would the husband of a metic *epikleros* be selected? Apollodorus—always ready to cite a law for his purposes—suggests in his suit against Stephanus that his mother was an *epikleros* and so improperly married to Phormion ([Dem.] 46. 19). But his mother Archippe, even if an 'adopted' citizen, was most likely not a native Athenian.[14] How likely is it that her father's male relatives (the male members of his *anchisteia*, first on the paternal and then on the maternal side), who in *Athenian law* would be responsible for her marriage, could ever have been called upon by the polemarch or an Athenian court to marry her instead? Would they be in Athens to protest the marriage in the first place? Given the importance of family connections in both the raising and settling of disputes over

[12] See Harrison 1968: 189–90.

[13] For these terms, see Patterson 1981: 151–67. Private arbitration, however, apparently gave the metic an opportunity to have his disputes settled by his peers; see the case of Theodotus in Demosthenes 23 discussed below.

[14] For Archippe's status and identity, see Whitehead 1986; Carey 1991; E. Cohen 1992: 102–6; and Hunter 1994: 197 n. 25.

property, status, and inheritance,[15] what indeed was the substance of the justice provided to metics in such situations? The hollowness of this seemingly broadly protective formal structure is underscored when we remember that the metic could own no land in Attica—all of which gives the polemarch's responsibility for metic *kleroi* and *epikleroi* a certain air of unreality.

The question of the size and extent of metic kinship structures is an important one, even if not a resolvable one, for any evaluation of metic legal status and access. How permanent or transient was the metic population in Athens? The Athenian kindred was legally defined as extending to the sons of cousins, a web of family relationship including three generations (i.e. a son of a cousin is the grandson of a father's brother, father's sister, mother's brother or mother's sister). Would a metic be likely to have such kin in Athens? Lysias tells the Athenian jury that his father had lived in Athens for thirty years, implying that this was a significant period of time—an especially long period of time, he says, in which to live without doing or suffering any wrong (Lys. 12. 4). But the extent to which Lysias and his brothers had an established kindred beyond their immediate family of siblings and their households is unclear. When protesting the violent and unlawful treatment of his brother Polemarchus, Lysias says that although his family had three houses, the Thirty did not allow Polemarchus' funeral to be conducted from any of them (18)—suggesting that each of the three sons of Cephalus had a house, one of which might have been the paternal house. From the speech against Neaera in the Demosthenic corpus, we also know that Lysias' mother, in her old age, lived in the same *oikia* with Lysias and his wife, who was the daughter of Brachyllus and also Lysias' own niece. But who was Brachyllus? It would also be interesting to know something of the family connections of Eratosthenes' wife (from whom the gold earrings were so violently taken) (12). Was this also a marriage within close kin? And who was Cephalus' wife? Did she move with him to Athens or marry him as part of the metic community of Athens? In sum, while it is possible to put together a few pieces of the metic *anchisteia* of Lysias, the limited character of the kin connections of even this well established metic is evident.[16]

[15] See above, n. 3.

[16] Note also that when immediate family members are prevented from clothing the corpse of Polemarchus, it is friends (*philoi*) who come to his aid and provide a cloak (12. 18).

Finally, on the issue of metic transiency, it is interesting that in the *Laws* Plato limited his resident aliens to a maximum stay of twenty years from the time of registration, beginning for a metic son at the age of fifteen (850b–c). This may or may not suggest that such length of residence was typical for metics in Plato's Athens, but it is evident that Plato was concerned to prevent the metics putting down roots in his new city. A limit of twenty years, even if generous to the individual, would certainly prevent the development of significant kin connections within and between metic families.

The significance of the relative shallowness of metic kinship structures suggested here for the security and quality of metic life is evident when we consider the law on homicide. Before discussing the polemarch's responsibility for metic justice in chapter 58, Aristotle explained the categories of homicide and the jurisdiction for each. 'Charges of unintentional homicide,' he noted, 'conspiracy to kill, and the killing of a slave, metic, or foreigner are heard by the Court of the Palladion' (*Ath. Pol.* 57. 3). There is legal recognition and legal recourse here, but hardly symmetry. The murder of a metic is not distinguished from the murder of a foreigner or slave; and within this category of homicide there is apparently no distinction between intentional or unintentional killing.[17] The murder of a metic, like that of a slave or an itinerant foreigner, can be no more serious than the unintentional killing of an Athenian citizen; it drew at most the penalty of exile. Further, since the responsibility for prosecution rested on a family member (i.e. the victim's nearest male kin), the metic's lack of rootedness in the Athenian polis might make even such prosecution and punishment of the killer difficult. So in Demosthenes 47, a former slave who was killed by the speaker's opponents (as they tried to seize his household property) had no known relative who could bring a suit against her murderers—and the murder went unpunished and unprosecuted (Dem. 47. 68–73). It would seem inherently unlikely that this woman, or any metic who entered that status via slavery, would have had the supporting net of kindred specified by Athenian law as the class of potential prosecutors or 'pursuers' of the murderer. In what sense did a slave have an *anchisteia*? Even a foreigner living in Athens with wife and children might be at risk for such legal 'invisibility' if his sons were not yet of an age to press

[17] See Whitehead 1977: 93–4.

the 'suit for murder' (*dike phonou*) for non-Athenians. Thus, the protection given the metic's person in Athenian law appears not only unequal but also dangerously hollow. And this, of course, is only looking at the level of legal structure and procedure; confronting in person a citizen jury, citizen witnesses, or citizen opponents would also have presented practical difficulties and anxieties for the metic litigant.

In sum, although the Athenian court system provided access to judicial processes to the resident foreigner and although the protection of the metic's person and property fell within the domain of public officials, most particularly the polemarch, nonetheless the profoundly different basis of participation of the metic in the social organization of the Athenian polis—no tribe, no deme, and for most aliens a minimal *anchisteia*—would have significantly undermined that access and protection within a judicial system in which kin, family, deme, and tribe played an essential role. Lack of significant family connections would also have fostered the popular view of the metic as someone without real ties, and so without loyalty, to the city. Any claim of metic loyalty, such as that articulated by Lysias in his speech against Eratosthenes (see below), would be made in the face of real suspicion that most metics were quite the opposite.

If we turn now from structures to actions, i.e. to specific cases, the significance of the metics' lack of rootedness in Athenian society for what Whitehead calls the 'ideology' of the Athenian metic comes into sharp focus. First, it should be emphasized that the number of metics, so identified, who appear in surviving Athenian orations is small. Discounting general references (for example, Lysias' statement that since the Athenians honoured 'the metics' who came to the aid of the city, they should definitely punish the citizen Philo who betrayed it (31. 29)), there are not more, and probably fewer, than twenty clearly identified metics making an appearance in surviving orations. The figure of course may be somewhat misleading, since in these speeches there are certainly foreigners who could be metics, but who are referred to only by their own citizen or ethnic affiliation. It could be that Artemo from Phaselis, Nausicrates from Carystus, or Antipater from Citium was in fact enrolled as a *metoikos* in Athens, but none is so identified in the oration in which he makes an appearance.[18]

[18] See Dem. 35. 10, 32.

The pool of metics in court is small but nonetheless illuminating. A closer look at a selection of twelve metics, two women and ten men, with their legal stories, adds force as well as detail to the essentially negative picture of their status drawn by Whitehead. The twelve selected here are hardly a homogeneous group; they include the wealthy Lysias and an *isoteles* named Theodotus (alone among metics his 'tax free' status is, it seems, a point of pride) as well as the merchant Cephisiades (described by his citizen opponent as 'an impotent metic') and the former slave and prostitute, Neaera. Such diversity of identity, however, does not qualify the stark reality of alien metic status. When the speaker of Lysias 22 begins his interrogation with 'Are you a metic?' (5), this was not intended to make the defendant feel at home.

Within the diverse group, only one metic is speaking for himself and only one is prosecuting an Athenian. This is, of course, the orator Lysias who, on behalf of his dead brother Polemarchus, prosecuted Eratosthenes during the latter's *euthuna*. I leave that drama and Lysias' story for last. All the other metics in court are either defendants or 'minor players' of one sort or another. Together they present an ideological background against which Lysias' speech *Against Eratosthenes* can be viewed.

1. In Demosthenes' speech *Against Aristogiton* (25), Zobia is an apparently independent metic woman who befriended and protected Aristogiton (when he broke out of prison) only to have him later 'drag her off to the auction-place of the *metoikion*' when she reminded him of her service. 'And if', says the speaker, 'her *metoikion* had not happened to be recorded, she would, because of him, have been sold' (57). A close call indeed—and a revealing indication for the speaker of Aristogiton's baseness and for us of the precariousness of metic status, particularly for a woman.
2. Neaera, the defendant in [Demosthenes] 59, experienced something similar at one point in her long career as an independent working woman when Phrynion, her former partner, tried to carry her off by force from the house of Stephanus, her current partner and *prostates*. The two men submitted their quarrel to arbitration, with the result that Neaera was declared 'free and mistress of herself' (*kuria hautes*)—and also (however this is to be understood) that she should 'be with' (*suneinai*)

each of the men, who now would be *philoi*, on alternate days (46). To be 'mistress of herself' is for Neaera a position of neither respect nor security.

3. The story of Pancleon, an alleged metic, would-be Plataean, and the target of Lysias 23, provides another view of the riskiness of life for the metic at the margins of Athenian society. According to the speaker, Pancleon was a troublesome fellow who had been injuring him 'for a long time' (2). So, 'supposing him to be a metic', the speaker summoned him before the polemarch. Pancleon, however, responded by claiming to be a Plataean and thus an Athenian citizen. Not to be put off, the speaker went to the cheese market where the Plataeans were known to meet and made enquiries. No one, he claims, knew of a Plataean of that name, but one person did say that a slave by the name of Pancleon had recently run away. Then, some days later the speaker himself happened to witness this same Plataean attempting to seize Pancleon. There was a fight, and only with the assurance of witnesses that Pancleon had a brother who could establish his freedom did everyone go home. On the next day, the speaker returned again to the agreed-upon spot only to find not a brother proving Pancleon's freedom but a woman asserting that he belonged to *her* and that she would not allow him to be taken away by anyone else. (It would seem that this was some sort of ruse to rescue Pancleon. The woman's identity is not provided.) In the midst of this confusion, says the speaker, Pancleon's companions carried him off. After adding a few other details, such as that Pancleon had taken up metic status in Thebes, an unlikely choice for a Plataean, the speaker rests his case.

4. Lysias' brief and incomplete speech on behalf of the metic Callias, charged with *hierosulia* on the testimony of his own slaves, reveals a different segment of metic society. The speaker claims to be drawn to speak in Callias' behalf because of the seriousness of the penalty (death) and because Callias was his and his father's *philos*. And there were many agreements (*sumbolai*) between them (5. 1). The mention of friendship and of family connections is certainly calculated to create sympathy and perhaps also to extend those protective relationships to Callias himself. Finally, the speaker's strong warning

about the dangers of encouraging slave accusations is also intended to emphasize to the Athenian jurors that Callias, a slave-owner who has done many 'good things' for the city, is from this perspective at least 'one of us'.

5. The anonymous grain dealers, on the other hand, who are accused in Lysias 22 of manipulating to their advantage the grain market by, it seems, buying more than the legal limit, are without doubt (in the speaker's mind) 'the enemy within'. Lysias 22 is not a neglected text; I do not intend to add here to the discussion of the specific laws which the merchants are said to have broken or of the economic and political background of their case in the 380s.[19] Instead, I want to point out the basis of the hostile construction of their status and character by the speaker, a former member of the boule, who, he says, had earlier spoken out against their summary execution. The speaker claims that he is only interested in the enforcement of Athenian law and so, as a law-respecting citizen, is unwilling to sentence the merchants without a trial. However, a more cynical view would be that he was interested in exposing the case to larger public view and to popular judgement so that it would be the Athenian people themselves who took action, not the council alone. In any case, the speaker is no friend of metics and his rhetoric does them no honour. After calling forward one of the defendants and abruptly asking, 'Tell me, are you a metic?' (5)—again not a polite or respectful way to begin—the speaker obtains the admission that this metic had, in fact, bought beyond the legal limit. From this point, in the speaker's mind and rhetoric, the case was or should have been closed. The metics' defence, that they bought up more grain on the advice of the Athenian magistrates and in good will towards the Athenians in order to keep the price low, is incompatible with what the speaker knows about metic character. Although in the Athenian imagination at least there was such a thing as the good metic, the speaker knows that the real world is different. The ideal (and imaginary) metic was the mythical Parthenopaeus, one of the 'seven against Thebes', whom Euripides described in the *Suppliants* as a metic in Argos: 'He was an Arcadian, but came to Inachus' streams and

[19] See Todd 1993: 316–20.

grew up in Argos. Reared there, he avoided—as befits the immigrant foreigner—making trouble or arousing jealousy in the city . . . he stood in the ranks like a native Argive and defended our land. He rejoiced when the city prospered, and sorrowed in its adversities' (890–900).[20] But the grain merchants are not like Parthenopaeus. The interests of the grain merchants, says the speaker, are 'the opposite of other men's; they make most profit when, on some bad news reaching the city, they sell their corn at a high price. And they are so delighted to see your disasters that they either get news of them in advance of anyone else, or fabricate the rumour themselves' (14).[21] And far from defending Athens like a native son, the grain merchants are themselves 'besieging' the city (15). The speaker concludes by insisting that both the Athenians and the grain importers have suffered because of the crimes of these men—men whose isolation and vulnerability as aliens in the Athenian court are now starkly apparent.

Three additional metic defendants are found in two speeches of Hyperides. After a look at the interesting case of the 'Egyptian' Athenogenes, I will be more brief about the other two, who are simply mentioned in passing by the orator.

6. Hyperides 3 was composed for a young Athenian named Epicrates who it seems was the victim of both love and a major financial swindle. (The story has a definite Menandrian flavour.) Having fallen in love with a young slave boy, the son of the slave Midas, who in turn was the manager of the perfume shop owned by Athenogenes, Epicrates was convinced by Antigone (the persuasive mistress of Athenogenes) to buy Midas and his *two* sons—and then free whomever he wanted. Epicrates did so, paying 40 minae and receiving not only the three slaves but the perfume shop in the bargain. Unfortunately, the bargain also included the slaves' debts which ran to some 5 talents, for which he as their owner was now responsible. When Athenogenes, a 'speechwriter' and a 'man of the agora' and 'most of all' an Egyptian, would not

[20] Tr. Whitehead 1977: 37. 'As befits the immigrant foreigner' translates *ὡς χρὴ τοὺς μετοικοῦντας ξένους* (892).

[21] Tr. Lamb.

relent, Epicrates went to court. Hyperides constructs an argument based on the principle of fairness and appeals to several 'laws of Solon', such as that invalidating a will made under the 'influence of a woman' (17). *A fortiori*, it follows that Epicrates' encumbering of his estate with such a debt, taken on under the influence of Antigone, should also be invalid.

In attempting to arouse sympathetic indignation among the jurors, Hyperides, however, does *not* actually call Athenogenes a metic or draw attention to that status. In fact, he alludes to the fact that Athenogenes' family has been in the perfume business in Athens for three generations (19).[22] Could it be that the man is what his name implies—perhaps a citizen of recent origin such as the wealthy and litigious Apollodorus, son of Pasion—and that the epithet 'the Egyptian' used by Hyperides is more ethnic name-calling or reference to his profession than fact?[23] The question is not decisively solved by Hyperides' reference in chapter 33 to the law which forbade metics to leave the city in time of war, since earlier (chapter 29) he had cited the law as simply ordering the arrest of the man who moved to another city in wartime. If Athenogenes were in fact a metic who had illegally left town to take up residence in Troezen, it is odd that Hyperides does not press the point with more force. In any case, Hyperides is certainly attempting to call into question Athenogenes' loyalty—both to the laws of Athens and to the polis itself. 'If a man', says Epicrates, referring to Athenogenes, 'has been vicious in his private life and given up hope of the city's safety [i.e. by leaving Athens for Troezen], if he has deserted you and expelled the citizens from the town of his adoption [i.e. Troezen, which gave Athenogenes citizenship], will you not punish him when he is in your power?' (35). Athenogenes' lack of loyalty to Athens, whether as wayward citizen or disloyal resident guest, made him unworthy of the protection of Athenian law.

[22] If Athenogenes is a metic, then his three-generation family business is, I think, the longest known metic residence in Athens.

[23] For a discussion of the family and business of Pasion, the slave who became a banker and then an Athenian citizen, see E. Cohen 1992: 61–110.

7. and 8. Two metic defendants are mentioned in passing by Hyperides in another oration (4) but are not participants in the case at hand—the defence of a certain Euxenippus in an *eisangelia* charging that he had misrepresented the dream he had had while sleeping in the temple of Amphiaraus in Oropos. Hyperides disputes the use of *eisangelia* in such a case, insisting that the procedure should be reserved for more weighty crimes. The situation now, he says, is laughable. 'Diognides and Antidorus the metic are impeached on a charge of hiring out flute-girls at a higher price than that fixed by law, Agasicles of Piraeus because he was registered in Halimus, and Euxenippus because of the dreams which he claims to have had' (3). Antidorus is identified as a metic (typically, we might think, engaged in market activities) and Agasicles is usually taken to be that same metic or foreigner who was prosecuted by a client of Dinarchus for fraudulent entry in the deme register of Halimus (Whitehead 1977: 50, 53). Could it be that, from the point of view of the Athenian citizen, a charge of *xenia* against a metic was considered of a weight similar to the improper hiring-out of flute girls? Perhaps this is another example of the conscious slighting of the 'worthless metic', suggesting that his crimes are not worthy of the most serious public procedures, even though he himself deserves the extreme penalty of enslavement for encroaching on citizen privilege.

9. We might expect that metics would figure significantly in cases involving commerce and maritime trade, since this is an area of Athenian life in which they are traditionally thought to have been active—and an area of Athenian law that is thought to have been especially open and 'hospitable' to metic businessmen and to foreigners in general.[24] But it is notably hard to identify securely the metics in these cases. Possibly, as suggested earlier, some of the foreigners identified by ethnic or foreign citizenship are in fact registered metics,[25] but are not identified as such because the speaker considers the distinction insignifi-

[24] On metics in commerce, see E. Cohen 1992 and also 1973; Millett 1991: 224–9.

[25] Given the likelihood that Athenian law in the fourth century required foreigners to register as metics after a short period of residency, perhaps one month (see Hansen 1991: 117), it is probable that some of these foreigners were indeed metics. But again, they apparently preferred not to be so identified.

cant or pejorative. It is striking, as Whitehead notes, that 'the only unambiguous status-designation in *all* these speeches . . . is Theodotus the "*isoteles*"' (a metic paying equally with the citizens), who serves as an arbitrator in Demosthenes 34 (18, 44) and a witness in Demosthenes 35 (14), both of which concern maritime loans and involve several non-Athenians.[26] In addition to confirming Whitehead's point that the *isoteles* alone chose to identify himself with reference to his status in Athens (while the ordinary metic, perhaps including various litigants in these speeches, preferred to use his own ethnic identity), the figure of Theodotus '*isoteles*' and 'arbitrator' suggests that some non-Athenians in Athens may have preferred to try to settle their disputes among themselves, without entering into the processes of the Athenian judicial system. Theodotus, however, passes their case on to the *dikasterion*.

10. and 11. Two other metics who add further emphasis and colour to the emerging collective judicial portrait appear in another pair of Demosthenes' speeches. Neither metic is presented positively. Demosthenes 52 involves a suit brought by an Athenian against Apollodorus for sums wrongfully turned over to Cephisiades, a 'worthless' and 'impotent' metic (9, 25); and Demosthenes 58 includes a reference to Ctesicles 'the metic', a speech-writer to whom the speaker's opponent goes for help—'one villain to another' (19)—in fixing a trial.

While the image of Athenian judicial hospitality is becoming clear, there still remains the celebrated case of the metic Lysias' prosecution of Eratosthenes for the murder of his brother Polemarchus. Lysias' speech against Eratosthenes represents without doubt an exceptional case in exceptional circumstances, the turbulent years of the rule of 'The Thirty' and of the restoration of democracy in 403 BC. The speech is also exceptional in that it seems to be the only documented case of a metic prosecuting an Athenian citizen. When one reads the speech with an eye to the status of the metic in court, the overt humility of Lysias' presentation of his life story before a jury of Athenian citizens is striking, as is the detail with which he documents his own humiliation by Eratosthenes' associate Peison, who came to arrest him. The case is weighted against him by the status difference, and while it was

[26] Whitehead 1977: 49.

customary even for Athenian litigants to profess inexperience and humility in the face of the powerful Athenian jury, in the speech he wrote for himself, Lysias accentuates his reluctant litigation and his feelings of weakness: 'Now as for myself,' he says, 'having never engaged in any suit either on my own account or on that of others, I have now been compelled by what has occurred to accuse this man: hence I have been often overcome with a great feeling of despondency, from a fear lest my inexperience might cause me to fail in making a worthy and able accusation on my brother's and on my own behalf.'[27]

Lysias' projection of the image of 'humble metic' extends to his description of his own attempt to buy Peison off with a talent of silver. As he describes the scene:

> When he [Peison] had sworn, invoking annihilation upon himself and his children if he did not save me on receipt of the talent, I went into my bedroom and opened the money-chest. Peison noticed it and came in; on seeing its contents, he called two of his underlings and bade them take what was in the chest. Since he now had, instead of the agreed amount, . . . three talents of silver, four hundred cyzicenes, a hundred darics and four silver cups, I begged him to give me money for my journey; but he declared that I should be glad enough to save my skin.[28]

Lysias is a wealthy man, but in this scene he is first reduced to, and then stripped of, his visible wealth, the contents of his chest. What resources does the metic have in the face of such outrageous treatment by a citizen? He is left to beg Peison for travel money. Similarly, in this speech Lysias begs/beseeches the Athenian jury for justice. He acknowledges that he and his brother are metics but pleads that they have always been well-behaved and have caused no trouble (12. 20):

> This was not the treatment that we deserved at the city's hands, when we had produced all our dramas for the festivals, and contributed to many special levies; when we showed ourselves men of orderly life and performed every duty laid upon us; when we had made not a single enemy, but had ransomed many Athenians from the foe.

[27] Ch. 3, tr. Lamb. (. . . *διὰ τὴν ἀπειρίαν ἀναξίως καὶ ἀδυνάτως ὑπὲρ τοῦ ἀδελφοῦ καὶ ἐμαυτοῦ τὴν κατηγορίαν ποιήσομαι.*) Notice Lysias' use of the words *anaxios* and *adunatos*, quite similar to those used by Demosthenes in his portrayal of the metic Cephisiades in oration 52. 9 and 25. 3.

[28] 10–12, tr. Lamb.

Lysias and Polemarchus (and their father Cephalus) have, Lysias claims, lived out the Athenians' imaginary role of Parthenopaeus, but their lack of a real share in the polis and connection to its land and kinship groups (real or fictitious) undermines the success of their appeal. Whatever their contributions, as metics they are still subjected to the humiliating treatment at the hands of members of the Thirty—including standing by impotently while Polemarchus' wife is stripped of her gold earrings (19). The forced endurance of such hubristic treatment of a female family member is vivid evidence of the metic's lack of status within the citizen community.

In the first thirty-six chapters of his speech, Lysias details the injustice of his family's treatment by the Thirty and the crime of Polemarchus' death. But the speech does not stop there. Lysias moves in the last sixty-four chapters to a prosecution of Eratosthenes on behalf of the Athenian citizens themselves and turns his rhetoric to the wrongs that the Athenians have suffered at the hands of the Thirty (including Eratosthenes). A full two-thirds of the speech is devoted to proving to the Athenian jury that as a member of the Thirty, Eratosthenes has wronged *them* and so deserves their condemnation. If you won't take vengeance on behalf of a metic, Lysias seems to say, then at least take it on behalf of yourselves. All through this last part of the speech, Lysias seems careful to distinguish himself, the metic, from the privileged citizen jury,[29] and the speech ends with a stirring call for the citizens to take vengeance: 'You have heard, you have seen, you have suffered, you *have* him. Give judgement!'

Lysias' prosecution of Eratosthenes is thus a testimony to his courage—but hardly to the hospitality of the Athenian courts. The metic was a guest in Athens' courts, but an isolated and often lonely one. When Strepsiades is pursued and struck by his son Pheidippides in Aristophanes' *Clouds*, he immediately calls on his neighbours, family (*sungeneis*), and demesmen for help (1322). How often could a metic have made such an appeal with confidence of a response? Friends and neighbours could help (as they apparently did in the case of Polemarchus' unclothed corpse (18)), but how often did he or she have an *anchisteia* waiting in the wings to spring to the defence? The metic's lack of extended

[29] The one exception may be his reference to the democratic return in 403 in which he participated: 'When we had come into the Piraeus . . .' (53).

family relations meant a lack of both supporting witnesses and prosecutors on behalf of person and property. At the same time, the metic's lack of connection with family and kin led to the suspicion that he was not really a part of the community, that he could not be trusted. The result is Demosthenes' scornful reference to the metic as 'worthless' (52. 9) and the metic's own apparent reluctance to advertise that status or expose it in court. Thus while the hospitality of the Athenian courts may not have been as bad as that of Homer's Polyphemus, it seems likely that even a 'privileged' foreigner resident in Athens would have had second thoughts before actively entering into litigation in the popular courts. Without family, neighbours, and fellow citizens to act as both legal allies and judges, the metic was indeed *adunatos* within the Athenian judicial system, even if not in danger of being 'eaten alive'.

References

CAREY, C. 1991. 'Apollodorus' Mother: The Wives of Enfranchised Aliens in Athens', *CQ* 41: 84–9.

CLERC, M. 1893. *Les métèques athéniens*. Paris.

COHEN, D. 1991. *Law, Sexuality, and Society: The Enforcement of Morals in Classical Athens*. Cambridge.

—— 1995. *Law, Violence, and Community in Classical Athens*. Cambridge.

COHEN, E. E. 1973. *Ancient Athenian Maritime Courts*. Princeton.

—— 1992. *Athenian Economy and Society: A Banking Perspective*. Princeton.

FOXHALL, L. and A. D. E. LEWIS (eds.) 1996. *Greek Law in its Political Setting: Justifications not Justice*. Oxford.

GAUTHIER, P. 1972. *Symbola: Les étrangers et la justice dans les cités grecques*. Nancy.

HANSEN, M. H. 1991. *The Athenian Democracy in the Age of Demosthenes: Structure, Principles and Ideology*, tr. J. A. Crook. Oxford.

HARRISON, A. R. W. 1968. *The Law of Athens*, i: *The Family and Property*. Oxford.

HUMPHREYS, S. C. 1985. 'Social Relations on Stage: Witnesses in Classical Athens', *History and Anthropology* 1: 313–69.

—— 1986. 'Kinship Patterns in the Athenian Courts', *GRBS* 27: 59–62.

HUNTER, V. J. 1994. *Policing Athens: Social Control in the Attic Lawsuits*,

420–320 BC. Princeton.

MILLETT, P. 1991. *Lending and Borrowing in Ancient Athens*. Cambridge.

OBER, J. 1989. *Mass and Elite in Democratic Athens: Rhetoric, Ideology, and the Power of the People*. Princeton.

OSBORNE, R. G. 1985. *Demos: The Discovery of Classical Attika*. Cambridge.

PATTERSON, C. 1981. *Pericles' Citizenship Law of 451/0*. New York.

TODD, S. C. 1993. *The Shape of Athenian Law*. Oxford.

VON WILAMOWITZ-MOELLENDORFF, U. 1887. 'Demotika der attischen Metoeken', *Hermes* 22: 107–28, 211–59.

WHITEHEAD, D. 1977. *The Ideology of the Athenian Metic*. Cambridge.

—— 1986. 'Women and Naturalisation in Fourth-Century Athens: The Case of Archippe', *CQ* 36: 109–14.

6

'Whoring Under Contract': The Legal Context of Prostitution in Fourth-Century Athens[1]

Edward E. Cohen

Modern scholarship often proffers political explanations of Athenian civilization and institutions, interpretations focusing on the 'status' of individuals—'citizens' (*politai*), 'resident foreigners' (metics), or 'slaves'.[2] Even business activity has been explained not in economic terms, but as a manifestation of political power: according to a thesis dominant for decades, citizens uniformly lived on incomes derived from capital investments and property; only non-citizens worked personally and actively in trade and production.[3] Sexual activity also has been characterized as responsive

[1] Unless otherwise indicated or clear from the context, all chronological references in this article are BC. I rely principally here on the evidence of Athenian court speeches, rhetorical contrivances that virtually always present evidence tendentiously (and often dishonestly). Yet—because the presuppositions underlying litigants' claims are generally reliable—this material is often useful to the social historian. Since litigants' presentations were made to large juries—with persuasion the speaker's dominant motive—the presence of a general phenomenon may be confirmed by a claim that presupposes such a phenomenon, even if we cannot establish the truth of the speaker's factual assertion. See E. Cohen 1990: 178, 186–90; Millett 1991: 2; Todd 1990.

[2] See, for example, M. H. Hansen 1991: 86; de Ste Croix 1981: 42–94; Finley 1985: 45–8; Todd 1993: 173.

[3] Scholars have long accepted Hasebroek's claim, largely derived from Weber, of a fundamental economic division in the polis between the non-citizens (who were actively involved in trade and production) and citizen-*rentiers* living on income generated from property (especially real-estate, supposedly enjoyed by *politai* with monopolistic exclusivity and assumed to be the basic source of wealth in an agrarian and 'primitive' society). See Hasebroek 1978 (1933): 22, 28, 35; Weber, especially 1924 (1909): 32–3. But more recent studies have refuted this politically oriented thesis. See Millett 1983: 38 ('Hasebroek's comments . . . cannot be reconciled with the actual evidence'); M. V. Hansen 1984: 88, 92 n. 74. Cf. Oertel's earlier criticism (1928: 1624–5). Despite the frequently high heuristic value of Weber's conceptualizations, they are often counterproductive in analysing actual historical phenomena: see Aron 1950: 232–6; Veyne 1971: 173–5.

not to erotic, but to political considerations.[4] Metics, totally lacking political rights but often of high economic and social position, allegedly 'had few sexual rights' (Posner 1992: 41). In contrast, a citizen 'might do whatever he wished with a slave boy or foreigner' (D. Cohen 1991a: 182). While 'the sexual behavior of citizen women was regulated by laws' (Pomeroy 1975: 86), for non-citizens 'the conventions of sexual segregation and protection did not apply' (Just 1989: 144). Even the obtaining of sexual pleasure through active, insertive use of the penis reflects not biology or socially constructed behaviour (neither 'a universal category of the human psyche or a universal structure of patriarchal society') but a political 'image of the citizen body as masculine and assertive' (Halperin 1990: 102–3).

At the intersection of business and *eros*, the commercial exchange of sex for compensation—'prostitution'[5]—has likewise been assumed to be governed by juridical position. For both male and female citizens,[6] political status supposedly precluded their employment as prostitutes. Athenian *politai* were 'perpetually on the superordinate side of a series of hierarchical and roughly con-

[4] Contemporary scholarship, following Dover (1989 (1978): 60–8, 81–109) and Foucault (e.g. 1984: 47–62, 98–9), generally views the Greek conceptualization of sexuality as focused not on gender or genital differentiations but on politicized opposition between activity (inherently masculine) and passivity (demeaned as inherently feminizing). See Chirassi Colombo 1984: 110; Cantarella 1988: 35–78; Halperin 1990; Winkler 1990; Bremmer 1989: 8; Larmour et al. 1998: 23. But Loraux (1995 (1989): 250 n. 29) is 'not convinced'; for D. Cohen (1991a: 172), 'major issues remain'; for Davidson, the prevailing model is an 'absurd simplification' (1997: 25).

[5] Ancient Greek employs two principal clusters of words for persons and acts relating to prostitution, those cognate to *pernanai* ('to sell') and those cognate to *hetairein* ('to be a companion'). The terms are not synonymous. Thus, in the case of women, 'emotional attitude' might determine the difference between a *hetaira* ('sometimes nearer to "mistress" than to "prostitute"') and 'a common prostitute' (*porne*) (Dover 1989 (1978): 21). For male prostitutes, a differentiation between *pornos* and *hetairos* is often present, 'analogous to the distinction between the *porne* and the *hetaira*' (ibid.). For Aeschines (1. 51–2), promiscuity was the prime differentiation between the two forms of sexual labour. Discursive analysis finds the 'opposition . . . constituted along the axis of gift- vs. commodity-exchange, identified with the *hetaira* and the *porne* respectively' (Davidson 1994: 141–2). Cf. Davidson 1997: 117–27; Kurke 1997: 107–12; Reinsberg 1989: 80–6.

[6] Because women lacked direct political rights, scholars generally deny the title 'citizen' to the female relatives of Athenian male citizens. See Loraux 1993: 10, 119; Carey 1992: 26; Ober 1993: 134–5; Saxenhouse 1991. The Athenians disagreed: the feminine πολῖτις was in use parallel with the masculine πολίτης: see, for example, Dem. 57. 30, 43; 59. 107; Isae. 8. 43; Arist. *Pol.* 1275^{b}33, 1278^{a}28; Pl. *Laws* 814c. Cf. Eur. *El.* 1335. Note the parallel use at Athens of the feminine ἀστή: Dem. 57. 35, 36, 40, 43, 46, 54; 59. 108; Ar. *Thesm.* 541. See E. Cohen 1997.

gruent distinctions in status: master vs. slave, free vs. unfree, dominant vs. submissive, active vs. passive, insertive vs. receptive, customer vs. prostitute, citizen vs. non-citizen, man vs. woman' (Halperin 1990: 102–3). Since 'the body of a citizen is sacrosanct' (Winkler 1990: 48), 'male prostitutes . . . were presumably for the most part foreigners' (Dover 1989 (1978): 32). According to Keuls, female prostitutes confirmed the male citizen's 'privileges of free status, citizenship, money, class, and gender' (1985: 174). Here too a political criterion—the male citizen's right to the exclusive sexual use or protection of members of his own household—supposedly mandated foreign predominance in female prostitution.[7]

I intend to show, however, that commercial sex at Athens reflected economic and sexual determinants far removed from hierarchical considerations of status. In other trades and endeavours, citizens, free foreigners, and slaves are known to have worked at the same tasks without differentiation based on personal juridical status.[8] Prostitution similarly encompassed all segments of the population: the sale of sexual services by both men and women, including citizens, was a commonplace and lawful aspect of Athenian life.[9] Yet Athenian laws purported to provide widespread protection from sexual abuse for the entire resident population (free or slave, male or female, and especially for children). Partly as a result, there arose the practice of 'whoring under contract' (*kata synthekas hetairekenai*), which emphasized the mutuality and market egalitarianism underlying the sale of sex at Athens.

[7] Krenkel 1988: 1291: 'Female prostitution . . . was the province of slaves, freed persons, and foreigners.' Cf. Keuls 1985: 154 ('We know of hardly any women of the citizen class who practiced the trade.').

[8] See below, pp. 125–6.

[9] Ancient sources treat both male and female prostitution as routinely present. See, for example, Dem. 22. 61 (citizen prostitutes); *Ep*. 4. 11; Ar. *Plut*. 155; Xen. *Mem*. 1. 6. 13; Alexis, fr. 242; Antiphanes, fr. 210 (K–A); Ephippus, fr. 20; Eupolis *Philoi*, fr. 286 (K–A); Cratinus, fr. 4; Aeschin. 1; Lys. 3; and Dem. 59 *passim*. Cf. Diog. Laert. 2. 105. Cf. Keuls 1985: 153–205; Licht (Brandt) 1952 (1932): 329, 410, 436–40; Herter 1960; Krenkel 1978, 1988; McGinn 1989. (Although Harrison (1968: 37) infers from the charges set forth in Aeschin. 1 the existence of a γραφὴ ἑταιρήσεως, no prosecution under such a statute is known. Lipsius (1966 (1905–15): 436) correctly dismisses the possible existence of such a procedural category.)

AN ACADEMIC FANTASY: SEXUAL EXPLOITATION AS POLITICAL ENTITLEMENT

A prime tenet of contemporary scholarship is the belief that the majority of the residents of Attica were wantonly exploited sexually by the adult-male citizen minority[10]—a manifestation, for prevailing dogma, of the general 'oppression of noncitizen groups within the Polis' (Ober 1989: 5). Virtually without dissent, scholars insist that Athens prohibited only liaisons which violated the property rights of male citizens (such as their wives' adultery), couplings which might upset prevailing hierarchical arrangements (marriage between aliens and local residents, for example), and sexual relations which implied or articulated acceptance by male citizens of a submissive sexual role, as in the sale of erotic favours by a *polites*.[11] Yet the substantial protections against sexual abuse or exploitation provided by both Athenian law and communal practice were actually directed toward, and applied for the benefit of, Attica's entire residential population, citizen or foreigner, and (to some extent) even for the protection of slaves. Correspondingly, personal inclinations, private situations, and financial considerations—not political classification—for the most part determined individual involvement in the sexual market.

An Athenian law purported to protect every inhabitant of

[10] Vatin 1984: 27: 'Au total, les citoyens de plein droit sont une petite minorité sur le territoire, et règnent en toute souveraineté sur une population majoritaire.' Cf. Raaflaub 1983: 544 n. 93; 1980: 44–6; Schaps 1979: 96; Pomeroy 1975: 58; Keuls 1985: 12. From a male citizen body which he estimates at 30,000, M. H. Hansen extrapolates a total population of 300,000 or more (1991: 93–4). Cf. Gomme 1933: 26, 29; Ehrenberg 1969: 31; Ruschenbusch 1979: 146; 1981: 112; M. H. Hansen 1985: 67–9.

[11] See Just 1989: 146–8; Posner 1992: 38–44; Halperin 1990: 92–104; Winkler 1990; Keuls 1985: 153–299; Dover 1984 (1973): 148–9; 1974: 205–16; 1989 (1978); Foucault 1984; and Pomeroy 1975: ch. 5. The dependency inherent in male prostitution is supposedly incompatible with the 'hoplite' culture of a state conceptualized by its citizens as a military force of kinsmen, 'a warrior band in Republican form' (Rahe 1994: 32; cf. Sagan 1991: 353), and therefore inherently closed to non-kinsmen. But in the Athenian armed forces of the fourth century—contrary to the traditional reliance of the polis on its own members (cf. Arist. *Pol.* 1327ᵃ40–b8)—metics and slaves (and mercenaries, many of whom did not even reside in Attica: see McKechnie 1989: 79–100) constituted a significant portion of total personnel. For military service by metics, see Xen. *Vect.* 2. 2–3; Thuc. 2. 13. 7, 31. 1–2; 3. 16. 1; 4. 90; Lyc. 1. 16. Cf. Gerhardt 1935 (1933): 42–4; Diller 1937: 134. For service by slaves, see Hunt 1998: esp. 87–101, 121–43, 177–8.

Attica—'whether a child or a woman or a man, whether free or slave'—from sexual exploitation or abuse. Legislation cited by Demosthenes authorized a public prosecution (*graphe*) for *hubris* 'whenever someone intentionally insults the honour (*hubrizei*) of another, whether a child or a woman or a man, whether free or slave, or does something unlawful (*paranomon*) against any such person'.[12] The law thus prohibits 'the deliberate infliction of serious insult on another human being',[13] a broad coverage confirmed explicitly by other contemporary sources—including Demosthenes' prime rival, Aeschines, who independently cites the legislation in language virtually identical with that of Demosthenes.[14] Accordingly, there is 'general agreement [that] we possess the actual text of the law as it stood in the fourth century' (Fisher 1992: 36), the 'genuine law' (MacDowell 1990: 263)—albeit a text that in its wide protection of Attica's *Untermenschen* conflicts starkly with the allegedly unlimited right of male citizens to exploit Attica's residents. As a result of this contradiction, the law's 'plain meaning'—its extension of protection far beyond adult male citizens—has tended to be disregarded, or even dismissed as 'incoherent' or theoretically impossible.[15] Athenian legislation against *hubris*, however, was far from theoretical. Demosthenes notes that harsh punishment had actually been meted out in many cases involving victimization of slaves (21. 48–9). To mitigate the

[12] 21. 47: *ἐάν τις ὑβρίζῃ εἴς τινα, ἢ παῖδα ἢ γυναῖκα ἢ ἄνδρα, τῶν ἐλευθέρων ἢ τῶν δούλων, ἢ παράνομόν τι ποιήσῃ εἰς τούτων τινά . . .*

[13] Fisher 1995: 45. In accord: Todd 1993: 270, 379, following Fisher 1992: 36–82 and 1990: 126; D. Cohen 1991b; Lipsius 1966 (1905–15): 420–9; Morrow 1939: 38–41; Harrison 1968: 168, 172; MacDowell 1976; 1978: 129–32; Dover 1989 (1978): 34–9; Cantarella 1983; Cole 1984: 99. Ruschenbusch (1965) even sees *hubris* as inclusively covering all offences against the person. Gagarin, in contrast, finds *hubris* distinguished by the use of inordinate force or violence (1979: 232). For other interpretations, see Cairns 1996.

[14] Aeschin. 1. 15: *ἐάν τις ὑβρίζῃ εἰς παῖδα (ὑβρίζει δὲ δή που ὁ μισθούμενος) ἢ ἄνδρα ἢ γυναῖκα, ἢ τῶν ἐλευθέρων τινὰ ἢ τῶν δούλων, ἢ ἐὰν παράνομόν τι ποιῇ εἰς τούτων τινά, γραφὰς ὕβρεως εἶναι πεποίηκεν* . . . ('Whenever someone intentionally insults the honour (*hubrizei*) of a child (and indeed any man paying [for sex] does insult honour) or of a man or woman, or anyone, whether free or slave, or does something unlawful (*paranomon*) against any one of these, the law provides public prosecutions (*graphai*) for *hubris*.') Cf. Hyp. fr. *Mantitheus*. (The text of the 'law' preserved at Aeschin. 1. 16 is patently a forgery: MacDowell 1990: 263–4.)

[15] The enshrinement of slaves' rights, for example, leaves distinguished scholars grasping (unsuccessfully) for words: 'such a law would have had to envisage a situation involving the treatment of free men as if they were slaves, or citizens as if they were foreigners, or slaves (who are specifically mentioned as within the scope of the law) as if they were—what?' (Murray 1990: 140). 'Incoherent': Gernet 1917: 183–97.

lengthy legal delays endemic within the Athenian court system,[16] actions charging *hubris* had to be heard within thirty days after the day on which the charges were first brought (Dem. 21. 47)[17]—a virtually unique acceleration of process.[18] Should the prosecutor prevail, there was to be an immediate determination of penalties (Dem. 21. 47). Upon conviction, an offender was held in prison until payment of any fine that had been assessed[19]—an extraordinary remedy in a system where private litigants generally had to enforce court judgments without official assistance[20] and where even debts owed to the state often were allowed to languish for months before obligors—subject to no restraint—fled.[21] To avoid the chimera of a protection not practically available to those unable personally to vindicate their rights against a more powerful abuser, prosecution could be pursued by any Athenian *polites*[22]—in contrast to the usual requirement in a private action (*dike*) of suit by the victim directly or through his or her male representative (*kurios*).[23]

[16] For the systemic prevalence and causes of protracted and postponed litigation, see E. Cohen 1973: 10–12; Charles 1938: 9–10.

[17] In practice—as anticipated by the statute—state considerations could still sometimes delay prompt resolution of the charges: cf. Dem. 45. 4.

[18] MacDowell 1990: 266–7 refutes M. H. Hansen's claim (1981: 167–70) that requirement of trial within thirty days was not uncommon: no other provision for εἰσαγωγὴ τριάκοντα ἡμερῶν is known at Athens (although we do know of 'thirty-day cases' (τριακοσταῖαι δίκαι) from Naupactus (ML 20) and from Heraclea (*Inscriptions Juridiques Grecques* i. 12, Table II, ll. 26–7). Cf. Gofas 1979: 180 n. 21. For the δίκαι ἔμμηνοι at Athens, see E. Cohen 1973: 23–6; Vélissaropoulos 1980: 242–5.

[19] Dem. 21. 47: ἐὰν δὲ ἀργυρίου τιμηθῇ τῆς ὕβρεως, δεδέσθω ἐὰν ἐλεύθερον ὑβρίσῃ, μέχρι ἂν ἐκτείσῃ. Imprisonment thus was not automatically available in cases of transgressions against slaves.

[20] See Todd 1993: 144–5; Allen 1997: 34. In the case of *hubris*, the fine was paid to the state, not to the victim or prosecutor, thereby giving the polis a direct financial interest in extracting payment. See Dem. 21. 45.

[21] For the rarity of imprisonment as a procedural or punitive process at Athens, see E. Cohen 1973: 74–83; MacDowell 1990: 268; Hunter 1997. On the state's laxity even in cases involving public debtors, note the famous case of Demosthenes' father-in-law, Gylon (Dem. 28. 1–3; Aeschin. 3. 171; Davies 1971: 121).

[22] Dem. 21. 47: γραφέσθω πρὸς τοὺς θεσμοθέτας ὁ βουλόμενος Ἀθηναίων οἷς ἔξεστιν ('Let anyone who wishes, of those Athenians who are qualified, submit a *graphe* (writ of prosecution) to the Thesmothetae'). Some potential cases, however, may have been discouraged by the absence of monetary incentive for a voluntary prosecutor (ὁ βουλόμενος) and by the requirement (see Lipsius 1966 (1905–15): 243–4; Harrison 1968: 195 n. 1) that the prosecutor be an Athenian citizen. For *graphai* open also to prosecution by non-Athenians, see Dem. 59. 66 (Epaenetus 'certainly a foreigner' (Carey 1992: 121)); 59. 16; 21. 175; 24. 105; possibly 59. 52.

[23] Just 1985: 173 n. 8: 'κύριος, the head of the household to which (an Athenian woman) was attached'—an improvement over the traditional translation of *kurios* as guardian or 'master' (Wolff 1944: 46–7 n. 22). In fact, '*kyrieia* is a much fuzzier, less formalized institu-

Because of 'the centrality of *hubris* . . . in Athenian social relations' (D. Cohen 1991b: 171), this legislation potentially affected many aspects of Athenian behaviour. Yet its prime impact was felt in sexual contexts, for eroticized misconduct was a fundamental and frequent manifestation of *hubris*.[24] Of approximately five hundred occurrences of *hubris* or its cognates in the principal surviving Athenian prose authors, eighty-two incidents relate to sexual misconduct—more cases by far than those of any other typology.[25] Rape is repeatedly denominated as *hubris*.[26] In fact, Aristotle specifically warns rulers that of the various manifestations of *hubris*, sexual abuse of boys and girls and physical violation of individuals are most to be avoided (*Pol.* 1315^{a}14–16). (Aristotle significantly does not differentiate between male and female youngsters, or between freemen and slaves in cases of bodily violence.) Dinarchus even brands as *hubris* the Macedonians' assignment of Theban women and children to barbarian tents (Din. 1. 19, 24).

Erotic insult did not require physical contact. Alcibiades is said to have committed *hubris* against his wife by merely bringing other women into their home (Andoc. 4. 14, 15, 29). Nor did protection require 'citizenship'. Although Archippe, widow of the Athenian banker Pasion, appears never to have received Athenian *politeia*, her son Apollodorus brought on her behalf an action for *hubris* against his mother's second husband, the family's former slave.[27] Even women of low status might complain of *hubris*, as did Neaera, allegedly a foreign whore born into slavery, who charged the Athenian *polites* Phrynion with *hubris* for various indignities, including consensual intercourse with her in public (Dem. 59.

tion than social and legal historians have generally thought' (Foxhall 1996: 150). A woman could be even *αὑτῆς κυρία* (Dem. 59. 46), and some *kurioi* were merely public representatives of familial interests or of powerful females (cf. Hunter 1989a: 46–7; 1994: 9–13, 15–19).

[24] Despite Athenian law's harsh penalties against *hubris*, and the general recognition among specialists that the word denotes behaviour seriously injurious and subject to rigorous punishment, 'more "traditional" interpretations of *hubris*, still commonly found in scholarly discourse and perhaps even more commonly among the "chattering classes", see it as human arrogance, over-confidence or unawareness of the reasons for one's own good fortune' (Fisher 1995: 45–6).

[25] Even physical assault against free persons is reported less frequently. See D. Cohen 1991b: 172–3; MacDowell 1976; Fisher 1976; 1979.

[26] See D. Cohen 1991b: 175; Doblhofer 1994: *passim*; Dover 1989 (1978): 36.

[27] Dem. 45. 4. For Archippe's continuing status as an alien, see Carey 1991. Cf. E. Cohen 1992: 102–6; Whitehead 1986.

33–7). In homo-erotic situations, charges of *hubris* likewise could arise from an abuse of power that caused dishonour. The public slave Pittalacus brands as *hubris* the actions of the well-connected Athenian *politai* Hegesandrus and Timarchus who, as the denouement of a sexual triangle, had sadistically tied Pittalacus to a column and whipped him during a nocturnal revel. Although he had the support of *politai* who were prepared to act for him and who might have brought a public action for this *hubris*, the slave instead brought a private suit (*dike*) on his own behalf against his two citizen-tormentors (Aeschin. 1. 62). Indeed, from the varied evidence of Aeschines 1, Montuori has contended that *anyone* who prostituted a male slave could be charged with *hubris* (1976: 12–14).

But even those scholars who accept the law's explicit statement of protection for slaves and other dependants often assume the provision to have been meaningless in actual practice. Harrison, for example, considers (1968: 172) that there was not even a 'slender chance' that any outsider would actually prosecute an alleged act of *hubris* by a master against his slave.[28] Yet even our sparse knowledge of actual Athenian litigation provides numerous examples of third parties instituting actions on behalf of women, children, and other dependants, and even confirms Demosthenes' statement (21. 49) that offenders had actually been executed for acts of *hubris* against slaves. Dinarchus reports that at the Eleusinian festival the Athenian citizen Themistius had been put to death for *hubris* against a Rhodian lyre-girl, and that a certain Euthymachus had been executed for forcing an Olynthian slave woman into a brothel (Din. 1. 23).[29] Legal actions also appear to have been brought over the hubristic treatment of another enslaved Olynthian woman by Athenians at a Macedonian symposium after Philip's destruction of Olynthus,[30] although 'we do not know enough about these cases to know in what circumstances they did, or might, reach the courts' (Fisher 1995: 69–70). Even where the wrongdoing involved only allegation of financial mismanagement, third parties are known to have come forward. In Demosthenes 38, under a statute permitting 'anyone' to act on behalf of the alleged victims, a certain Nicidas, not otherwise involved or even known,

[28] Cf. Humphreys 1993: 5.

[29] Cf. Worthington 1992: 169. Demosthenes mentions by name a number of other persons executed for misdeeds at such religious gatherings (21. 175–81).

[30] Dem. 19. 196–8; Aeschin. 2. 4, 153–5.

denounced a guardian for mismanagement of an estate intended to benefit minor children.[31]

Legislation permitting 'anyone' to take action on behalf of an abused individual allowed persons otherwise lacking standing the opportunity to intervene on behalf of individuals to whom they were not directly related by blood—as Archedamus did when he charged Eupolis with having ravaged the estate of the son of Archedamus' wife by an earlier marriage (Isae. 7. 5–7). Friends frequently took an active role as arbitrators in reconciling various members of an *oikos*, in many cases effectively protecting dependent members of a household.[32] But total outsiders are also known to have come to the aid of dependent persons. When Neaera, an ex-slave staying in Megara, had been subjected to *hubris* by the Athenian citizen Phrynion (who claimed to be her master), she sought assistance from the Athenian *polites* Stephanus, whom she had only recently met. He responded to her appeal—for Stephanus the beginning of substantial litigation on her behalf, including defence of her freedom through a claim of *aphairesis* against Phrynion (Dem. 59. 37–40). Similarly, the slave Pittalacus was able to call on the influential *polites* Glaucon to vindicate his legal rights against harassment by the prominent Hegesandrus—who claimed that Pittalacus was his slave (Aeschin. 1. 62).

Athenian concern for the rights, especially the sexual sanctity, of dependents contrasts with modern Western societies' long history of ignoring or trivializing sexual abuse against minor and female family members (and against slaves, even where miscegenation statutes prohibited interracial sexual relations). But at Athens social structures and communal values (especially commitment to *philanthropia*) encouraged effective protection against the sexual abuse of children, slaves, and women.[33] Accordingly, Aeschines sets forth in considerable detail the extraordinarily strong Athenian laws against child abuse, which affected a wide circle of men who might have contact with children, but targeted with special rigour *kurioi* and other adult male family members.[34] Legal protection for slaves was

[31] Dem. 38. 23. For *phasis* as a procedure against κάκωσις οἴκου ὀρφανικοῦ, see Harpocration, s.v. φάσις; Arist. *Ath. Pol.* 56. 6.

[32] See, for example, Dem. 36. 15, 41. 14. Cf. Scafuro 1997: 131–5.

[33] Fisher 1995 skilfully explores the inherent tension between Athenian support for the authority of the *kurios*, and Athenian social concepts mandating protection for dependent persons.

[34] Note in particular the provisions against child prostitution at 1. 13; cf. the pedagogic

consonant with the recognition of *douloi* as integral members of the household.[35] In a ceremony analogous to that which greeted the entry of a bride, a newly purchased slave was welcomed into the *oikos* with an outpouring of figs, dates, and other delicacies intended to portend a 'sweet and pleasant' future.[36] The mistress of the house was expected (at least by Xenophon) to provide care for slaves who might become ill: not a single case is reported where a slave was abandoned because of old-age.[37] Although slaves were generally within the complete power of their *kurioi*, they were entitled even within the household to protection from *hubris*—just as Athenian parents had some discretion to deny even life to new-born children, but not to abuse their dependent children sexually (D. Cohen 1991b: 183).[38] And outside the household, relative to other inhabitants of Attica (free or slave), the Athenian *doulos* was under no legal obligation of subservience. For example, even the prominent Callipus, *proxenos* of the Heracleotes, pressing a claim at a bank, was dismissed by a slave functionary with the derisive 'And what business is it of yours?' (Dem. 52. 5–6). Athenian slaves who allegedly did not need even to yield on the street to a free person had no obligation to acquiesce in sexual *hubris* from outsiders.[39]

Within the *oikos*, the adult male citizen had little opportunity to function as a sexual predator. As Foxhall has shown (1994), following earlier work by Hunter (principally 1989a), the presence within many *oikoi* of more than a single generation often resulted in the senior female member's significant influence—sometimes

regulations set forth at 1. 9–11 and the penalties for procurement of free minors (προαγωγεία) at 1. 14.

[35] Slaves are explicitly included by Aristotle as members of the *oikos*, along with husband, wife, and children (*Pol.* 1253^{b}4–7). Indeed, the slave, as a member of the *oikos*, was frequently referred to as an *oiketes*.

[36] *Lexica Segueriana* 269. 9. Cf. Ar. *Plut.* 768 and schol.; Dem. 45. 74; Pollux 3. 77; Harpocration and *Suda*, s.v. καταχύσματα.

[37] Xen. *Oec.* 7. 24, 37; Pomeroy 1994: 223. Cf. de Ste Croix 1988: 25–6. Dem. 47. 55–6 tells of an elderly servant who after manumission had lived independently with her husband, but on his death, in need, had come back to her ex-master's family, who in turn professed an obligation to care for her.

[38] For the extent and context of infanticide at Athens, see Patterson 1985; Golden 1988; for slaves' protection from murder by their masters, see Antiph. 5. 48; schol. Aeschin. 2. 87; Harrison 1968: 171–2. For the flagrantly outrageous treatment required for *hubris* against a slave, see Fisher 1992: 40.

[39] See Xen. *Ath. Pol.* 1. 10: οὔτε ὑπεκστήσεταί σοι ὁ δοῦλος ('Nor will a slave stand aside for you'). Cf. Bechtle 1996.

even dominance. Late marriage for men (usually at about thirty) encouraged prolonged male adolescence and dependence; early marriage for women (often shortly after puberty) meant early social maturation—and most significantly, in many cases early widowhood. Such relatively young widows would have instructed their daughters, influenced their sons, and controlled household operations (Hunter 1989b). Hence, the Athenian phenomenon (described by Aeschines) of numerous naive young men of wealth whose widowed mothers actively managed the family property (1. 170). This phenomenon of the strong wife or widow is exemplified by the dominant familial influence of Cleoboule, mother of the Athenian leader Demosthenes,[40] and by the mother and wife of the wealthy and influential Lysias, who did not dare to bring his girl-friend, even chaperoned by her 'mother', to his own home (Dem. 59. 22). And even in cases where no mother or mother-in-law was present, the Athenian male was far from a domineering sexual exploiter. In Menander's *Plocium*, for example, the husband of Crobyle is portrayed as reduced to whining ineffectively after his wife has ejected from the house a servant-girl in whom he was interested (fr. 333–4 Koerte, 402–3 Kock). Because there survive no other detailed chronicles of the adult male's ability to take wanton sexual advantage of servile retainers, *Lysias* 1 is often cited as exemplar. But in this narrative, the 'master's' spouse locks him in his bedroom lest—his wife asserts—he renew his prior drunken 'attempt' at the household's servant-girl. With her *kurios* dominantly imprisoned, his wife can enjoy sex with her lover without interference! (Lys. 1. 11–13).

CONSENSUAL SEX: 'PROSTITUTION BY CONTRACT', NOT STATUS

'Now let me tell you how it happens that it has become the prevailing custom to say that persons have become prostitutes "under written agreement". One of our citizens . . . is said to have been a prostitute in accordance with a written contract deposited with Anticles. Now, since he was not a private person, but active in public affairs and a lightning-rod for attacks, he caused the city to become accustomed to this expres-

[40] See Dem. 27 and related speeches. Cf. Hunter 1989a: 43–6; Foxhall 1996: 144–7.

sion, and that's the reason why some people inquire if the (sexual) act has been "under written agreement".' (Aeschin. 1. 165)[41]

The prevalence of written agreements governing the commitments and entitlements of Athenian prostitutes and customers clashes with scholarly preconceptions that emphasize the controlling importance of juridical status—not private arrangements—in Athenian life. Indeed, some scholars recently have been questioning whether Athenian law even recognized 'contractual autonomy'—the right to enter into agreements legally enforceable without regard to a party's personal status.[42] And many economic historians passionately deny the applicability to Athenian society of conventional economic concepts—pricing mechanisms, market principles, supply-and-demand considerations.[43] For this school, vocational functions are 'embedded' in political and social arrangements, employment arrangements are 'conventional rather than market-determined', and compensation is 'remarkably undifferentiated'.[44] Consensual arrangements would have been meaningless in a society in which virtually every worker received a 'standard wage' of 1 drachma per day, and the assignment of labour functions accordingly reflected not monetary motivations, but a 'wider social context'.[45] In such an 'economy', employment as a prostitute might well have been determined by caste—a service function allocated to foreigners and slaves whose abject political

[41] *πόθεν οὖν ἴσχυκε καὶ σύνηθες γεγένηται λέγειν, ὡς κατὰ γραμματεῖον ἤδη τινὲς ἡταίρησαν, ἐρῶ. ἀνὴρ εἷς τῶν πολιτῶν . . . λέγεται κατὰ συνθήκας ἡταιρηκέναι τὰς παρ' Ἀντικλεῖ κειμένας· οὐκ ὢν ⟨δ'⟩ ἰδιώτης, ἀλλὰ πρὸς τὰ κοινὰ προσιὼν καὶ λοιδορίαις περιπίπτων, εἰς συνήθειαν ἐποίησε τοῦ λόγου τούτου τὴν πόλιν καταστῆναι, καὶ διὰ τοῦτο ἐρωτῶσί τινες, εἰ κατὰ γραμματεῖον ἡ πρᾶξις γεγένηται.*

[42] See Todd 1994. Cf. E. Cohen 1994.

[43] Cf., for example, Meikle 1995b; Finley 1985: 21.

[44] Finley 1985: 212 n. 19, 80. Anthropologists have developed models of primitive groups where production, distribution, and consumption are accomplished solely through familial or political relationships. In such societies, economic activity supposedly cannot occur without direct social significance; the economy thus is said to be 'embedded' in the society itself. See Polanyi, Arensberg, and Pearson 1957: 68; Polanyi 1944: 63–4; Wohl 1998: 215 n. 18; Lowry 1987: 2; Humphreys 1978: 152. Finley, following Weber's sweeping conceptualization (1924 (1909); 1921) of the subordination of economic considerations to politics in antiquity, argued that at Athens the economy was embedded in social relations and claimed that in such entities 'political rights' pre-empted 'economic interests' (1985: 80–1). Finley's view has been widely accepted.

[45] Stewart 1990: 65. A sampling of proponents of a standard wage at Athens (set by modern academic edict at 1 drachma per day): Burford 1972: 138; Himmelmann 1979; Gallo 1987: esp. 47, 58.

position rendered such work appropriate. But the Athens of reality was far different.

In fact, the prevailing economic model of 'undifferentiated' and 'standard' wages is itself internally inconsistent and empirically erroneous. Ampolo and Migeotte have demonstrated the absence of a 'fixed' or 'normal' price for grain.[46] Loomis has shown from an analysis of actual data that 'there was *no* standard wage at Athens' and that wage rates were more reflective 'of a market economy than the modern orthodoxy has held'.[47] In any event, a theoretically consistent, politically derived allocation of resources would have mandated higher wages for citizens than for other workers, but among *politai* an egalitarian treatment. However, the polis itself, in its own wage practices, pursued a policy totally inconsistent with any such expectation. It indiscriminately employed free foreigners, citizens, and slaves to perform similar services for similar compensation, but paid to its citizen functionaries quite varying compensation for differing tasks (see Arist. *Ath. Pol.* 62. 2). The compensation paid to a diverse group of 'skilled' and 'unskilled' workers—citizens, metics, slaves—at Eleusis in 329/8 and 327/6 likewise varied considerably, but according to trade and task, not pursuant to the political 'order' to which the worker belonged.[48] Again, without regard to 'status', the slaves, foreigners, and citizens working on construction of the Erechtheum between 409 and 407 were all paid precisely the same wage, a single drachma per day.[49] Political rights likewise appear to have played no role in the type of labour performed: we find, for example, nine citizens, twelve metics, and sixteen slaves working as masons.[50] The state's indiscriminate arrangements corresponded to the pattern prevailing in private businesses, where many slaves and many free residents of Attica—citizen and metic—worked in crafts

[46] Ampolo 1986: 146–7; Migeotte (forthcoming). Cf. Reger 1993: 312–14.

[47] Loomis 1997: 1 (his italics). Cf. Loomis 1998.

[48] *IG* II² 1672–3. A sampling of wages: workers carrying construction materials (such as bricks or wood), sifting plaster, mixing mortar, breaking clods, 2 dr. 3 obols per day (*IG* II² 1672–3. 28–30, 32–4, 44–6, 60–2); two sawyers, 3 dr. (perhaps aggregate pay for both: *IG* II² 1672. 159–60); workers laying bricks and working on wood, 2½ dr. (*IG* II² 1672. 26–8); workers laying roof tiles, 2 dr. (*IG* II² 1672. 110–11); architect, 2 dr. (*IG* II² 1672. 12); mason finishing stone and plasterer, 1 dr., 1½ obols each (*IG* II² 1672. 31–2).

[49] *IG* I³ 474–6. See Randall 1953; Paton 1927: 338–9, 380, 382, 398, 416.

[50] No slave sculptors or woodcarvers are attested, but citizens are not lacking: three *politai* and five metics appear as sculptors, but five metic woodcarvers outnumber a single citizen. See R. Osborne 1995: 30.

or trades,[51] while many slaves 'living independently', 'indistinguishable in dress and appearance from free men' (Fisher 1993: 53), often conducted their own businesses, retaining the net revenues after predetermined payments to their owners.[52] In some cases, these *douloi* even owned their own slaves.[53] Even within Athenian households, free women worked alongside domestic slaves at many tasks.[54]

Despite occasional assertions to the contrary,[55] there is no evidence for governmental controls on pricing or other aspects of the sexual economy.[56] Prices for sexual services largely reflected market factors—especially consumer preference. Consider Demosthenes 59, a presentation focused on Neaera, a woman (according to the plaintiff) long notorious as a whore but for decades passing as an Athenian *politis* ('female citizen')—an improbable (and therefore unpersuasive) accusatory coupling if prostitution were truly incompatible with 'citizenship'.[57] In fact, it is precisely the possibility of large numbers of female citizens becoming courtesans that Apollodorus hyperbolically warns against: *politides* lacking wealthy relatives to provide appropriate

[51] See Hopper 1979: 140; Finley 1981: 99; Ehrenberg 1962: 162; R. Osborne 1995: 30.

[52] For slaves maintaining their own households (δοῦλοι χωρὶς οἰκοῦντες), see E. Cohen 1998; Perotti 1974.

[53] See *IG* II² 1570. 78–9 with regard to [. . .]leides (whose name has been incompletely preserved). Ownership of slaves by persons themselves enslaved is not unique to Athens: in Rome, for example, slaves routinely owned other slaves—sometimes in large numbers. See Watson 1987: 95.

[54] See, for example, Ischomachus' wife at Xen. *Oec.* 7. 6.

[55] For example, Krenkel (1978; 1988: 1294, 1296) asserts that polis officials imposed a 'standard fee' of 4 drachmas on male prostitutes, unjustifiably generalizing from an isolated prostitute's claim for 4 drachmas (Aeschin. 1. 158). From the limitation on flute-girls' compensation (that he attributes to the *agoranomoi*—see following note), Krenkel incorrectly derives a general limitation on female prostitutes' 'charge for a single visit' (1988: 1294).

[56] Arist. *Ath. Pol.* 50. 2 does report that the *astunomoi* set a maximum fee of 2 drachmas for females who played reed-pipes, harps, and/or lyres. Even if we assume that these musicians 'might also be called on to provide sexual entertainment' (Rhodes 1981: 574), this is far from proof of a general limitation on the fees of female sexual workers. (On the 'fluidity' of female 'discursive categories', see Henry 1986: 147; Kurke 1997: 109; on the diversity and complexity of the sexual market for women in Athens, Davidson 1997: 74–6.) The limitation on compensation here seems intended to avoid brawls on the street from competing revellers: 'on the street the flute-girls really came into their element, in the *kômos*, a conga of revellers' (ibid.: 81), where 'Woman is present as musician, dancer, flutist, or parasol-bearer, not as hetaira' (Frontisi-Ducroux and Lissarrague 1990: 228).

[57] Whether Neaera herself actually was a former prostitute is beyond our knowledge, but the speaker's presupposition (that such a woman could pass for decades as an Athenian citizen) is significant—see n. 1 above. For the equation of πολίτιδες and Athenian 'citizens', see n. 6 above.

dowries will become prostitutes if the prohibition against marriage with foreigners (encouraging men to marry even poor *politides* of middling appearance) is not enforced (Dem. 59. 112–13). (In the early third century an Athenian *aste*, who was a prostitute, is in fact parodied by Antiphanes as having neither guardian nor kinsmen, and thus presumably lacking a dowry.[58]) Unenslaved women drew premium prices. The procuress Nicarete, herself a freedwoman, supposedly presented as her own offspring the child prostitutes whom she owned, including Neaera, who allegedly came whoring to Attica before reaching puberty. Nicarete's motivation: the 'highest prices' might be obtained from customers desiring to have sex with young girls whom they believed to be the free offspring of the woman providing the children's services.[59] But customers would also pay higher fees for sexual relations with women of seemingly bourgeois pretension living in a stable marital relationship[60]—a market phenomenon (also encountered in modern sexual commerce) of enhanced payment for denigration.[61] Indeed, the cultural significance at Athens of 'zero-sum competition' would have further enhanced the market attractiveness of free prostitutes, and especially of youths from established families: in the agonistic environment of Athens, only to the extent that sexual submission is felt to dishonour and humiliate a person or his/her 'household' is the purchaser's self-esteem and perceived self-worth enhanced.[62] The resultant willingness of customers to lavish huge sums on citizen prostitutes is exemplified by Simon, who supposedly con-

[58] Fr. 210 (K–A) (= Ath. 13. 29 (572a)). I am grateful to W. T. Loomis for calling this citation to my attention.

[59] Dem. 59. 19: *ἵν' ὡς μεγίστους μισθοὺς πράττοιτο τοὺς βουλομένους πλησιάζειν αὐταῖς ὡς ἐλευθέραις οὔσαις.*

[60] Dem. 59. 41: *τοὺς δὲ μισθοὺς μείζους ἐπράττετο τοὺς βουλομένους αὐτῇ πλησιάζειν, ὡς ἐπὶ προσχήματος ἤδη τινὸς οὖσα καὶ ἀνδρὶ συνοικοῦσα.*

[61] Psychological elements—especially of debasement and abuse—not directly related to genital sexuality are an important determinant of modern prostitutional compensation (Rosen 1982: 97; Pateman 1988: 259 n. 33). According to some observers, denigration is the essence of purchased eroticism: 'prostitution and pornography are acts of dominance expressed through sexuality' (Kitzinger 1994: 197). But purchased debasement does not lack ideological defence: sado-masochistic lesbian groups valorize what others consider to be the 'dehumanization of sexual relations' involved in customers' frequent choice of 'abusive' satisfactions. See Barry 1995: 69–73, 79–90; Leidholdt 1990: ix; Goode 1978: 72. The continued erotic centrality of power within ostensibly egalitarian female relationships has evoked considerable analytical concern (see Kitzinger 1991; 1994; Hoagland 1988; Lobel 1986).

[62] On the centrality of 'zero-sum' competition in Athenian culture, see Gouldner 1965: 49; Dover 1964: 31; Winkler 1990: 178; D. Cohen 1995: 63.

tracted to pay the *polites* Theodotus 300 drachmas—when his own possessions amounted to only 250 drachmas![63] But this desire to prevail—to enhance oneself by debasing another—could easily lead to the would-be predator's victimization. Neaera supposedly would entice a 'wealthy but unknowledgeable foreigner' into a sexual relationship, after which her 'husband' Stephanus, as an outraged cuckold, would extract a considerable cash settlement from the victim (Dem. 59. 41). Similarly in Hyperides 3, Antigone (a former prostitute, now a brothel-operator) in a complex contractual arrangement allegedly defrauds a young *polites*, Epicrates. She and her metic confederate, Athenogenes, sell an entire perfumery operation to Epicrates, who had no interest in the business but lusted after the son of the slave, a *doulos* 'living independently' who operated the enterprise. By purchasing the business and freeing the slaves, Epicrates hoped to gain the slave boy's gratitude and goodwill (Hyp. 3. 6).

For the *hetairoi* of Athens, contractual arrangements for sexual services—whether directly explicit, as in Lysias 3, or constructed with greater complexity, as in Hyperides 3—were the norm. Aeschines—contrary to his own litigational interest (he was unable to provide written confirmation of his charges of prostitution

[63] Lys. 3. 22–4. Lysias 3 identifies Theodotus as a Plataean, and hence presumably an Athenian *polites*. But Dover (1989 (1978): 32–3) has claimed that Theodotus was of 'marginal citizenship status', since some Plataeans may have been denied *politeia* when the Athenians, prior to 427, bestowed their 'citizenship' on the Plataeans and their descendants. However, the relevant decree (preserved at Dem. 59. 104) makes no mention of any exceptions, and explicitly provides not for 'marginal citizenship status' but for full equality with all other Athenians. (On the authenticity of Dem. 59. 104, see Carey 1992: 139; M. Osborne 1981–3: ii. 13–16; Lambert 1993: 115–16.) Although the original grantees could not hold certain administrative and religious offices, their descendants were fully eligible for such positions: the 'young Plataean Theodotus' (as Dover calls him) some thirty-five years later was necessarily such a scion. In any event, potential challenges based on defects in individual entitlement at the time of the original decree would have been precluded by the rider of Nicomenes attached in 403 to the resolution renewing the 'citizenship law' of Pericles, specifically forbidding evaluation of the qualifications of those who had been accepted as *politai* before 403/2 (schol. Aeschin. 1. 39; cf. Dem. 57. 30). Lysias 23 demonstrates that after 403 a Plataean's claim to Athenian 'citizenship' could be rebutted only by a showing that the claimant was in fact not a Plataean or of Plataean descent: see E. Cohen 1994: 146–9. Lamb has puzzled over the speaker's allusion to 'this child, who was capable of giving information under torture' (Lamb's Loeb translation of §33): 'If Theodotus was a *free* Plataean, he would have the same rights as an Athenian citizen, and could not be subjected to torture' (1930: 86 n. a.). Cf. Carey 1988. But Gagarin (1996: 2) has shown that 'clearly *βάσανος*, in some uses at least, is not the same thing as its common modern translation, "torture"', 'in the orators it sometimes retains the simple sense of a "test" (Andoc. 1. 30; Isae. 9. 29). . . an interrogation'.

against Timarchus)—acknowledges that male prostitutes were often said to work 'under written contract'.[64] References to such contractual arrangements were so commonplace that the phrase 'whoring under contract' (*syngraphe*)—a usage popularized by a prominent *polites* who had worked as a prostitute—had become idiomatic in local discourse (Aeschin. 1. 165). Requests were routinely anticipated in court proceedings for written confirmation of commercial sexual acts.[65] As with written agreements for other commercial undertakings, contracts for sexual services appear on occasion even to have been deposited for safeguarding with third persons,[66] and prostitutional obligations, as was the case with other contractual arrangements, were undertaken with a panoply of witnesses to confirm the agreements.[67]

Even female courtesans are known to have entered into elaborate contractual commitments. In Plautus' *Asinaria*, an adaptation of a Hellenic original,[68] there is presented, in comic version, but at considerable length, a contract in writing (termed *syngraphus*, the Latin rendering of the Greek *syngraphe*), providing for Philaenium, daughter of Cleareta, to spend her time exclusively with the Athenian Diabolus for a period of one year at a price of 2,000 drachmas, a 'gift' paid in advance.[69] The contract contains extended provisions of humorous paranoia—for example, Philaenium is not even to gaze upon another man and must swear only by female deities. Similar Greek contractual arrangements with

[64] Loeb translation of *κατὰ γραμματεῖον* (Adams 1919): for *grammateion* as written contract, see Lys. 32. 7 ('*τὰ γράμματα* would include the contracts relating to the loans': Carey 1989: 214). Cf. *P. Oxy*. 1012, fr. 9 ii. 15. For the relevant text (Aeschin. 1. 165), see n. 41 above. For the distinction between *hetairoi* and *pornoi*, see above n. 5.

[65] Aeschin. 1. 160: *ἐὰν δ' ἐπιχειρῶσι λέγειν ὡς οὐχ ἡταίρηκεν ὅστις μὴ κατὰ συγγραφὰς ἐμισθώθη, καὶ γραμματεῖον καὶ μάρτυρας ἀξιῶσί με τούτων παρασχέσθαι* . . . ('If they shall undertake to say that no man has been a prostitute who has not been hired under a written contract, and they urge me to produce written documentation and witnesses . . .'). Cf. 1. 165: *ἐρωτῶσί τινες εἰ κατὰ γραμματεῖον ἡ πρᾶξις γεγένηται* ('some men ask if the act has been done pursuant to written documentation').

[66] Aeschin. 1. 165: *λέγεται κατὰ συνθήκας ἡταιρηκέναι τὰς παρ' Ἀντικλεῖ κειμένας·* ('He is said to have been a prostitute in accordance with a contract deposited with Anticles'). For safekeeping of maritime loan agreements, for example, see Dem. 34. 6; 56. 15.

[67] Aeschin. 1. 125: *ἀγοραῖα τεκμήρια*. Without witnesses, even written agreements were unrecognized and unenforceable until very late in the fourth century. See Thomas 1989: 41–5; Pringsheim 1955.

[68] For the validity of the use of Roman comic material as evidence for Athenian legal and social practices, see Scafuro 1997: 16–19; Paoli 1976: 76–7.

[69] Lines 751–4: Diabolus Glauci filius Clearetae | lenae dedit dono argenti viginti minas, | Philaenium ut secum esset noctes et dies | hunc annum totum.

courtesans are alluded to in a number of other Plautine comedies and in a work of Turpilius (who seems often to have adapted plays from Menander).[70] From Athenian sources, we know directly of the complex financial arrangements made by the *hetaira* Neaera in Corinth with the Athenian Phrynion—and with Timanoridas the Corinthian, Eucrates of Leucas, and other of her 'lovers'.[71] The same woman later, acting on her own behalf in a private arbitration proceeding at Athens, reached agreement with two Athenian patrons requiring mutual consent for any alteration in the terms governing allocations of property and obligations of maintenance undertaken in exchange for her provision of sexual services to both men (Dem. 59. 45–6). Although these arrangements are presented by the courtesan's opponent without comment and with-out invective (in a speech otherwise replete with personalized contumely directed at the *hetaira*), modern scholarship has been horrified. For the editor of the only commentary on the speech available in English, the contractual provisions are 'a further indication of her degraded life that she can be shared in this way . . . passed back and forth daily like an object' (Carey 1992: 110–11).

Such reactions reflect, at least in part, the chasm between Athenian and modern conceptualizations of prostitution. Contemporary Western thought and governmental regulation largely continue to 'embed' prostitution within prevailing social, political, and religious values that see prostitution as morally degenerate and humanly exploitative, a selling of one's self rather than a contracting out of a particular type of labour for a set period in exchange for money and/or other consideration.[72] In contrast with the

[70] See Plaut. *Merc.* 536ff.; *Bacch.* fr. 10 and 896ff.; Turpilius Com. fr. 112 (Ribbeck). Cf. Schonbeck 1981: 150–1 and 203 n. 73; Herter 1960: 81 nn. 193 and 194.

[71] Dem. 59. 29–32.

[72] See, for example, Barry 1995: 220–42; Rosen 1982; Walkowitz 1980. Neither of the two principal Athenian clusters of words for persons and acts relating to prostitution—those cognate to *pernanai* ('to sell') and those cognate to *hetairein* ('to be a companion') (above, n. 5)—inherently denominate prostitution as a sale of sexual services alone or as a sale of the body itself. Scholars, however, have generally interpreted and translated both terms as though they both carried the solitary meaning, in Dover's words, of 'sale of one's own body': Dover 1989 (1978): 20. But cf. Henry (1996), who explicitly deems prostitution an exchange of 'sexual service' for 'other resource'. Greek usage is equivocal: cf. Aeschin. 1. 29: 'ἡταιρηκώς'· τὸν γὰρ τὸ σῶμα τὸ ἑαυτοῦ ἐφ' ὕβρει πεπρακότα ('to be a prostitute: one who has sold his own body for *hubris*'); 1. 31: καταγελάστως μὲν κεχρημένου τῷ ἑαυτοῦ σώματι ('who has used his own body despicably'); 1. 40: πωλεῖν αὐτὸν προῃρημένος . . . ἐχρήσαντο

Athenian use of written contract to provide for the individualized sale of sexual services (in a society where written contracts are believed to have been relatively unimportant[73]), prevailing modern juridical theory rejects prostitution as within the ken of employment contracts, denying that 'the prostitution contract is exactly like—or is one example of—the employment contract . . . . A prostitute does not . . . contract out use of *sexual services*'.[74]

But consensual arrangements for sexual services did not evoke moral outrage at Athens. Prostitution enjoyed the goodwill of the goddess Aphrodite, divinity of sex: 'in ancient Greece prostitutes clearly functioned as mediators of Aphrodite's power, their sexual skills a sort of "technology" that canalized her potent force.'[75] Attic law, furthermore, mandated the recognition of 'whatever arrangements either party willingly agreed upon with the other',[76] and some written contracts explicitly provided for the priority of such private agreements even over laws and decrees.[77] The Athenian government not only tolerated prostitution by *politai*—it sought to share in the revenues! Each year the boule delivered to private tax-collectors a list of prostitutes subject to the occupational levy

τῷ σώματι ⟨τῷ⟩ Τιμάρχου ('they used the body of Timarchos . . . who had chosen to sell himself'); 1. 51: ἡταιρηκέναι . . . ἐπὶ μισθῷ δὲ τὴν πρᾶξιν ποιούμενος ('to be a prostitute . . . doing the act for pay').

[73] See, for example, Thomas 1992: 89, 149; Harris 1989: 68–70. But, as Stroud argues persuasively (1998: 45–8), new evidence and fresh consideration suggest that *syngraphai* may have been used more frequently and earlier than has been acknowledged.

[74] Pateman 1988: 191 (her emphasis). Cf. Richards 1982: 115, 121; Ericcson 1980: 335–66; McIntosh 1978: 54.

[75] Thornton 1997: 152. For prostitutes as devotees and beneficiaries of Aphrodite, see, for example, Paus. 8. 6. 5; 10. 15. 1; Ath. 588c, 590e.

[76] Dem. 56. 2: τοῖς νόμοις τοῖς ὑμετέροις (sc. Ἀθηναίοις) οἳ κελεύουσι, ὅσα ἄν τις ἑκὼν ἕτερος ἑτέρῳ ὁμολογήσῃ κύρια εἶναι. Similarly: Dem. 42. 12; 47. 77; Hyp. 3. 13; Din. 3. 4; Pl. *Symp.* 196c.

[77] The maritime-loan document preserved at Dem. 35. 10–13, the sole surviving text of an actual Athenian sea-finance agreement, provides explicitly that as to the matters encompassed therein, 'nothing else has greater validity than (this) contract' (κυριώτερον δὲ περὶ τούτων ἄλλο μηδὲν εἶναι τῆς συγγραφῆς). This clause is characterized in the text of Dem. 35. 39 as giving the contract priority over laws and decrees: ἡ μὲν γὰρ συγγραφὴ οὐδὲν κυριώτερον ἐᾷ εἶναι τῶν ἐγγεγραμμένων, οὐδὲ προσφέρειν οὔτε νόμον οὔτε ψήφισμα οὔτ' ἄλλ' οὐδ' ὁτιοῦν πρὸς τὴν συγγραφήν· ('for the written agreement does not permit anything to have greater validity than the provisions set forth therein in writing, nor that any law or decree or anything at all take priority over the written contract'). (On the authenticity of this document, see Purpura 1987: 203–6.) A similar provision was found in the written agreement which is the subject of litigation in Demosthenes 56 (see §26). Cf. *IG* XII 7. 27, 67, and 76.

on courtesans (Aeschin. 1. 119).[78] The names of citizens must have been found routinely among those listed, for Timarchus' defenders, seeking to show that he had not prostituted himself, argued that his name was absent from these lists (Aeschin. 1. 119)—a nugatory contention if the names of *politai* had not regularly appeared on the annual registers. Indeed, one *polites* engaged in prostitution, the orphan Diophantus, in seeking to collect 4 drachmas owed as payment for a sex act, even sought the active aid of the archon (who was charged with protecting minors who had lost their fathers) (Aeschin. 1. 158).

Athenian moral outrage, however, was reserved for forms of labour, in particular, 'gainful employment', 'useful labour', 'the work ethic', that are extolled under modern socialism and capitalism.[79] Although many free Athenians were engaged in a great variety of occupations, unable or unwilling to attain the philosophically expressed ideal of leisurely dedication to cultural and social activities, Athenians abhorred extended labour for a single employer.[80] Employment by a master for brief periods, a day or two, might have been acceptable to a few citizens,[81] but prolonged service was intolerable. In Aristotle's words, 'the nature of the free man prevents his living under the control of another'.[82] Because prostitution was often promiscuous, involving numerous customers for short periods of time, or at least might be pursuant to negotiated terms memorialized in writing, personal provision of sexual services was not inherently incompatible with Athenian values. The contractual arrangements of Theodotus

[78] From the time of Caligula (first century AD) to the late fifth century, the Romans likewise imposed a tax on prostitutes (and on pimps): see McGinn 1989.

[79] The academic inclination to view ancient societies through modernizing lenses has a long and deleterious pedigree. 'We are badly in need of comparative studies which overcome the tendency to base judgment on the standards of the nineteenth and twentieth centuries, which in fact constitute the exception in terms of universal history' (Nippel 1985: 419).

[80] While 'metic-status was autonomous, ambiguous, and did not "naturally" gravitate either down toward slaves or up toward citizens' (Whitehead 1977: 115), metics of free Greek origin would likely have harboured the same attitudes as Athenian citizens toward 'servile' employment. Aeschin. 1. 42 emphasizes that Timarchus was under no financial pressure to work as a prostitute.

[81] Although most of those standing daily for hire at Colonus Agoraeus in Athens were slaves, some might have been free men: see Pherecrates, fr. 134 (Edmonds 256 = K-A 142). Cf. Fuks 1951: 171–3.

[82] Arist. *Rhet.* 1367^{a}32: ἐλευθέρου γὰρ τὸ μὴ πρὸς ἄλλον ζῆν. It was not manual labour itself, but dependence on a master that was despised. See Isae. 5. 39. Cf. Isoc. 14. 48; Dem. 57. 45; Xen. *Mem.* 2. 8. 1–5. See also Humphreys 1993: 10.

and Neaera reflected this liberating ideal, as did the avoidance by free persons of sexual labour in a brothel[83] or financial work in a bank.[84]

Antagonism to work under a master should not be confused with antipathy to labour itself.[85] But in the fourth century a sector of Athenian opinion did object to any form of endeavour that, violating Athenian traditions of self-sufficiency and non-monetary reciprocity, sought monetary aggrandizement through exchange of services or goods, or that promoted non-traditional, especially flagrant, expenditures. Aeschines' speech against Timarchus invokes an Athenian law that prohibited participation as a speaker in the Assembly by those who had, *inter alia*, accepted compensation for sex, wasted family assets or inheritances, or had failed to provide for a parent.[86] Aeschines emphasizes Timarchus' dual economic crimes: although financially able to pursue the Athenian ideal of self-sufficiency, in order to palliate his addiction to excessive consumption (expensive meals, luxurious women, and gambling), Timarchus had enslaved himself by accepting compensation for sexual services, and had wasted his paternal estate (Aeschin. 1. 42, 75–6, 154).

In the monetized economy of fourth-century Athens, conservative opinion yearned for an earlier period when services were provided not as a commodity to be paid for, but more 'naturally' through the self-sufficiency of households.[87] In the *Politics*,

[83] Prevailing scholarship assumes that 'houses' were staffed by servile labour. Krenkel 1988: 1295: 'slave boys were forced into prostitution; they would ply their trade in brothels and in private lodgings called stegoi by Aeschines (1. 36)'. Cf. Davidson 1997: 83–91.

[84] For the operation of *trapezai*—even at the highest levels of financial responsibility and remuneration—exclusively by slaves and family members, see E. Cohen 1992: 70–82.

[85] For the distinction, and an analysis of its historical basis, see Wood 1988: 126–45, esp. 139.

[86] Aeschin. 1. 28–32: '*δοκιμασία ῥητόρων· ἐάν τις λέγῃ ἐν τῷ δήμῳ τὸν πατέρα τύπτων ἢ τὴν μητέρα, ἢ μὴ τρέφων, ἢ μὴ παρέχων οἴκησιν*', *τοῦτον οὐκ ἐᾷ λέγειν* . . . '*ἢ τὰς στρατείας μὴ ἐστρατευμένος* . . . *ἢ τὴν ἀσπίδα ἀποβεβληκώς*' . . . '*ἢ πεπορνευμένος ἢ ἡταιρηκώς*' . . . '*ἢ τὰ πατρῷα κατεδηδοκώς, ἢ ὧν ἂν κληρονόμος γένηται*' . . . '*δοκιμασίαν μέν ἐπαγγειλάτω Ἀθηναίων ὁ βουλόμενος, οἷς ἔξεστιν*' ('Scrutiny of Official Speakers: If someone should speak in the Assembly who beats his father or mother, or does not support them, or does not provide lodging for them', (the law) does not permit (him) to speak . . . 'nor someone who has avoided military service' . . . 'or has thrown away his shield' . . . 'or has been a prostitute or a courtesan' . . . 'or has wasted his family's estate, or that of which he has been heir' . . . 'let anyone who wishes, of those Athenians who are qualified, challenge his Scrutiny'). Beyond participation in the Assembly, a number of other positions of honour or opportunity were also foreclosed to prostitutes: Aeschin. 1. 19–20.

[87] 'Naturally': *κατὰ φύσιν* (Arist. *Pol.* 1258^{b}1).

Aristotle notes the relatively recent development of a new type of economic activity which had adversely affected traditional values and methods.[88] The 'monied mode of acquisition' (*khrematistike ktetike* (*tekhne*))[89] had arisen from the new dominance of economic activity by persons motivated by profit considerations ('making money from one another').[90] This individualistic pursuit of profit reflected society's new functioning through the exchange of goods and services for money, a process superseding the prior system of household production/consumption supplemented by barter based on social and political relations. Although Aristotle longs for the former arrangement, its replacement by impersonal coined money is what he actually portrays—and rues.[91] Modern scholars likewise sharply differentiate the nature of economic activity at Athens in the fourth century from that prevailing earlier.[92] While coinage of high value (useful only for settling large transactions) was introduced into mainland Greece by the late sixth century,[93] and

[88] Aristotle sees the introduction of coinage as the precondition to the development of retail trade (*τὸ καπηλικόν*), but explicitly separates an earlier, 'simple' state of this trade from the profit-seeking, complex market activity existing in his own time: *πορισθέντος οὖν ἤδη νομίσματος ἐκ τῆς ἀναγκαίας ἀλλαγῆς θάτερον εἶδος τῆς χρηματιστικῆς ἐγένετο, τὸ καπηλικόν, τὸ μὲν πρῶτον ἁπλῶς ἴσως γινόμενον, εἶτα δι' ἐμπειρίας ἤδη τεχνικώτερον, πόθεν καὶ πῶς μεταβαλλόμενον πλεῖστον ποιήσει κέρδος* ('once a supply of money came into being, for the necessities of exchange, that other form of money-making arose—commercial trade—at first perhaps arising simply, then through experience becoming more sophisticated, [focusing on] whence and how trade [*lit.* (an item) being exchanged] will yield the most profit') (*Pol.* 1257^{b}1–5).

[89] *χρηματιστική*, an adjective, is derived from the noun *χρῆμα*, which carried a dual meaning of 'money' or of 'property' (goods, chattels, etc.). When applied to the fourth-century market, as in the Aristotelian phrase *ἡ κτητικὴ χρηματιστικὴ* (*τέχνη*) (*Pol.* 1256^{b}40–1), the monetary notation is clearly present. Cf. Humphreys 1993: 12: '*chrematistike*, the art of money-making'.

[90] Arist. *Pol.* 1258^{b}1–4: *τῆς δὲ μεταβλητικῆς ψεγομένης δικαίως* (*οὐ γὰρ κατὰ φύσιν ἀλλ' ἀπ' ἀλλήλων ἐστιν*). For Aristotle's view on the appropriate role of money, see *Eth. Nic.* 1133^{a}19–29, 1133^{b}10–28.

[91] Aristotle, however, recognized the dichotomy between focus on the ideal (*περὶ τῆς μελλούσης κατ' εὐχὴν συνεστάναι πόλεως*: *Pol.* 1325^{b}36–8), and recognition of actual phenomena (*τῶν γιγνομένων διὰ τῆς αἰσθήσεως*: 1328^{a}20–1).

[92] Polanyi et al. 1957: 67 ('in Aristotle's writings we possess an eyewitness account . . . of incipient market trading at its very first appearance in the history of civilization'). Cf. Meikle 1995a: 153–6 (critical of Finley 1970); von Reden 1995: 105–6; Davies 1971: 38–87. Mossé explicitly connects fourth-century developments in commercial banking with 'l'apparition d'une mentalité nouvelle en contradiction avec l'ethique de la cité' (1972: 143).

[93] Von Reden (1995: 171–94) dates 'the establishment of state coinage in the proper sense' to the introduction of the Athena/owl pieces late in the sixth century. Vickers 1985, opposing the general preference for a sixth-century attribution, dates the earliest Athenian 'owls' to sometime between 479 and 462. For the *opinio communis*, see Karweise 1991;

became widespread in the fifth,[94] only in the fourth century were there substantial issues of fractional coinage appropriate for retail trade,[95] and only after 350 did Athens produce a regular bronze coinage.[96] A torrent of recent studies has explored the revolutionary impact of this dissemination of coined money, which was a catalyst for the resultant commoditization of wealth and economic activity, a process that culminated ultimately in the detached monetary transactions of fourth-century Athens.[97]

A law purportedly limiting the political activity of men selling sexual services (or violating other traditional standards of economic conduct) must therefore be seen in the context of conservative objection to all profit-making endeavour.[98] According to Aristotle, many oligarchic states absolutely prohibited citizens from engaging actively in business.[99] Aristocratic thought also condemned as inherently incompatible with 'citizenship' all 'banausic' pursuits—production or trading of goods, labour for monetary compensation, even professional acting or musical performances.[100] Theophrastus is dismissive not only of operating brothels, but even of innkeeping (and tax-collection!).[101] Plato joins as disreputable prostitution, shoemaking, and fish-marketing (*Charm.* 163b). Xenophon finds the commercialization of sex no less disgusting than charging for education (*Mem.* 1. 6. 13). And prostitution was the paradigmatic commercial exchange of sex for compensation.

Howgego 1995: 2–6; Kroll 1997: 175 (who considers von Reden's chronology improperly late).

[94] Rutter 1981. Cf. Howgego 1995: 6–8; Kraay 1976: 317.

[95] Kraay 1964. In Asia Minor, and in a few cities in southern Italy and Sicily, there may have been significant earlier issues of fractional coins (see Kim 1994; 1997; Price 1968; 1979).

[96] Kroll 1979: 24. In the areas to the north and west of the Black Sea, Stancomb 1993 traces a similar monetary development betwen the mid-sixth and mid-fourth centuries.

[97] For the 'fundamental difference between the social consequences of exchange based on coinage on the one hand and on gift exchange on the other' (von Reden 1997: 154) and similar paradigmatic economic alterations, see Kurke 1994: 42; Seaford 1994: 199. Cf. Gill, Postlethwaite, and Seaford 1998; von Reden 1995; Steiner 1994; Kurke 1989. The cultural independence of money is analysed critically, from an anthropological perspective, in Bloch and Parry 1989.

[98] '[T]he trade of Athens, its monetary commercialism, its naval policy, and its democratic tendencies . . . were hated by the oligarchic parties of Athens' (Popper 1950: 173, with regard to the fifth century).

[99] χρηματίζεσθαι (*Pol.* 1316^{b}3–5). Cf. Ober 1991: 125.

[100] On the virulent opposition to *banausia*, see, e.g., Arist. *Pol.* 1337^{b}18–22; 1258^{b}25–7, 33–9; 1260^{a}41–b2; 1277^{a}36–7; 1277^{b}33–1278^{a}13; 1277^{a}32–b7; 1341^{b}8–18. Cf. Humphreys 1978: esp. 148–9.

[101] *Char.* 6. 5. Aeschines is likewise critical of the business of brothel-keeping (1. 188).

Although the Athenian state did not ban this business, the existence of a law forbidding such economic activity by its political leaders, albeit often dismissed as a 'dead letter',[102] gave Aeschines the opportunity to strike at Demosthenes through the indictment of Timarchus.

But Athens was not monolithic, and such views—even where legitimated by the force of traditional law (*patrios nomos*)—could coexist with the reality of a 'city [that] lived entirely by cash transactions', an Athens whose *politai* were 'farmers, fishermen, shopkeepers, market gardeners and small craftsmen' (Humphreys 1978: 148), and prostitutes. We need not be discomfited by the dissonance reflected in the persistence of legislative disincentives to citizen prostitution alongside the widespread, lawful purchase of sex from citizen prostitutes. Athenian culture was 'fraught with ambivalence, ambiguity and conflict' (D. Cohen 1991a: 21). Although classicists and ancient historians have long been in thrall—albeit often without conscious recognition—to 'functionalist' doctrines that stress the 'social solidarity', 'structural equilibrium', or 'cultural uniformity' of societies,[103] a striving for theoretical consistency necessarily obliterates the discontinuities, contradictions, and unintegrated deviations that are inherent in complex and dynamic civilizations.[104] Aristotle may have nostalgically preferred an Athens where citizens did not sell their sexual services (or other commodities and skills) for profit. But that was not the Athens of reality, and even Aristotle (although not an Athenian citizen) accepted compensation for services.

[102] Cf. Davidson 1997: 252: 'The real figures of authority, the real "leaders" of the city were the *rhêtores*, those who made speeches in the Assembly . . . everyone was assumed to be eligible unless challenged. Such challenges were issued very rarely. I know of only one certain example in the whole history of the democracy . . . Timarchus.' But even Timarchus (prior to his politically motivated indictment) for years was openly active in the Assembly (even holding public office). See Dover 1989 (1978): 19.

[103] See Leach's early criticism (1965: 7) of British anthropologists' adherence to functional ideology. Cf. D. Cohen 1995: 9–13.

[104] Cf. Keiser 1986; Rueschemeyer 1984: 134; Bourdieu 1977: 98. Dougherty properly urges us 'to read the multiplicity of narratives that represent Athenians as Athenians in such a way that we preserve their contradictions' (1996: 251). The Athenians were well aware of the complexity, and inconsistency, of their civilization, especially in sexual mores: see Pl. *Symp*. 182a7–9 ('in other *poleis* erotic conventions are easy to understand and well-defined, but at Athens they are *poikilos*'—complex, intricate, many-hued).

References

Adams, C. D. (ed.) 1919. *The Speeches of Aeschines*. Cambridge, Mass.

Allen, D. 1997. 'Imprisonment in Classical Athens', *CQ* 47: 121–35.

Ampolo, C. 1986. 'Il pane quotidiano delle città antiche fra economia e anthropologia', *Opus* 5: 143–51.

Aron, R. 1950. *La philosophie critique de l'histoire, essai sur une théorie allemande de l'histoire*. Paris.

Barry, K. 1995. *The Prostitution of Sexuality*. New York.

Bechtle, G. 1996. 'A Note on Pseudo-Xenophon, *The Constitution of the Athenians* 1. 11', *CQ* 46: 564–6.

Bloch, M. and J. Parry (eds.) 1989. *Money and the Morality of Exchange*. Cambridge.

Bourdieu, P. 1977. *Outline of a Theory of Practice*, tr. Richard Nice. Cambridge.

Bremmer, J. 1989. 'Greek Pederasty and Modern Homosexuality', in J. Bremmer (ed.), *From Sappho to De Sade: Moments in the History of Sexuality*. London. 1–14.

Burford, A. 1972. *Craftsmen in Greek and Roman Society*. London.

Cairns, D. L. 1996. '*Hybris*, Dishonour, and Thinking Big', *JHS* 116: 1–32.

Cantarella, E. 1983. 'Spunti di riflessione critica su *hybris* e *timê* in Omero', in P. Dimakis (ed.), *Symposion 1979 (Akten der Gesellschaft für Griechische und Hellenistische Rechtsgeschichte)*. Cologne. 85–96.

—— 1988. *Secondo Natura*. Rome.

Carey, C. 1988. 'A Note on Torture in Athenian Homicide Cases', *Historia* 37: 241–5.

—— (ed.) 1989. *Lysias: Selected Speeches*. Cambridge.

—— 1991. 'Apollodorus' Mother: The Wives of Enfranchised Aliens in Athens', *CQ* 41: 84–9.

—— (ed.) 1992. *Apollodoros Against Neaira [Demosthenes] 59*. Warminster.

Charles, J. F. 1938. *Statutes of Limitations at Athens*. Chicago.

Chirassi Colombo, I. 1984. 'L'Inganno di Afrodite', in *I labirinti dell'Eros*. Florence. 109–21.

Cohen, D. 1991a. *Law, Sexuality, and Society: The Enforcement of Morals in Classical Athens*. Cambridge.

—— 1991b. 'Sexuality, Violence, and the Athenian Law of *Hubris*', *G&R* 38: 171–88.

—— 1995. *Law, Violence and Community in Classical Athens*. Cambridge.

Cohen, E. E. 1973. *Ancient Athenian Maritime Courts*. Princeton.

—— 1990. 'Commercial Lending by Athenian Banks: Cliometric

Fallacies and Forensic Methodology', *CP* 85: 177–90.
—— 1992. *Athenian Economy and Society: A Banking Perspective*. Princeton.
—— 1994. 'Status and Contract at Athens', in G. Thür (ed.), *Symposion 1993 (Akten der Gesellschaft für Griechische und Hellenistische Rechtsgeschichte)*. Cologne. 141–52.
—— 1997. 'The *Astoi* of Attika: Nationality and Citizenship at Athens', in G. Thür and J. Vélissaropoulos-Karakostas (eds.), *Symposion 1995 (Akten der Gesellschaft für Griechische und Hellenistische Rechtsgeschichte)*. Cologne. 57–94.
—— 1998. 'The Wealthy Slaves of Athens: Legal Rights, Economic Obligations', in H. Jones (ed.), *Le monde antique et les droits de l'homme*, Actes de la 50e session de la société Fernand de Visscher pour l'histoire des droits de l'antiquité. Brussels. 105–29.
—— (forthcoming). 'Equal Employment Opportunity at Athens: Prostitution not the "Special Preserve of Foreigners"', in P. Cartledge, L. Foxhall, and E. E. Cohen (eds.), *Kerdos: The Economics of Gain in the Ancient Greek World*. London.
Cole, S. G. 1984. 'Greek Sanctions Against Sexual Assault', *CP* 79: 97–113.
Davidson, J. N. 1994. 'Consuming Passions: Appetite, Addiction and Spending in Classical Athens', D.Phil. Diss., Oxford University.
—— 1997. *Courtesans and Fishcakes: The Consuming Passions of Classical Athens*. London.
Davies, J. K. 1971. *Athenian Propertied Families, 600–300 BC*. Oxford.
—— 1981. *Wealth and the Power of Wealth in Classical Athens*. Salem, N.H.
Diller, A. 1937. *Race Mixture among the Greeks before Alexander*. Urbana, Ill.
Doblhofer, G. 1994. *Vergewaltigung in der Antike: Beiträge zur Altertumskunde* 46. Stuttgart.
Dougherty, C. 1996. 'Democratic Contradictions and the Synoptic Illusion of Euripides' *Ion*', in J. Ober and C. Hedrick (eds.), *Demokratia: A Conversation on Democracies, Ancient and Modern*. Princeton. 249–70.
Dover, K. J. 1964. 'Eros and Nomos', *BICS* 9: 31–42.
—— 1974. *Greek Popular Morality in the Time of Plato and Aristotle*. Berkeley.
—— 1984 (1973). 'Classical Greek Attitudes to Sexual Behaviour', in J. Peradotto and J. P. Sullivan (eds.), *Women in the Ancient World: The Arethusa Papers*. 143–57. (Originally published in *Arethusa* 6: 59–73.)
—— 1989 (1978). *Greek Homosexuality*. London.
Ehrenberg, V. 1962. *The People of Aristophanes: A Sociology of Old Attic Comedy*. New York.

—— 1969. *The Greek State*, 2nd edn. London.

ERICCSON, L. 1980. 'Charges against Prostitution: An Attempt at a Philosophical Assessment', *Ethics* 90: 335–66.

FINLEY, M. I. 1970. 'Aristotle and Economic Analysis', *Past and Present* 47: 3–25 (reprinted in Finley 1974: 26–52).

—— (ed.) 1974. *Studies in Ancient Society*. London.

—— 1981. *Economy and Society in Ancient Greece*, ed. B. D. Shaw and R. P. Saller. London.

—— 1985. *The Ancient Economy*, 2nd edn. Berkeley.

FISHER, N. R. E. 1976. '*Hubris* and Dishonour', pt. 1, *G&R* 23: 177–93.

—— 1979. '*Hubris* and Dishonour', pt. 2, *G&R* 26: 32–47.

—— 1990. 'The Law of *hubris* in Athens', in P. Cartledge, P. Millett, and S. C. Todd (eds.), *Nomos: Essays in Athenian Law, Politics, and Society*. Cambridge. 123–45.

—— 1992. *Hybris*. Westminster.

—— 1993. *Slavery in Classical Greece*. London.

—— 1995. '*Hybris*, Status, and Slavery', in A. Powell (ed.), *The Greek World*. London. 44–84.

FOUCAULT, M. 1984. *Histoire de la sexualité*, ii: *L'Usage des plaisirs*; iii: *Le Souci de soi*. Paris. (Tr. into English by R. Hurley as *The History of Sexuality*, ii: *The Use of Pleasure*; iii: *The Care of the Self*. New York, 1985–6.)

FOXHALL, L. 1994. 'Pandora Unbound: A Feminist Critique of Foucault's *History of Sexuality*', in A. Cornwall and N. Lindisturre (eds.), *Dislocating Masculinity: Comparative Ethnographies*. London. 133–46.

—— 1996. 'The Law and the Lady', in L. Foxhall and A. D. E. Lewis (eds.), *Greek Law in its Political Setting: Justifications not Justice*. Oxford. 133–52.

FRONTISI-DUCROUX, F. and F. LISSARRAGUE 1990. 'From Ambiguity to Ambivalence: A Dionysiac Excursion through the "Anakreontic" Vases', in D. M. Halperin, J. J. Winkler, and F. I. Zeitlin (eds.), *Before Sexuality: The Construction of Erotic Experience in the Ancient Greek World*. Princeton. 211–56.

FUKS, A. 1951. '*Kolonos misthios*: Labour Exchange in Classical Athens', *Eranos* 49: 171–3.

GAGARIN, M. 1979. 'The Athenian Law against *Hybris*', in G. W. Bowersock, W. Burkert, and M. C. J. Putnam (eds.), *Arktouros: Hellenic Studies presented to Bernard Knox*. Berlin and New York. 229–36.

—— 1996. 'The Torture of Slaves in Athenian Law', *CP* 91: 1–18.

GALLO, L. 1987. 'Salari e inflazione: Atene tra V e IV sec. A.C.', *ASNP* iii 17. 1: 19–63.

GERHARDT, P. 1935 (1933). *Die attische Metoikie im vierten Jahrhundert*. Dissertation, Königsberg.

GERNET, L. 1917. *Recherches sur le développement de la pensée juridique et morale en Grèce. Étude sémantique.* Paris.

GILL, C., N. POSTLETHWAITE, and R. SEAFORD (eds.) 1998. *Reciprocity in Ancient Greece.* Oxford.

GOFAS, D. 1979. 'Les "emmenoi dikai" à Thasos', in A. Biscardi (ed.), *Symposion 1974 (Akten der Gesellschaft für Griechische und Hellenistische Rechtsgeschichte).* Cologne. 175–88.

GOLDEN, M. 1988. 'Did the Ancients Care When Their Children Died?', *G&R* 35: 152–63.

GOMME, A. W. 1933. *The Population of Athens in the Fifth and Fourth Centuries* BC. Oxford.

GOODE, E. 1978. *Deviant Behavior: An Interactionist Approach.* New York.

GOULDNER, A. 1965. *Enter Plato: Classical Greece and the Origins of Social Theory.* New York.

HALPERIN, D. M. 1990. *One Hundred Years of Homosexuality and Other Essays on Greek Love.* New York.

HANSEN, M. H. 1981. 'Two Notes on the Athenian *dikai emporikai*', in P. Dimakis (ed.), *Symposion 1979 (Akten der Gesellschaft für Griechische und Hellenistische Rechtsgeschichte).* Cologne. 167–75.

—— 1985. *Demography and Democracy.* Copenhagen.

—— 1991. *The Athenian Democracy in the Age of Demosthenes: Structures, Principles and Ideology*, tr. J. A. Crook. Oxford and Cambridge, Mass.

HANSEN, M. V. 1984. 'Athenian Maritime Trade in the 4th Century BC: Operation and Finance', *C&M* 35: 71–92.

HARRIS, W. V. 1989. *Ancient Literacy.* Cambridge.

HARRISON, A. R. W. 1968–71. *The Law of Athens*, 2 vols. Oxford.

HASEBROEK, J. 1978 (1933). *Trade and Politics in Ancient Greece*, tr. L. M. Fraser and D. C. MacGregor. London.

HENRY, M. M. 1986. '*Ethos, Mythos, Praxis*: Women in Menander's Comedy', *Helios* n.s. 13/2: 141–50.

—— 1996. 'Secular Prostitution', in *OCD* 3rd edn. 1264.

HERTER, H. 1960. 'Soziologie der antiken Prostitution im Lichte der heidnischen und christlichen Schriftum', *Jahrbuch für Antike und Christentum* 3: 70–111.

HIMMELMANN, N. 1979. 'Zur Entlohnung künstlerischer Tätigkeit in klassischen Bauinschriften', *Jahrbuch des deutschen Archäologischen Instituts* 94: 127–42.

HOAGLAND, S. L. 1988. *Lesbian Ethics: Toward New Value.* Palo Alto.

HOPPER, R. J. 1979. *Trade and Industry in Classical Greece.* London.

HOWGEGO, C. 1995. *Ancient History from Coins.* London.

HUMPHREYS, S. C. 1978. *Anthropology and the Greeks.* London.

—— 1993. *The Family, Women and Death: Comparative Studies*, 2nd edn. Ann Arbor.

HUNT, P. 1998. *Slaves, Warfare and Ideology in the Greek Historians.* Cambridge.

HUNTER, V. J. 1989a. 'Women's Authority in Classical Athens', *EMC/CV* 33: 39–48.

—— 1989b. 'The Athenian Widow and Her Kin', *Journal of Family History* 14: 291–311.

—— 1994. *Policing Athens: Social Control in the Attic Lawsuits, 420–320 BC.* Princeton.

—— 1997. 'The Prison of Athens: A Comparative Perspective', *Phoenix* 51: 296–326.

JUST, R. 1985. 'Freedom, Slavery and the Female Psyche', in P. A. Cartledge and F. D. Harvey (eds.), *Crux: Essays in Greek History presented to G. E. M. de Ste Croix*. London. 169–88.

—— 1989. *Women in Athenian Law and Life*. London.

KARWEISE, S. 1991. 'The Artemisium Coin Hoard and the First Coins of Ephesus', *Revue belge de numismatique et de sigillographie* 137: 1–28.

KEISER, R. 1986. 'Death Enmity in Thull: Organized Vengeance and Social Change in a Kohistani Community', *American Ethnologist* 13: 489–505.

KEULS, E. C. 1985. *The Reign of the Phallus: Sexual Politics in Ancient Athens*. New York.

KIM, H. S. 1994. 'Greek Fractional Silver Coinage: A Reassessment of the Inception, Development, Prevalence, and Functions of Small Change during the Late Archaic and Early Classical Periods', M.Phil. Diss., Oxford University.

—— 1997. Oral Communication at Conference on 'Kerdos: The Economics of Gain in the Ancient Greek World'. Cambridge, 28–30 May 1997.

KITZINGER, C. 1991. 'Feminism, Psychology and the Paradox of Power', *Feminism and Psychology: An International Journal* 1/1: 111–29.

—— 1994. 'Problematizing Pleasure: Radical Feminist Deconstructions of Sexuality and Power', in H. L. Radtke and H. J. Stam (eds.), *Power/Gender: Social Relations in Theory and Practice*. London. 194–209.

KRAAY, C. M. 1964. 'Hoards, Small Change and the Origin of Coinage', *JHS* 84: 76–91.

—— 1976. *Archaic and Classical Greek Coins*. London.

KRENKEL, W. A. 1978. 'Männliche Prostitution in der Antike', *Das Altertum* 24: 49–55.

—— 1988. 'Prostitution', in M. Grant and R. Kitzinger (eds.), *Civilization of the Ancient Mediterranean: Greece and Rome*. New York. 1291–7.

KROLL, J. H. 1979. 'A Chronology of Early Athenian Bronze Coinage, *ca.* 350–250 BC', in O. Mørkholm and N. M. Waggoner (eds.), *Greek*

Numismatics and Archaeology: Essays in Honor of Margaret Thompson. Wetteren. 139–54.

—— 1997. Review of S. von Reden, *Exchange in Ancient Greece* (London, 1995), *AJA* 101: 175–6.

KURKE, L. 1989. '*Kapelia* and deceit', *AJP* 110: 535–44.

—— 1994. 'Herodotus and the Language of Metals', *Helios* 22: 36–64.

—— 1997. 'Inventing the *Hetaira*: Sex, Politics, and Discursive Conflict in Archaic Greece', *Cl. Ant.* 16: 106–50.

LAMB, W. R. M. (ed.) 1930. *Lysias*. Cambridge, Mass.

LAMBERT, S. D. 1993. *The Phratries of Attica*. Ann Arbor.

LARMOUR, D., P. MILLER, and C. PLATTER 1998. 'Situating *The History of Sexuality*', in D. Larmour, P. Miller, and C. Platter (eds.), *Rethinking Sexuality: Foucault and Classical Antiquity*. Princeton. 3–41.

LEACH, E. 1965. *Political Systems of Highland Burma*, 2nd edn. Boston.

LEIDHOLDT, D. 1990. 'Introduction', in D. Leidholdt and J. G. Raymond (eds.), *Sexual Liberals and the Attack on Feminism*. New York. ix–xvii.

LICHT, H. (P. BRANDT) 1952 (1932). *Sexual Life in Ancient Greece*, ed. L. H. Dawson, tr. J. Freese. New York.

LIPSIUS, J. H. 1966 (1905–15). *Das attische Recht und Rechtsverfahren*, 3 vols. Hildesheim.

LOBEL, K. 1986. *Naming the Violence: Speaking Out about Lesbian Violence*. Washington, D.C.

LOOMIS, W. T. 1997. 'A Standard Athenian Wage?' Presentation to New England Ancient History Colloquium, at Brown University, 3 March 1997.

—— 1998. *Wages, Welfare Costs and Inflation in Classical Athens*. Ann Arbor.

LORAUX, N. 1993. *The Children of Athena: Athenian Ideas about Citizenship and the Division between the Sexes*, tr. C. Levine. Princeton.

—— 1995 (1989). *The Experiences of Tiresias: The Feminine and the Greek Man*. Princeton.

LOWRY, S. T. 1987. *The Archaeology of Economic Ideas: The Classical Greek Tradition*. Durham, N.C.

MACDOWELL, D. M. 1976. '*Hubris* in Athens', *G&R* 23: 14–31.

—— 1978. *The Law in Classical Athens*. London.

—— (ed.) 1990. *Demosthenes, Against Meidias (Oration 21)*. Oxford.

MCGINN, T. A. J. 1989. 'The Taxation of Roman Prostitutes', *Helios* 16: 79–111.

MCINTOSH, M. 1978. 'Who Needs Prostitutes? The Ideology of Male Sexual Needs', in C. Smart and B. Smart (eds.), *Women, Sexuality and Social Control*. London. 53–64.

MCKECHNIE, P. 1989. *Outsiders in the Greek Cities in the Fourth Century* BC. London.

MEIGGS, R. 1972. *The Athenian Empire*. Oxford.

MEIGGS, R. and D. LEWIS (eds.) 1969. *A Selection of Greek Historical Inscriptions*. Oxford.

MEIKLE, S. 1995a. *Aristotle's Economic Thought*. Oxford.

—— 1995b. 'Modernism, Economics, and the Ancient Economy', *PCPS* 41: 174–91.

MIGEOTTE, L. (forthcoming). 'Quelques aspects légaux et juridiques de l'affermage des taxes en Grèce ancienne', in *Symposion 1997 (Akten der Gesellschaft für Griechische und Hellenistische Rechtsgeschichte)*.

MILLETT, P. 1983. 'Maritime Loans and the Structure of Credit in Fourth-Century Athens', in P. Garnsey, K. Hopkins, and C. R. Whittaker (eds.), *Trade in the Ancient Economy*. Berkeley. 36–52.

—— 1991. *Lending and Borrowing in Ancient Athens*. Cambridge.

MONTUORI, M. 1976. 'Su Fedone di Elide', *Atti dell'Accademia Pontaniana* n.s. 25: 1–14.

MORROW, G. R. 1939. *Plato's Law of Slavery in its Relation to Greek Law*. Urbana, Ill.

MOSSÉ, C. 1972. 'La vie économique d'Athènes au IVème siècle. Crise ou renouveau?', in F. Sartori (ed.), *Praelectiones Patavinae*. Rome. 135–44.

MURRAY, O. 1990. 'The Solonian Law of Hubris', in P. Cartledge, P. Millett, and S. C. Todd (eds.), *Nomos: Essays in Athenian Law, Politics and Society*. Cambridge. 147–65.

NIPPEL, W. 1985. '"Reading the Riot Act": The Discourse of Law Enforcement in 18th Century England', *History and Anthropology* 1: 401–26.

OBER, J. 1989. *Mass and Elite in Democratic Athens*. Princeton.

——'Aristotle's Political Sociology: Class, Status, and Order in the *Politics*', in C. Lord and D. K. O'Connor (eds.), *Essays on the Foundations of Aristotelian Political Science*. Berkeley and Los Angeles. 112–35.

—— 1993. 'The *Polis* as a Society: Aristotle, John Rawls and the Athenian Social Contract', in M. H. Hansen (ed.), *The Ancient Greek City-State*. Copenhagen. 129–60.

OBER, J. and C. HEDRICK (eds.) 1996. *Demokratia: A Conversation on Democracies, Ancient and Modern*. Princeton.

OERTEL, F. 1928. Review of J. Hasebroek, *Staat und Handel im alten Griechenland*, *Deutsche Literaturzeitung* 49: 1618–29.

OSBORNE, M. J. 1981–3. *Naturalization in Athens*, 4 vols. Brussels.

OSBORNE, R. G. 1995. 'The Economics and Politics of Slavery at Athens', in A. Powell (ed.), *The Greek World*. London. 27–43.

PAOLI, U. E. 1976. *Altri studi di diritto greco e romano*. Milan.

PATEMAN, C. 1988. *The Sexual Contract*. Cambridge.

PATON, J. M. (ed.) 1927. *The Erechtheum*. Cambridge, Mass.

PATTERSON, C. 1985. '"Not Worth the Rearing": The Causes of Infant Exposure in Ancient Greece', *TAPA* 115: 103–23.

PEROTTI, E. 1974. 'Esclaves *ΧΩΡΙΣ ΟΙΚΟΥΝΤΕΣ*', in *Actes du colloque 1972 sur l'esclavage. Annales littéraires de l'Université de Besançon* 163. Paris. 47–56. (Translation of 'Una categoria particolare di schiavi attici, i *χωρὶς οἰκοῦντες*', *Rendiconti dell' Istituto Lombardo di Scienze e Lettere* 106 (1972): 375–88.)

POLANYI, K. 1944. *Origins of Our Time: the Great Transformation*. New York.

POLANYI, K., C. M. ARENSBERG, and H. W. PEARSON (eds.) 1957. *Trade and Markets in the Early Empires*. New York.

POMEROY, S. 1975. *Goddesses, Whores, Wives, and Slaves: Women in Classical Antiquity*. New York.

—— 1994. *Xenophon Oeconomicus: A Social and Historical Commentary*. Cambridge.

POPPER, K. R. 1950. *The Open Society and Its Enemies*. Princeton.

POSNER, R. A. 1992. *Sex and Reason*. Cambridge, Mass.

PRICE, M. J. 1968. 'Early Greek Bronze Coinage', in C. M. Kraay and G. K. Jenkins (eds.), *Essays in Greek Coinage Presented to Stanley Robinson*. Oxford. 90–104.

—— 1979. 'The Function of Early Greek Bronze Coinage', *Atti del VI Convegno del Centro Internazionale di Studi Numismatici: Napoli 17–22 aprile 1977*. Supplement to *Atti dell'Istituto Italiano di Numismatica* 25: 351–65.

PRINGSHEIM, F. 1955. 'The Transition from Witnessed to Written Transactions in Athens', in *Aequitas und Bona Fides: Festgabe für A. Simonius*. Basel. 287–97.

PURPURA, G. 1987. 'Ricerche in tema di prestito marittimo', *Annali del Seminario Giuridico dell' Università di Palermo* 39: 189–337.

RAAFLAUB, K. A. 1980. 'Des freien Bürgers Recht der freien Rede: Ein Beitrag zur Begriffs- und Sozialgeschichte der athenischen Demokratie', in W. Eck et al. (eds.), *Studien zur Antiken Sozialgeschichte: Festschrift F. Vittinghoff*. Kölner historische Abhandlungen 28. Cologne. 7–57.

—— 1983. 'Democracy, Oligarchy, and the Concept of the "Free Citizen" in Late Fifth-Century Athens', *Political Theory* 11: 517–44.

RAHE, P. A. 1994 (1992). *Republics Ancient and Modern: The Ancien Régime in Classical Greece*. Chapel Hill.

RANDALL, R. H., Jr. 1953. 'The Erechtheum Workmen', *AJA* 57: 199–210.

REDEN, S. VON 1995. *Exchange in Ancient Greece*. London.

—— 1997. 'Money, Law, and Exchange: Coinage in the Greek Polis',

JHS 117: 154–76.

REGER, G. 1993. 'The Public Purchase of Grain on Independent Delos', *Cl. Ant.* 12: 299–334.

REINSBERG, C. 1989. *Ehe, Hetärentum und Knabenliebe im antiken Griechenland*. Munich.

RHODES, P. J. 1981. *A Commentary on the Aristotelian Athenaion Politeia*. Oxford.

RICHARDS, D. A. J. 1982. *Sex, Drugs, Death and the Law: An Essay on Human Rights and Decriminalization*. Totowa, N.J.

ROSEN, R. 1982. *The Lost Sisterhood: Prostitution in America, 1900–1918*. Baltimore.

RUESCHEMEYER, D. 1984. 'Theoretical Generalization and Historical Perspective in the Comparative Sociology of Reinhard Bendix', in T. Skocpol (ed.), *Vision and Method in Historical Sociology*. Cambridge. 129–69.

RUSCHENBUSCH, E. 1965. '*Hybreos Graphe*: ein Fremdkörper in athenischen Recht des 4. Jahrhunderts v. Chr.', *ZRG* 82: 302–9.

—— 1979. *Athenische Innenpolitik im 5 Jahrhundert v. Chr.: Ideologie oder Pragmatismus?* Bamberg.

—— 1981. 'Noch Einmal die Bürgerzahl Athens um 330 v. Chr.', *ZPE* 44: 110–12.

RUTTER, N. K. 1981. 'Early Greek Coinage and the Influence of the Athenian State', in B. Cunliffe (ed.), *Coinage and Society in Britain and Gaul: Some Current Problems*. London. 1–9.

SAGAN, E. 1991. *The Honey and the Hemlock: Democracy and Paranoia in Ancient Athens and Modern America*. New York.

DE STE CROIX, G. E. M. 1981. *The Class Struggle in the Ancient Greek World from the Archaic Age to the Arab Conquests*. London.

—— 1988. 'Slavery and Other Forms of Unfree Labour', in L. J. Archer (ed.), *Slavery and Other Forms of Unfree Labour*. London. 19–32.

SAXENHOUSE, A. 1991. 'Aristotle: Defective Males, Hierarchy, and the Limits of Politics', in M. L. Shanley and C. Pateman (eds.), *Feminist Interpretations and Political Theory*. University Park, Penn. 32–52.

SCAFURO, A. 1997. *The Forensic Stage*. Cambridge.

SCHAPS, D. M. 1979. *Economic Rights of Women in Ancient Greece*. Edinburgh.

SCHONBECK, H.-P. 1981. *Beiträge zur Interpretation der plautinischen 'Bacchides'*. Düsseldorf.

SEAFORD, R. 1994. *Reciprocity and Ritual*. Oxford.

STANCOMB, W. 1993. 'Arrowheads, Dolphins, and Cast Coins in the Black Sea Region', *Classical Numismatic Review* 18/3: 5.

STEINER, D. T. 1994. *The Tyrant's Writ*. Princeton.

STEWART, A. 1990. *Greek Sculpture*. New Haven.

STROUD, R. S. 1998. *The Athenian Grain-Tax Law of 374/3 BC*. Hesperia Supplement 29. Princeton.

THOMAS, R. 1989. *Oral Tradition and Written Record in Classical Athens*. Cambridge.

—— 1992. *Literacy and Orality in Ancient Greece*. Cambridge.

THORNTON, B. S. 1997. *Eros: The Myth of Ancient Greek Sexuality*. Boulder, Colo.

TODD, S. C. 1990. 'The Purpose of Evidence in Athenian Courts', in P. Cartledge, P. Millett, and S. C. Todd (eds.), *Nomos: Essays in Athenian Law, Politics and Society*. Cambridge. 19–39.

—— 1993. *The Shape of Athenian Law*. Oxford.

—— 1994. 'Status and Contract in Fourth-Century Athens', in G. Thür (ed.), *Symposion 1993 (Akten der Gesellschaft für Griechische und Hellenistische Rechtsgeschichte)*. Cologne. 125–40.

—— 1997. 'Status and Gender in Athenian Public Records', in G. Thür and J. Vélissaropoulos-Karakostas (eds.), *Symposion 1995 (Akten der Gesellschaft für Griechische und Hellenistische Rechtsgeschichte)*. Cologne. 113–24.

VATIN, C. 1984. *Citoyens et non citoyens dans le monde grec*. Paris.

VÉLISSAROPOULOS, J. 1980. *Les nauclères grecs*. Geneva.

VEYNE, P. 1971. *Comment on écrit l'histoire. Essai d'épistémologie*. Paris.

VICKERS, M. 1985. 'Early Greek Coinage: A Reassessment', *Num. Chron.* 45: 108–28.

WALKOWITZ, J. R. 1980. *Prostitution and Victorian Society: Women, Class and the State*. Cambridge.

WATSON, A. 1987. *Roman Slave Law*. Baltimore.

WEBER, M. 1924 (1909). *Agrarverhältnisse im Altertum*. Tübingen.

—— 1921. 'Die Stadt', *Archiv für Sozialwissenschaft* 47: 621–772. (Reprinted in *Wirtschaft und Gesellschaft* (Tübingen 1922)); ET *The City*, tr. and ed. D. Martindale and G. Neuwirth (Glencoe, Ill. 1958).)

WHITEHEAD, D. 1977. *The Ideology of the Athenian Metic*. Cambridge.

—— 1986. 'Women and Naturalisation in Fourth-Century Athens: The Case of Archippe', *CQ* 36: 109–14.

WINKLER, J. J. 1990. 'Laying Down the Law: The Oversight of Men's Sexual Behavior in Classical Athens', in D. M. Halperin, J. J. Winkler, and F. I. Zeitlin (eds.), *Before Sexuality: The Construction of Erotic Experience in the Ancient Greek World*. Princeton. 171–209.

WOHL, V. 1998. *Intimate Commerce: Exchange, Gender, and Subjectivity in Greek Tragedy*. Austin.

WOLFF, H. J. 1944. 'Marriage Law and Family Organization in Ancient Athens', *Traditio* 2: 43–95. (Reprinted in *Beiträge zur Rechtsgeschichte Altgriechenlands und des hellenistisch-römischen Ägypten*. Weimar, 1961. 155–242.)

Wood, E. M. 1988. *Peasant-Citizen and Slave: The Foundations of Athenian Democracy*. London.

Worthington, I. 1992. *A Historical Commentary on Dinarchus: Rhetoric and Conspiracy in Later Fourth-Century Athens*. Ann Arbor.

7
The Scrutiny of New Citizens at Athens

Bruce G. Robertson

In Athens of the fifth and fourth centuries BC, the full status of the citizen was not ascribed at birth. The citizen assemblies that resulted from such an arrangement—with toddlers ranged alongside seniors—were never more than the dream of philosophers.[1] Instead, a male of Athenian parents inched towards citizen status in a series of loosely connected rites that incorporated him into increasingly larger social units:[2] his father accepted him as a newborn into the family at the *amphidromia*;[3] then he was introduced to his father's phratry, first as a child and later as an adolescent;[4] and as a young adult, or ephebe, he acquired membership in his local government, or deme, and thereby membership in the state, through an institution called the *dokimasia*, roughly translated 'scrutiny'.[5] This chapter will discuss the last of these rites. Its first part will show that the *dokimasia* was understood, among other things, as a qualitative assessment of the prospective citizens' physical maturity, and the second part will explore the implications of this for the Athenians' understanding of their bodies.

To be sure, this rite did not mark the last transformation in political status. In fact, following the *dokimasia*, the newly enrolled demesmen underwent two years of military training as *epheboi* and only then were they enrolled in assembly registries and thus

I would like to thank the editors of this volume and Mark Golden for their helpful criticism and guidance.

[1] Heraclitus 22B 121 D-K (=Diog. Laert. 9. 2); cf. Strabo 14. 1. 25. This reference and a good general discussion on the matter may be found in Golden 1994.

[2] See Garland 1990: 197–8.

[3] See Pl. *Tht.* 160e and schol.; Eubulus 150 (Hunter); *Lexica Segueriana* 207. 13; Phot. s.v. ἀμφιδρόμια; *Suda* s.v. ἀμφιδρόμια; schol. Ar. *Lys.* 757.

[4] See Garland 1990: 179–80 and Lambert 1993: 165–75.

[5] Arist. *Ath. Pol.* 42. 1; Rhodes 1981: 497–502; 1972: 171–4.

allowed to address their fellow citizens in the assembly.[6] Furthermore, the jurors and legislators, or *nomothetai*, of Athens were drawn exclusively from those over thirty years of age,[7] and other privileges accrued to those in later age classes.[8] But these later stages differ from the scrutiny of youths in two important regards. First, the citizen apparently acquired the later age status passively, as do, for instance, citizens of Western countries who are granted franchise on their eighteenth birthday. In contrast, the scrutiny of the ephebes was an activity through which the prospective citizen had to pass successfully in order to acquire the status of citizen. Secondly, however diminished were the rights of those who freshly passed their *dokimasia*, it was this event to which the Aristotelian *Constitution of the Athenians* and the Athenians themselves in their forensic speeches refer as the beginning of life as a citizen.[9]

Let us begin then with the account of the scrutiny in the *Constitution of the Athenians*. I provide below Rhodes's (1984) translation because it expresses well the common approach to this event. I will later return to and revise both the translation and the approach once we have considered further evidence.[10]

Men belong to the citizen body if they are of citizen parentage on both sides, and they are registered as members of their demes at the age of eighteen. When they are registered, the deme members take a vote about them on oath, first to decide whether they have reached the age prescribed by the law (if they decide they have not, the candidates return to the ranks of the boys), and secondly to decide whether they are free men and born as prescribed by the laws. Then, if they reject a man as unfree, he appeals to the jury-court, and the deme members choose five of their own number as prosecutors: if he is found to have been unjustly registered, the state sells him as a slave; if he wins the case, the deme members are obliged to register him. After this, the council scrutinizes those who have been registered, and if anyone is found to be below the

[6] On the evidence for this practice and for its starting date, see Rhodes 1981: 494–5 and Hansen 1991: 89, 100.

[7] Jurors: Arist. *Ath. Pol.* 63. 3; legislators taken from the year's heliasts: Dem. 24. 21. Hansen explores the demographic implications of these rules, 1991: 89, 91.

[8] Some magistracies were open only to those older than thirty-nine years (Arist. *Ath. Pol.* 42. 2), and men over fifty had the privilege of addressing the assembly first (Aeschin. 1. 23; 3. 4). Men in their last year of military service (notionally fifty-nine years old): Arist. *Ath. Pol.* 53. 4; sixty years old (women): Dem. 43. 62.

[9] Dem. 27. 5; 30. 6; Isoc. 7. 37; Lys. 10. 31; 21. 1; 32. 9.

[10] Below, p. 160.

age of eighteen it punishes the deme members who have registered him. (Arist. *Ath. Pol.* 42. 1–2, tr. Rhodes 1984)[11]

The *dokimasia*, then, was an event at which the assembled demesmen accepted the citizen upon assenting to the veracity of his claim to be, first, properly born and, secondly, of a certain age. Disputed cases could be appealed, and the decisions of the demes were audited by the council, or boule. In short, according to Rhodes's translation, the *dokimasia* was a formal process involving facts and procedures to ascertain those facts.

Our only other contemporary source for this event is Aristophanes, and his contribution, if, as I argue, it is to be taken seriously, puts the *dokimasia* in a different light. As the jury-crazed Philocleon of Aristophanes' *Wasps* lists the benefits of being a politically active senior adult, he includes some less savoury advantages, including the opportunity to gaze upon the private parts of those undergoing the *dokimasia*.[12] In assessing this evidence we must admit that Aristophanes is a comic poet, bent on making us laugh, not on improving our understanding of his society. Is this comic remark evidence for what really happened or simply flight-of-fancy? First, I note that this is part of a comic list recited at high speed, allowing the audience to consider each for only a split second. All the other listed advantages derive from the duties and privileges of a politically active adult, such as deciding cases involving inheritance (583–6) or receiving jury pay (605–10). What is outrageous and thus funny is that Philocleon consistently gains personal advantage from these hallowed roles. Secondly, nudity was a common feature of Greek social activity, from the seventh century on. It was particularly common where youth were involved, as in athletic competition or in initiation rites (Bonfante 1989: 551–5). I thus conclude with the text's modern com-

[11] *μετέχουσιν μὲν τῆς πολιτείας οἱ ἐξ ἀμφοτέρων γεγονότες ἀστῶν, ἐγγράφονται δ' εἰς τοὺς δημότας ὀκτωκαίδεκα ἔτη γεγονότες. ὅταν δ' ἐγγράφωνται, διαψηφίζονται περὶ αὐτῶν ὀμόσαντες οἱ δημόται, πρῶτον μὲν εἰ δοκοῦσι γεγονέναι τὴν ἡλικίαν τὴν ἐκ τοῦ νόμου, κἂν μὴ δόξωσι, ἀπέρχονται πάλιν εἰς παῖδας, δεύτερον δ' εἰ ἐλεύθερός ἐστι καὶ γέγονε κατὰ τοὺς νόμους. ἔπειτ' ἂν μὲν ἀποψηφίσωνται μὴ εἶναι ἐλεύθερον, ὁ μὲν ἐφίησιν εἰς τὸ δικαστήριον, οἱ δὲ δημόται κατηγόρους αἱροῦνται πέντε [ἄν]δρας ἐξ αὐτῶν, κἂν μὲν μὴ δόξῃ δικαίως ἐγγράφεσθαι, πωλεῖ τοῦτον ἡ πόλις· ἐὰν δὲ νικήσῃ, τοῖς [δ]ημόταις ἐπάναγκες ἐγγράφειν. μετὰ δὲ ταῦτα δ[οκ]ιμάζει τοὺς ἐγγραφέντας ἡ βουλή, κἄν τις δόξ[ῃ] νεώτερος ὀκτωκαίδεκ' ἐτῶν εἶναι, ζημιοῖ τ[ο]ὺς δημότας τοὺς ἐγγράψαντας* (Arist. *Ath. Pol.* 42. 1–2).

[12] *παίδων τοίνυν δοκιμαζομένων αἰδοῖα πάρεστι θεᾶσθαι.* (Ar. *Vesp.* 578).

mentators that at some point in the process of the *dokimasia* the candidates were naked (MacDowell 1971: 210; Sommerstein 1983: 192), and that Aristophanes' joke is that those who swore the heliastic oath were getting a cheap thrill from what should be a solemn ceremony.

How can we reconcile this nudity with the function of the *dokimasia* described in Aristotle's text? Rhodes and Sommerstein take the position that least disrupts the common impression of the *dokimasia* as a procedure that confirms facts. They suggest that in exceptional circumstances alone the physical maturity of the prospective citizen could be entered as evidence for his age (Rhodes 1981: 499; Sommerstein 1983: 192). Philocleon is a juror, and although the *Constitution of the Athenians* only mentions questions of citizenship being appealed to a jury, Rhodes (1981: 500) and others suggest that questions of age might have been, too. One can well imagine a father stripping his son in that forum in order to win the case. On this view, the *dokimasia* proper remains an assessment of a formal quantitative criterion, namely age determined by years from birth, and only when a dispute arose and the matter went to the courts would the polis entertain a qualitative criterion, that is, age determined by physical maturity.

MacDowell's notes on this passage go further in integrating a bodily examination into the process. Since the pool of politically active adults to which Philocleon belonged also provided the councillors who reviewed all decisions on age, he suggests that 'the councillors evidently must have inspected the youths in the nude to judge from their physical development if they were adult' (MacDowell 1971: 210).[13] According to MacDowell, then, it was not the occasional tough case in which the physical development of the youth was applied as evidence for his age, but rather this was the means by which the councillors routinely determined if candidates had met the age requirement.

The extent to which the *dokimasia* was understood as a verification of the ephebe's age through an objective record of years from birth or as a subjective assessment of his maturity is crucial to the role of the institution. The candidate's definition of his situation would differ vastly depending on how he understood he was being assessed. In the first case, he would have understood the *dokimasia*

[13] See also MacDowell 1990: 370 *ad* Dem. 21. 154, where his position is much like p. 159 below.

as a process which verifies that which he already was, namely, someone who had lived a certain number of years. Errors of fact might be possible and cause temporary embarrassment or inconvenience, but they would not alter the candidate's true situation. If, on the other hand, the candidate understood that the criterion of age was assessed through his physical attributes, his adulthood was not something which he already possessed before the *dokimasia*, but rather something which the *dokimasia* itself conferred upon him. In this case, to be returned 'into the ranks of the boys', in Aristotle's ominous phrase, was not an administrative foul-up: it was a public and complete repudiation of his claim to be an adult.

The evidence we have looked at so far cannot resolve the issue. By stating that they were registered as members of their demes at the age of eighteen, Aristotle's text (particularly in the translation given) strongly suggests that the criterion is objective. Aristophanes, on the other hand, introduces an element of physical scrutiny which would be unnecessary if the criterion were wholly and at all times objective. To explore the issue further I shall briefly examine first how citizens recorded and expressed their own and each other's ages and, second, how the citizens understood what happened to them at the *dokimasia*.

RECKONING AGE IN ATHENS

In modern Western democracies, age is perceived as an objective fact within the context of several cultural practices and institutions. Birth certificates which record the date of birth are, of course, essential; but the numerical chronography we employ greatly facilitates the calculation of one's age from that document. Furthermore, the celebration of the birthday in some Western countries marks the transition from one age number to the next. Increasingly, these age groups are also conceived of numerically: the teen years, thirty-somethings, those over sixty-five, and so on. Finally, our large bureaucracies and private administrations frequently employ numerical age and date of birth as means of identification.

These cultural institutions and practices support our concept of age. What forensic scientists call physiological age is, in our understanding, an illusion; and chronological age is an objective property of self, like one's place of birth or parentage. Thus knowledge of one's age is basic self-knowledge. Furthermore, knowledge of another's age is part of knowing another, and if we misread someone else's chronological age from physiological signs, we quickly memorize the correct, that is, chronological, value.

The situation in ancient Athens was, of course, very different. The chronography of the state (wherein years were labelled with the name of the man who was the eponymous archon during that year) did not facilitate the calculation of age: one had to know the name of the archon in whose year the birth took place and recall the archon list perfectly to get within a year of the correct chronological age.[14] For the measurement of time within a year, two incompatible official calendars were in use simultaneously (Bickerman 1968: 34–8). Indeed, what evidence we have for Greek birthdays makes no mention of the number of years which have passed in our manner.[15]

The Athenian state and its private organizations which did employ calendars appear not to have recorded dates of birth. As far as we can tell, at Athens the state itself only registered citizens following the *dokimasia* and thus was not itself equipped with official information on the age of its *prospective* citizens. However, most (if not all) prospective citizens were part of a phratry before the *dokimasia*.[16] Were the phratries administered in such a way as to identify their members by age or provide the demes with accurate information about the age of their members? Each phratry followed its own rules, and therefore what follows is, if anything, an excessively tidy account of the situation. Nevertheless, it seems that the prospective citizen's first association with his phratry was in childhood, when his father introduced him to it in a rite called the *meion*; in what appear to be the teenage years he underwent another process, the *koureion*, and after this there might be a *diadikasia*, a word which we might also translate as 'scrutiny'.[17] It

[14] *IG* I³ 1031 is our best example of the archon lists, which were said to have been published near the prytanium (schol. Ar. *Pax* 1183). Though at least one person claimed to be able to recite their content (Pl. *Hp. mai.* 285e3–6), it seems that they were rarely used outside of official documentation (Shrimpton 1995: 50–1).

[15] On birthdays, see Schmidt 1910.

[16] Lambert (1993: 31–57) most recently makes the case for all citizens being members of phratries.

[17] Ancient commentators thought these rites were the same event: schol. Ar. *Ran.* 798; *Etym. Magn.* 533. 37 s.v. κουρεῖον. Since the *koureion* is mentioned of an adolescent in Isae. 6. 22 and there is other evidence of some official association with *phrateres* in youth (Ar. *Ran.*

was not required that either of the first two events take place after a fixed year of the youth's life. In some cases the earlier rite took place in the first year of the infant's life (Andoc. 1. 125–6 *megas pais*; Dem. 43. 11, 57. 54 *paidion*); in others, when the child has reached the age of three or four (*P Oxy*. 2538, fr. 1, col. 2. 23–8, schol. Pl. *Ti*. 21). And indeed, the age of the candidate was not part of the father's oath.[18] From all our sources regarding the administration of citizen organizations, there is no evidence that documents were kept to record the age of prospective citizens.

In fact, it appears that fundamental differences in mentality underlie the differences in record-keeping between modern Western states and ancient Athens. Hunter argues in a discussion of time in Herodotus and Thucydides that the Athenians conceived of time as a relative sequence of events, as did the inhabitants of early modern Europe (1982: 316–19). In his study of the Nuer, Evans-Pritchard observes that his subjects also understood time as a relative sequence, either of ecological events or of the communal experiences of the tribe and its ceremonies (1940: 104–5).These latter sorts of relative temporal landmarks appear to have been the primary means of measuring age at Athens. Lambert points out that the decree of the phratry of the Demotionidae does not specify the age at which the new member's scrutiny takes place; rather, it is to be 'in the year following the *koureion*', suggesting that the age of the candidate at that point was variable (Lambert 1993: 167). Similarly, the phrase 'to mature for two years (presumably after adolescence)' (*epi dietes heban*), which appears in various references to maturity (Aeschin. 3. 122; Isae. 10. 12; *lex apud* Dem. 46. 20), is further evidence of a flexible, relative approach to describing the age of prospective citizens.

The evidence from the age-classes of ancient athletic competitions also points away from reliable, absolute chronological reckoning.[19] Athletic age-classes were given names that were vague such as 'the Pythian boys' (*paides Puthikoi*) or ones that referred to physiological development such as 'the beardless ones' (*ageneioi*). As Golden notes (1998: 106), modern attempts to derive from these names consistent chronological age-classes fail to explain all the

420–4), it is assumed that the distinction of these rites is by age and the latter is the *meion*: see Lambert 1993: 161–78. Scrutiny: *IG* II^2 1237. 26.

[18] The content of the oath is given in Isae. 8. 19.

[19] For a general discussion of athletic age-classes, see Golden 1998: 104–23.

evidence. Whether the main criterion for athletic age-classes was chronological age (Golden 1998: 106) or physical development (Frisch 1988), it was a matter of impressions and sometimes open to debate. Pindar records that Epharmostus won at wrestling in the *ageneioi* class against a field of older competitors (*Ol.* 9. 88–90). Furthermore, as Xenophon reports, Agesilaus succeeded in arranging for an Athenian child who was a borderline case ('the largest of the boys') to compete among the boys (*paides*), again at Olympia (Xen. *Hell.* 4. 1. 40; Plut. *Ages.* 13. 3). Here the criteria surely were subjective, for there is no hint that Agesilaus' influence-peddling was an act of outright fraud.[20]

Furthermore, it appears that even evidence offered in court for the age at which one underwent civic rites was shaky. In a fragmentary Attic speech recovered from a papyrus, the speaker attempts to prove that he is the legitimate son of the man he calls father, probably to lay claim to an inheritance or to defend himself against the charge of being a foreigner acting as a citizen. He offers witnesses to his introduction to a phratry with these words: 'first then I shall put before you witnesses of how he brought me to the members of the phratry when I was three or four years of age' (*P Oxy.* 2538, fr. 1, col. 2. 23–8).[21] Thus he and his witnesses did not intend to specify the age at which he was introduced. Either the speaker is unable to attain consensus from his witnesses or he does not feel that the precise age mattered.

We should conclude, then, that Athenian society did not place anywhere near the same amount of emphasis on expressing age in absolute and precise chronological terms as our modern Western societies do. The use of precise dating by archon year (i.e. with the phrase *ep' archontos* or, simply, *archontos*) in the forensic corpora of Demosthenes, Isaeus, and Lysias confirms this. Such archon dates are not rare; on the contrary, transactions, verdicts, public achievement, even marriages are ascribed archon years.[22] Almost all of

[20] For another approach to this matter, see Golden 1990: 67–9.

[21] *πρῶ]τον μὲν | οὖν ὡς εἰσήγαγέ | με εἰς τοὺς φράτε- | ρας ἔ[τ]η γεγονόντα | τρ[ία] ἢ | τέτταρα μάρ- | τυρας ὑμῖν παρέξομαι·* (*P Oxy.* 2538, fr. 1, col. 2. 23–8).

[22] Athletic victory: Dem. 59. 33; citizenship: Dem. 46. 13; commercial voyage: Dem. 49. 60; council membership: Dem. 47. 44; death: Dem. 46. 13; *dokimasia*: Lys. 21. 1; financial transaction: Dem. 37. 6; 49. 6, 28, 30, 44, 59, 62; Lys. 7. 9; liturgies: Lys. 21. 1, 3, 4; marriage and divorce: Dem. 30. 15; office: Dem. 18. 155; prosecution: Dem. 30. 17; punishment: Dem. 24. 138; supposed criminal act: Lys. 7. 11; taxation: Dem. 22. 44; trial: Dem. 49. 22; Lys. 17. 3; vote in Assembly: Dem. 50. 4 (with day); 58. 28; war and peace: Dem. 59. 37 (and two years before 59. 36); Lys. 19. 28; Isae. 6. 14.

these events are ones that the polis or private parties documented and thus dated (the only exception to my mind is the supposed cutting of the olive-stump which the plaintiff dates by archon year in Lys. 7. 11). Nevertheless, there is not a single example of an individual stating the archon year of his or anyone else's birth.

The following three examples show how claims of chronological age were instead made relative to important communal events. In his speech *Against Eubulides*, Demosthenes' client argues for his citizenship partly on the basis of his father's birth before the archonship of Euclides when, it is claimed, the rules became stiffer. After calling witnesses, he claims nothing more specific than simply that his father was born before the crucial year (57. 30). In Isaeus' speech *On the Estate of Ciron*, the speaker states the opposite, that he and his siblings were born after the archonship of Euclides, this time without calling witnesses to the fact (8. 43).[23] Presumably it was self-evident. The most specific statement of age comes from Isaeus' *On the Estate of Philoctemon*:

> Fifty-two years have passed since the Sicilian expedition, reckoning from the date of its departure in the archonship of Arimnestus; yet the elder of these two alleged sons of Callippe and Euctemon has not yet passed his twentieth year. If these years are deducted, more than thirty years still remain since the Sicilian expedition; so that Callippe, if she were thirty years of age, ought to have been no longer under a guardian, nor unmarried and childless, but long ago married, given in marriage either by her guardian, according to the law, or else by an adjudication of the court. (Isae. 6. 14, tr. E. S. Forster)

Here the speaker gives an upper limit to the age of the elder of his rival claimants to the inheritance: 'not yet beyond twenty years' (6. 14). It is part of a rough calculation of the age at marriage of the mother of his rivals; and the other piece of information he requires is the date of the Sicilian expedition, since, apparently, his rivals claim she was under their grandfather's guardianship, since her father had left Athens to serve in the fleet on that expedition and had died on the voyage. The speaker provides an absolute archon date to the political event, the flotilla to Sicily, but applies relative dates when dealing with the ages of his fellow citizens.[24]

[23] *ἐὰν γὰρ ἐξαπατηθῆτε ὑμεῖς πεισθέντες ὡς ἡ μήτηρ ἡμῶν οὐκ ἦν πολῖτις, οὐδ' ἡμεῖς ἐσμεν· μετ' Εὐκλείδην γὰρ ἄρχοντα γεγόναμεν* (Isae. 8. 43).

[24] Observe also how the speaker at Lys. 10. 4 provides his age when his father died at the hands of the Thirty. Though the numbers are corrupt, it is clear that he calculates it from

In two instances orators apparently provide incorrect ages, perhaps intentionally and in order to improve their cases. In *Against Timarchus* Aeschines states that he and his opponent's lover, Misgolas, are contemporaries and both in their forty-fifth year (1. 49). Harris (1988: 213) argues that Aeschines, by stating that Misgolas is his coeval and then drawing attention to his own grey hair, attempted to convince his audience that Timarchus was sufficiently younger than Misgolas to make it plausible that the two were lovers, despite the fact that in the very same speech (1. 109) evidence is provided that Timarchus served on the boule of 361/0 BC and was, therefore, at least a contemporary of the other two. Similarly, in his speech *Against Midias* Demosthenes claims he is thirty-two years old in 347/6 BC, and Midias 'perhaps fifty years old, or a little less' (Dem. 21. 154). Other evidence from his speeches suggests he was five years older than he claims (below, p. 162). As Harris writes (1989: 123–4), the earlier age suits Demosthenes' purposes in the context: the greater the difference in their ages, the more shocking is Midias' poor liturgical record as compared to the speaker's.

Thus the institutions of Athens and the attitudes of its citizens to time and age produced a situation wherein the date of birth of a citizen was not common knowledge: it did not constitute a social fact. It should not surprise us, then, that in three cases Athenians profess a remarkable ignorance of each other's chronological age. In Plato's *Lysis*, two young men argue about their respective ages:

I said: Son of Demophon, which of you is older?
It is a point in dispute between us, he replied.
Then you must also argue, I said, as to which of you two is the nobler.
Yes, to be sure, he said.
And moreover, which is the more beautiful, likewise . . .

(Pl. *Lys*. 207b–c)[25]

Similarly, Mantitheus, a client of Demosthenes who speaks in a trial where the ages of the plaintiff and defendant are of great importance, makes the remark: 'None of you knows age measured

his current age and the number of years since the restoration of the democracy, not, as we would, from the year of his birth.

[25] *ὦ παῖ Δημοφῶντος, ἦν δ' ἐγώ, πότερος ὑμῶν πρεσβύτερος; ἀμφισβητοῦμεν, ἔφη. οὐκοῦν καὶ ὁπότερος γενναιότερος, ἐρίζοιτ' ἄν, ἦν δ' ἐγώ. πάνυ γε, ἔφη. καὶ μὴν ὁπότερός γε καλλίων, ὡσαύτως* . . . (Pl. *Lys*. 207b–c).

in years, since I will say that mine is greater and he his; but all of you know how to calculate justice' (39. 29).[26] We are inclined, of course, to believe that he feigns ignorance because the evidence is not on his side (Carey and Reid 1985: 186–7). But Mantitheus' claim is much stronger than that: he states that to others, age measured in years is not within the realm of knowledge, but rather is a sort of opinion. If Demosthenes did not believe that this was at least one fairly widely held approach to chronological age, he was engaged in a risky strategy: to claim that a jury could not know that which they believed they could know would have been dangerous indeed. Finally we should note that Athenian gravestones almost never provide chronological information about the deceased: only one such epitaph includes the archonship of birth or of death (*IG* II^2 6217).

So far it has been shown that the Athenian concept of age was not an objectively verifiable and wholly chronological fact as it is in modern Western societies. It has not, however, been discussed how the Athenians did conceive age; this is the more complex question, and only a brief outline of an answer can be provided here. To begin with how age was measured, we should not ignore the fact that the chronological criterion was certainly used at times. After all, when Aristotle ascribed years to physiological events in the developing body (e.g. to puberty: *Hist. an.* 581^{a}31), he must have been referring to chronological, not physiological, years, since the latter would be a tautology. On the other hand, on the evidence presented, the Athenians did not apply the chronological criterion with the precision we do today. As a result, age was, as Mantitheus suggests, something about which one can have an opinion rather than true knowledge, in Plato's terms *doxa*, not *episteme*. As such, the memories of those who could remember a child's birth and had observed his physiological development and had a general impression of his physiological age made the crucial contribution towards establishing an Athenian citizen's age.

The one piece of anecdotal evidence regarding the distinction between men and boys supports this interpretation. When his son was being pressured to pay taxes as an adult because of his great height, Iphicrates remarked, 'If you consider tall boys men, you

[26] *ἔτι δ', ὦ ἄνδρες Ἀθηναῖοι, τὸν μὲν τῶν ἐτῶν χρόνον οὐδεὶς οἶδεν ὑμῶν (ἐγὼ μὲν γὰρ ἐμοὶ πλείονα, οὗτος δ' ἑαυτῷ φήσει), τὸν δὲ τοῦ δικαίου λόγον ἅπαντες ἐπίστασθε* (Dem. 39. 29).

must vote that short men are boys' (Arist. *Rhet.* 1399^{a}35, tr. J. H. Freese).[27] It might be supposed that, since Iphicrates excluded stature as a criterion, he wished chronological age to be the sole determining factor. In that case, the very fact that his fellow citizens employed one standard and Iphicrates argued for a different one shows that age was not an objectively established social fact. It is more likely, however, that chronological age was not what he had in mind. Iphicrates complained about the use of height *alone* to determine age; for him height was not the only way to form an impression of physiological age. Iphicrates was appealing for a more comprehensive approach to assigning age-class than merely measuring the candidates, agreeing with Xenophon that 'in the case of those who have attained their growth although they are still young, there yet appears that freshness which betrays their lack of years' (*Cyr.* 1. 4. 3, tr. W. Miller).[28]

Let us now return to the text of Aristotle's *Athenian Constitution* with this matter in mind.[29] The crucial passage is the one in which he describes how the demesmen vote on prospective citizens (42. 1–2); I shall here explain the structure of the passage and provide different English wording in order to emphasize key points which are obscured in Rhodes's translation. In this section, Aristotle uses two parallel clauses introduced by 'first if' (*proton men ei*) and 'secondly if' (*deuteron d' ei*). What differs in these clauses is the verb used to denote the matter in question. Regarding free birth, the verbs 'to be' (*einai*) and 'to be born' (*gignesthai*) are used. That is, the demesmen vote on the fact of free birth. Indeed, later in the passage the verb 'to be' (*einai*) is used when the demesmen reject the prospective citizen's claim.[30] Compare this with the verb used in the first conditional clause, the one regarding age. Here Aristotle says the demesmen vote 'if they appear to have reached the age' (*ei dokousi gegonenai ten helikian*). Later he repeats, 'if they do seem so'. In both cases the word 'to appear' or 'to seem' (*dokeo*) is used. Indeed later in the passage the same verb is used of the boule's

[27] *ὁ Ἰφικράτης, τὸν υἱὸν αὐτοῦ, νεώτερον ὄντα τῆς ἡλικίας, ὅτι μέγας ἦν λειτουργεῖν ἀναγκαζόντων, εἶπεν ὅτι εἰ τοὺς μεγάλους τῶν παίδων ἄνδρας νομίζουσι, τοὺς μικροὺς τῶν ἀνδρῶν παῖδας εἶναι ψηφιοῦνται* (Arist. *Rhet.* 1399^{a}35).

[28] *ὅσοι νέοι ὄντες μέγεθος ἔλαβον, ὅμως ἐμφαίνεται τὸ νεαρὸν αὐτοῖς ὃ κατηγορεῖ τὴν ὀλιγοετίαν* (Xen. *Cyr.* 1. 4. 3).

[29] See the Greek text in n. 11 above.

[30] *ἔπειτ' ἂν μὲν ἀποψηφίσωνται μὴ εἶναι ἐλεύθερον*: 'if they vote that he is not freeborn . . .'

decision on the candidate's age. The alternating use of these words supports the conclusion we drew from the forensic speeches: age was a matter of appearance and opinion.[31]

Thus Aristotle's text confirms that these two criteria were known in different ways. Parentage was considered, as it is today, a verifiable and knowable fact of identity because there were institutions and practices preceding the *dokimasia* and involving the prospective citizen which publicly asserted that fact. The oath which the father or his witnesses swore before the phratry asserted it,[32] and the scrutiny which the phratry conducted sanctioned it as truth (Isae. 7. 16). Age, on the other hand, was a matter of opinion because it had not yet been tested and recorded; that, in part, was the role of the *dokimasia*. Indeed, of our contemporary sources, only Aristotle unambiguously ascribes a precise age expressed in terms of years to the moment when an Athenian should present himself for his *dokimasia*. The many other references to the *dokimasia* use phrases comprising terms of maturity, particularly *pais*, 'child', and *aner*, 'adult male'. 'To be judged into the company of adults', 'to depart from the children', or simply 'to become a man', these are the terms of the Athenians (Goldhill 1987: 67). Following this rite, the state recorded the ephebes (Arist. *Ath. Pol.* 53. 4) and mature citizens (*Ath. Pol.* 53. 5, 7) by age-class (not actual age) under the name of the archon and eponymous hero of their enrolment year.[33]

To return to our original question, we should conclude that the *dokimasia* was a subjective assessment of the candidate's maturity, not a verification of established facts. This in turn puts Aristophanes' text in a new light. He refers not to an exceptional incident wherein the demesmen were forced to inspect the body of the youth but rather to a necessary part of the initiation ritual. In addition to the ritual functions of nudity in such an initiation rite (Bonfante 1989: 551–2), it was also an important means by which the demesmen formed an opinion about the maturity of a group of candidates.

Before considering the implications this has for Athenians' understanding of their bodies in society, I wish briefly to outline how this approach to the *dokimasia* bears on two prosopographical

[31] Garland 1990: 180 briefly notes the use of *dokein*.

[32] Isae. 7. 16 (adult adoption); 8. 19 (*meion*); Dem. 57. 54 (?*meion*).

[33] For these age-classes in use, see n. 8 above.

problems. The first of these is Demosthenes' date of birth.[34] In his speech *Against Aphobus*, Demosthenes says he was seven years old when his father died (27. 4) and that he became an adult ten years after that (27. 6). Ten plus seven does not equal eighteen, and, as a result, several scholars have suggested that what is meant in the text of Aristotle (*Ath. Pol.* 42. 1) is that men were registered as members of their demes in 'the eighteenth year of life' rather than 'when they were eighteen years old'. Golden (1979) has shown that this cannot be so, and suggests that since the process took place only once a year to cover an entire year's worth of candidates, some of them might have been seventeen, like those schoolchildren born in December who are, in November, six years old and not seven like most of their classmates in the Canadian school system.[35] I agree that the year's candidates for the *dokimasia* arrived as cohorts, but I suggest that these cohorts did not comprise boys born exactly within a year-long period, but were roughly hewn from the friendships, games, and contests of youth, wherein a similarity in physical and mental maturity counts for more than the number of years and months lived; in such cohorts variations of chronological age up to perhaps two years are of little consequence.

Finally, scholars have noted that there is an unusually large number of ephebes who share the same age-class and patronym (Sekunda 1992: 329–30). In a recent article Hansen suggests two explanations for these apparently over-populous twins. First, he points out that it is not altogether rare for the period between the birth of two consecutive children to one mother to be less than a year (Hansen 1994: 304). However, if we retain the rigid chronological age-classes, closely spaced births do little to solve the problem. If the ephebes undergoing *dokimasia* comprised only those born in one year, there is a low probability that two boys born twelve or even eleven months apart would be part of the same age-class, since this would only be true if their mother delivered the first child in the first month or two of the year.[36]

[34] For a bibliography on this question, see Golden 1979: 25 n. 1.

[35] The problem with this approach is the absence of evidence for records of cohorts of the youth before their *dokimasia* compared to the rich evidence for such records after it. The school administrators in, for instance, Ontario have enough difficulty enforcing the age-classes despite their certain knowledge of a student's age; in ancient Athens, on current evidence, such a system would be untenable.

[36] If we distribute the 3% of births that took place within a year of each other evenly

Hansen's second explanation is that 'brothers who were close in age to one another may, for all practical purposes, have been treated as twins' (Hansen 1994: 304). This begs the question of how age was assessed, and I think we can now do better: chronological age simply was not the sole criterion. Some brothers who were close to one another in age did not undergo the *dokimasia* at the earliest opportunity after the eighteenth anniversary of their births or even in step with any putative age-class based precisely on the number of years and months lived; rather, the two were part of the same cohort since one appeared as much a man as the other, and the two progressed through the ephebate together.

SCRUTINY AND ATHENIAN POLITICAL IDEOLOGY

The final part of this chapter explores some of the ways in which a *dokimasia* based (at least in part) on physical maturity might contribute to the social structure and ideology of Athens. Building on the work of Halperin (1990) and Hunter (1992), I shall argue that the *dokimasia* was a political rite which reinforced the ideology of a citizen's body.

First, we should consider and, I believe, reject a simpler possible function of the *dokimasia*. According to the *Constitution of the Athenians*, the two years that directly followed the *dokimasia* (42. 2–5) were a form of military service, which naturally required physically healthy and mature participants. It might be suggested that a scrutiny of age organized along the lines I suggested above was a means of weeding out those who would be unable to fulfil their roles; furthermore, the scrutiny would be likely to accept candidates who, on other criteria, might be considered under-age but who seemed likely to provide good service. However, we know of no cases of rejection on the basis of age by which to test this theory. Furthermore, the Athenian polis did not consider physical capability a condition of citizenship. Rather, there were persons in the citizen population with handicaps that would exclude them from active military duty, and if such persons met a

among the ninth, tenth, and eleventh month, the proportion of births that take place in the same calendar year is only 0.26%.

needs requirement, they received welfare payments (Arist. *Ath. Pol.* 49. 4; Lys. 24; Philochorus *FGrH* 328 F 197b). Thus it seems that the *dokimasia* did not simply sort out potential candidates for the ephebate.

Since we have no evidence of a failed *dokimasia*, we should consider how the experience of that vast majority, the successful candidates, contributed to the culture of Athens. Imagine the adolescent who is soon to be enrolled in his father's phratry and who a little later will undergo the *dokimasia*. There, he knows, he will appear alongside his friends, and the senior members of the deme will accept him or return him to the children, based on how well he embodies their idea of an eighteen-year-old or, simply put, a man. In such contexts, a low rate of failure has little effect on the coercive power of the examination.

Modern professional examinations provide a useful analogy for the age requirement at the *dokimasia*. In both cases, those who have acquired a particular status assess candidates for that status according to a set of criteria over which the examiners have the power of interpretation. Furthermore, the candidate seeks out the interpretation and attempts to live up to it, and by this means the values of the status group are transmitted. A medical student, for instance, strives for four years to understand what the criterion of 'good bedside manners' means to her instructing physicians while they constantly measure her and rate her progress. Similarly, the young Athenian male would consider, first, what his examiners, that is, the majority of his male elders, believe it means to be a citizen male and reach maturity (*he helikia*) and, secondly, how he might achieve it.

We are in a good position to assess the cultural representations of young adulthood that would influence our candidate. The surviving material remains from Athens provide an abundance of images of the young adult; these express the Athenian—and, indeed, Greek—ideal of a slim, well-toned, supple body in action.[37] As an example, I provide an image of Harmodius from the statue-group of Harmodius and Aristogiton by Critius and Nesiotes (Fig. 1), a model of the politically active youth if ever there was one.[38] It was not only in art that the prospective citizen apprehended this

[37] See Stewart 1997: 63–85.

[38] See Brunnsåker 1971 and, now, Stewart 1997: 70–4 for the date and history of the work.

Figure 1: The ideal citizen's body: statue of Harmodius by Critius and Nesiotes. Photograph courtesy of Deutsches Archäolog. Institut.

ideal: he saw his seniors naked in athletic competition, and in exercise (Stewart 1997: 26–7). Nakedness—ideally, beautiful nakedness—was, in Bonfante's terms, the 'costume' of the male citizen, which distinguished him from women and slaves (1989: 551).

Furthermore, through facilities for exercise the polis provided our prospective citizen with the means of acquiring this costume. It regulated gymnasia so they might be safe and congenial environments for him. Prodicus was ejected by the gymnasiarch of the Lyceum for discussing matters inappropriate for young ears, perhaps in the late fourth century ([Pl.] *Eryxias* 399a). According to the Old Oligarch, the polis even built palaestrae for the common citizen's use ([Xen.] *Ath. Pol.* 2. 10). In such places, the ideal Athenian youth regularly underwent an experience similar to the *dokimasia*. Stripped, as he would be on the big day, he exercised under the gaze of his seniors, who took a keen interest in his physical maturation (Ar. *Nub.* 972–8; 1015–20) and discussed the degree to which he and his friends were maturing and met the ideal (Pl. *Prt.* 309a).

There is, then, one important difference between the modern professional candidate and the prospective Athenian citizen. The former believes she is being judged against an ideal of competency, the latter, I suggest, against an ideal of the body. Why, we might ask, this criterion; why not, for instance, that knowledge of the laws which Aeschines says a youth has by the time he becomes an adult (1. 18) or the ability to speak sensibly, which is an important distinction in Greek thought between young and old (Golden 1994: 376–8)? To this question we can apply—with some adjustments—the recent efforts of today's sociologists to place the body in its modern social context. In a survey of this work, Shilling unearths the consensus that social relations, inequalities, and oppressions guide the biological progression that is a human body. As a result, he says, 'The social reproduction of society also involves the *social reproduction of appropriate bodies*' (Shilling 1993: 125, his emphasis). For our purposes, the most interesting such appropriate body is that of the modern social élites as described by Bourdieu. First, Bourdieu points out how different classes produce bodies appropriate to their station. The lower classes, since they must use their bodies as tools, treat them as a means to an end, and thus value physical power; the dominant classes treat their bodies as an ongoing project, with emphasis either on the body's 'intrinsic functioning' or—more appropriate to our project—'on the appearance as a perceptible configuration . . . i.e. the body for others' (Bourdieu 1984: 212–13). More specifically, today's dominant classes aim less for total muscle bulk than for the slim muscular body which produces effect through its posture, gestures, etc. Thus the bodily forms acquire symbolic values reflecting the underlying social inequalities which produced them. (For instance, the muscle-bound and tattooed male body carries great symbolic weight in some automobile repair-shops but not on the campus.) Secondly, Bourdieu (1984: 206) points out that moulding our bodies in this way is a form of labour, and so he refers to the resulting physique as *body capital.* The dominant classes expend more labour on their physique and produce a bodily form that has greater exchange-value. The lower classes have to be more pragmatic and can employ theirs only for wage-labour. The dominant classes deprecate such an exchange and prefer more abstract, and ultimately more valuable, forms of exchange, principally using their bodies' pleasing form and comportment to form social ties.

One may have doubts, as I do, about whether Bourdieu's work can, as his terms suggest, be grafted on to historical materialist sociology or if it is in fact an idealist approach that makes use of Marxist terminology. Nevertheless, I think he well exposes the way in which class inequalities affect how we treat our bodies and the manner in which the resultant bodies legitimize and perpetuate such inequalities. I propose that the Athenian citizen's body depicted in art, formed in the palaestra, and approved in the *dokimasia* similarly reinforced and legitimized the inequalities in Athenian society and had a symbolic value similar to the body of the dominant classes today. The primary differences are first that this body was understood as a symbol of social status—citizen vs. non-citizen—not of class, and secondly that Athens formally and publicly recognized the symbol in ritual, namely the *dokimasia*.

Aristotle's apology for slavery in the first book of the *Politics* nicely illustrates the symbolic value of bodies in classical Athens. First, he confirms that the ideal expressed in art was commonly understood as a symbol of relations of power. He states, 'this is certainly clear, that if persons were born as distinguished only in body as are the statues of the gods, everyone would say that those who were inferior deserved to be these men's slaves' (1254^{b}34–5).[39] Furthermore, in a description of nature's role in the development of physiques, he shows the ideology of the citizen's body in action:

> The intention of nature therefore is to make the bodies also of freemen and of slaves different—the latter strong for necessary service, the former erect and unserviceable for such occupations, but serviceable for a life of citizenship. (Arist. *Pol.* 1254^{b}29–30, tr. H. Rackham)[40]

Aristotle contrasts his image of the slave with that of a poised and supple citizen, and he considers these physiques products of a different natural purpose for the body, not of the different labour that moulded the potential of each body. Such is the strength of an ideology built on bodies: because the body is a product of both

[39] *τοῦτό γε φανερόν, ὡς εἰ τοσοῦτον γένοιντο διάφοροι τὸ σῶμα μόνον ὅσον αἱ τῶν θεῶν εἰκόνες, τοὺς ὑπολειπομένους πάντες φαῖεν ἂν ἀξίους εἶναι τούτοις δουλεύειν* (Arist. *Pol.* 1254^{b}34–5).

[40] *βούλεται μὲν οὖν ἡ φύσις καὶ τὰ σώματα διαφέροντα ποιεῖν τὰ τῶν ἐλευθέρων καὶ τῶν δούλων, τὰ μὲν ἰσχυρὰ πρὸς τὴν ἀναγκαίαν χρῆσιν, τὰ δ' ὀρθὰ καὶ ἄχρηστα πρὸς τὰς τοιαύτας ἐργασίας, ἀλλὰ χρήσιμα πρὸς πολιτικὸν βίον* (Arist. *Pol.* 1254^{b}29–30).

nature and society, the body moulded by *social* inequalities becomes a symbol of *natural* inequalities, and this in turn legitimizes and perpetuates the social inequalities which differentially mould the citizen and slave bodies.

The most obvious of these inequalities is the daily labour to which Aristotle assigns the slave and the free. Xenophon, too, considers the ideal body to be the product of a proper civic life and agricultural work. Banausic labour, performed stooping over a fire, destroys the body and saps the individual of civic virtues, he says (*Oec.* 4. 2–4), and in some states citizens were not allowed to perform such work (*Oec.* 6. 4–10). Ideally, it seems, the citizen's body should reflect not only his *status*, but also imply a difference in *class* between himself and others in the polis.

Athens did not in this way attempt to enforce distinctions of class for its citizens and non-citizens, but it did create other inequalities with important effects on the bodies of the citizen and slave. Citizens enjoyed access to palaestrae and gymnasia, but a law of Solon expressly forbade slaves to exercise in these facilities (Plut. *Sol.* 1. 3). Aeschines reports the law in his speech *Against Timarchus*:

> Your fathers, when they were laying down laws to regulate the habits of men and those acts that inevitably flow from human nature, forbade slaves to do those things which they thought ought to be done by free men. 'A slave,' says the law, 'shall not take exercise or anoint himself in the wrestling-schools.' It did not go on to add, 'But the free man shall anoint himself and take exercise'; for when, seeing the good that comes from gymnastics, the lawgivers forbade slaves to take part, they thought that in prohibiting them they were by the same words inviting the free. (Aeschin. 1. 138, tr. C. D. Adams)[41]

As Mactoux states, the prohibition demarcated the centres of athletic activity as places that identify the citizen: 'l'absence d'esclaves qualifie une partie de l'espace matériel de la cité à travers les actes symboliques qui sont les exercices gymniques' (1988: 340–1). In such places the youth trained to represent their city in hoplite battle or in panhellenic athletic competition. Such exercises were more than symbolic acts, though; their performance also

[41] *οἱ γὰρ πατέρες ἡμῶν, ὅθ' ὑπὲρ τῶν ἐπιτηδευμάτων καὶ τῶν ἐκ φύσεως ἀναγκαίων ἐνομοθέτουν, ἃ τοῖς ἐλευθέροις ἡγοῦντο εἶναι πρακτέα, ταῦτα τοῖς δούλοις ἀπεῖπον μὴ ποιεῖν. "δοῦλον," φησὶν ὁ νόμος, "μὴ γυμνάζεσθαι μηδὲ ξηραλοιφεῖν ἐν ταῖς παλαίστραις." καὶ οὐκέτι προσέγραψε· "τὸν δ' ἐλεύθερον ἀλείφεσθαι καὶ γυμνάζεσθαι." ὁπότε γὰρ οἱ νομοθέται τὸ καλὸν τὸ ἐκ τῶν γυμνασίων κατιδόντες ἀπεῖπον τοῖς δούλοις μὴ μετέχειν, τῷ αὐτῷ ἡγοῦντο, ᾧ ἐλείνους ἐκώλυον, τοὺς ἐλευθέρους προτρέπειν* (Aeschin. 1. 138).

ideally moulded the participant into a lasting representation of the citizen's identity. He was the opposite in body as well as status to the slave, whose nude body as it appears on Attic painted vases was lacking all the distinguishing definition of the citizen's (Bonfante 1989: 555–6).

Such, in any case, was the ideology. We should wonder if those who were not among the propertied class of Athens were in practice able to make any more use of these facilities than the city's slaves. After all, regular devotion to athletic activity was traditionally the privilege of the wealthy few in Athens as elsewhere (Golden 1998: 157–63). It seems, though, that athletic activity was among those prerogatives of the élites that the democracy wrested from their control and made communal (Ober 1989: 259–66). The Old Oligarch tells us that the demos built many palaestrae for its own enjoyment, and he complains that the common crowd (*ochlos*) uses these more than do the wealthy few ((Xen.) *Ath. Pol.* 2. 10). There was also a tale told of Themistocles visiting the illegitimates (*nothoi*) whose habit it was to exercise at the Cynosarges (Plut. *Them.* 1. 1). Whatever we make of these illegitimates appearing before the citizenship laws of Pericles, it seems this passage also reflects a tradition in which the dispossessed of Athens made use of its athletic facilities. Indeed the Old Oligarch reports that the demos had ended respect for the privilege of the young and rich to devote themselves to sport ((Xen.) *Ath. Pol.* 1. 13). Of course, not every citizen achieved the ideal. Nevertheless, I imagine that an even occasional use of the facilities allowed less-wealthy youths to believe that they were striving towards the ideal and hence participating in it. In this way, what had been the body of the élite seems by the fifth century to have been understood as the body of the citizen.[42]

For this reason, many rights and responsibilities of citizenship were understood with reference to the body. In particular, Hunter has shown how the different treatment of citizen and slave in law

[42] As in other questions regarding status and class in Athens, here the metic raises interesting questions. Foreigners were not barred from athletic facilities at Athens. Prodicus of Ceos apparently frequented the gymnasia ((Pl.) *Eryxias* 399a), though the offence that he gave while there suggests that foreigners in particular entered these spaces precariously. The wealthy metic residing in Athens might have considered it prudent to deter his boys from spending time at such public facilities. In any case, whatever efforts the metic's male children might privately have made to form themselves, their bodies would never formally be acknowledged and thus would never wear the citizen's costume of public nudity.

and penal practice was an expression of the ideology of a citizen's body. Slaves could be tortured for judicial information; citizens could not (Hunter 1992: 278). Citizens could not be confined or maltreated, but whipping and branding were the favoured punishments of the errant slave (Hunter 1992: 279–81). In Halperin's memorable formulation (1990: 96), 'at the boundaries of a citizen's body the operation of almost all social and economic power halted'.

If others could not treat a citizen's body as a slave's, neither could the citizen himself. An Athenian law stipulated that any citizen who performed sexual acts for pay was subject to separation from many of the privileges of citizenship (Aeschin. 1. 3, 13–14, 19). In his analysis of this law in a chapter entitled 'The Democratic Body', Halperin notes that to subject one's body to sexual domination was submitting to the very maltreatment against which the citizen's body provided protection (1990: 96–7). Halperin, following Aeschines' interpretation (1. 29–32), suggests that the polis viewed this as the act of one who would sell any aspect of his autonomy, and whom the polis could not trust in its deliberative roles. In order to explain why accepting money for sex was penalized among citizens, Halperin's analysis must import categories of sexual activities that are degrading to the citizen (1990: 96); to him, as to Aeschines, prostitution entails *hubris*. No doubt this was commonly the case (Dover 1978: 103), but the law makes no such assumptions. I therefore believe we still need to explain the wrongdoing in accepting payment for *any* sort of sexual activity, even that to which, under other circumstances, the polis might turn a blind eye.

The wrongdoing, I suggest, was not necessarily in the sorts of acts the recipient performed, but in the fact that he used the beauty of his body in a commercial exchange. The attractive body of the citizen was the result of a great amount of labour both on the part of the citizen himself and society as a whole, and the citizen was meant to use this physical capital to create social bonds through pederastic courtship, friendship, and the like. To exchange the citizen's body for cash was understood as liquidating a valuable inherited asset, tantamount to squandering a patrimony which, not coincidentally, was another sort of behaviour punished by diminished status (Aeschin. 1. 30).

Furthermore, the *dokimasia* was a formal and ritualized certification of a citizen's body. Osborne has examined the role of such periodic conventional events, or rituals, in forming a cohesive citizenry (1994: 8–9). His observations certainly apply to the *dokimasia*, during the yearly performance of which all citizens played formal roles of either arbiter or embodiment of bodily excellence: whatever the true nature of the candidate's physique, his elders on this occasion stated that he in turn embodied the ideals of the citizen. More importantly, however, the *dokimasia* repeated a lifelong pattern of ritual scrutiny whereby he gained access to position and status. In particular, the ritual acceptance of an individual on grounds of his physical form brings to mind the very first instance of this pattern, the *amphidromia*, wherein a father ritually accepted a child—also on the basis of physical form—into that smallest social unit of the city, the *oikos*, or household. To know that one's body was consciously accepted, not simply tolerated, by the *oikos* and later the deme was the assurance that this particular ritual pattern provided the Athenian citizen.

In summary, the *dokimasia* was part of a group of institutions and representations that guided the prospective and mature citizen's attitude towards his body. In particular, the *dokimasia* was the annual rite that formally declared that each citizen's body represented an ideal shared by, and exclusive to, the collected citizens, the polis. In this way it supported the ideological distinction between citizen and slave. Even if the ideology centred around the ephebe's body, the *dokimasia* put the power of shaping that ideology in the hands of his seniors. Returning to Aristophanes' old juror, we now might suspect that his delight is not only in viewing the bloom of his deme's youth, but also in wielding the power which is the prerogative of his age: just as jury duty gave him authority over the judicial—and at times, political—process, participation in the *dokimasia* gave him the power to reconstruct the civic ideology in the next generation.[43]

I conclude by presenting a possible depiction of this interplay between the young and old on a fourth-century Attic funerary stele from the Ilissos river (Athens, Nat. Mus., inv. no. 896; Fig 2).

[43] Thus while the ideal citizen body was that of a fit and healthy young adult, this should not be interpreted as evidence for a 'youth culture' at Athens (see Garland 1990: 206–7) any more than the general admiration of a Marilyn Monroe proves a culture centred on women in the USA of the mid-twentieth century. In both cases, the admired individuals conform to an ideal which neither they nor their social group controls.

Figure 2: The young, the old, and scrutiny: Athenian funerary stele, fourth century BC. Photograph courtesy of Deutsches Archäolog. Institut.

The monument presents three stages of life, but the artistic centre of the piece is the youth. Naked and muscular, he faces the viewer, alluring with the beauty and grace of his form. To his right, however, is an older man who holds his chin with his thumb and forefinger. He ponders the youth, neither in awe of his form, nor disinterested. Perhaps he is in mourning. Perhaps, though, this is a moment of that assessment, that measuring-up of the youth against an ideal which constructed the citizen's body.[44] On this grave marker is *dokimasia* chosen to typify the relations between young and old and, more importantly, the continuation of the polis' ideology beyond even death itself?

[44] Professor Timothy McNiven of the Ohio State University kindly informed me by private correspondence that in his database of 16,000 gestures on Attic vases this gesture appears twenty-three times in mourning scenes and fifty times in contexts where someone is contemplating something.

References

Bickerman, E. J. 1968. *Chronology of the Ancient World*. London.

Bonfante, L. 1989. 'Nudity as a Costume in Classical Art', *AJA* 93: 543–70.

Bourdieu, P. 1984 (1979). *Distinction: A Social Critique of the Judgement of Taste*, tr. Richard Nice. London.

Brunnsåker, S. 1971. *The Tyrant-Slayers of Kritios and Nesiotes: A Critical Study of the Sources and Restorations*, 2nd edn. Stockholm.

Carey, C. and R. A. Reid (eds.) 1985. *Demosthenes: Select Private Speeches*. Cambridge.

Dover, K. J. 1978. *Greek Homosexuality*. Cambridge, Mass.

Evans-Pritchard, E. E. 1940. *The Nuer: A Description of the Modes of Livelihood and Political Institutions of a Nilotic People*. Oxford.

Frisch, P. 1988. 'Die Klassifikation der *Παῖδες* bei den griechischen Agonen', *ZPE* 75: 179–85.

Garland, R. 1990. *The Greek Way of Life*. London.

Golden, M. 1979. 'Demosthenes and the Age of Majority at Athens', *Phoenix* 33: 25–38.

—— 1990. *Children and Childhood in Classical Athens*. Baltimore.

—— 1994. 'Children's Rights, Children's Speech and *Agamemnon*', in R. Osborne and S. Hornblower (eds.), *Ritual, Finance, Politics: Athenian Democratic Accounts Presented to David Lewis*. Oxford. 371–83.

—— 1998. *Sport and Society in Ancient Greece*. Cambridge.

Goldhill, S. 1987. 'The Great Dionysia and Civic Ideology', *JHS* 107: 58–76.

Halperin, D. 1990. *One Hundred Years of Homosexuality*. London.

Hansen, M. H. 1991. *The Athenian Democracy in the Age of Demosthenes: Structure, Principles and Ideology*, tr. J. A. Crook. Oxford.

—— 1994. 'The Number of Athenian Citizens *Secundum* Sekunda', *EMC/CV* 13: 299–310.

Harris, E. M. 1988. 'When Was Aeschines Born?', *CP* 83: 211–15.

—— 1989. 'Demosthenes' Speech against Meidias', *HSCP* 92: 117–36.

Hunter, V. J. 1982. *Past and Process in Herodotus and Thucydides*. Princeton.

—— 1992. 'Constructing the Body of the Citizen: Corporal Punishment in Classical Athens', *EMC/CV* 11: 271–91.

Lambert, S. D. 1993. *The Phratries of Attica*. Ann Arbor.

MacDowell, D. M. (ed.) 1971. *Aristophanes' Wasps*. Oxford.

—— (ed.) 1990. *Demosthenes, Against Meidias (Oration 21)*. Oxford.

Mactoux, M.-M. 1988. 'Lois de Solon sur les esclaves et formation d'une société esclavagiste', in T. Yuge and M. Doi (eds.), *Forms of*

Control and Subordination in Antiquity. Leiden. 331–54.

Ober, J. 1989. *Mass and Elite in Democratic Athens*. Princeton.

Osborne, R. G. 1994. 'Introduction', in R. G. Osborne and S. Hornblower (eds.), *Ritual, Finance, Politics: Athenian Democratic Accounts Presented to David Lewis*. Oxford. 1–21.

Rhodes, P. J. 1972. *The Athenian Boule*. Oxford.

—— 1981. *A Commentary on the Aristotelian Athenaion Politeia*. Oxford.

—— (tr.) 1984. *Aristotle: The Athenian Constitution*. London.

Schmidt, W. 1910. 'Genethlios hemera', *RE* 7: 1135–49.

Sekunda, N. V. 1992. 'Athenian Demography and Military Strength 338–322 BC', *ABSA* 87: 311–55.

Shilling, C. 1993. *The Body and Social Theory*. London.

Shrimpton, G. 1995. 'Time, Memory, and Narrative in Thucydides', *Storia della Storiografia* 28: 47–54.

Sommerstein, A. (ed.) 1983. *Aristophanes' Wasps*. Warminster.

Stewart, A. 1997. *Art, Desire, and the Body in Ancient Greece*. Cambridge.

8

Epilogue: Some Trends in Recent Work on Athenian Law and Society

Mark Golden

This book provides evidence for how much the study of Greek law has changed since the days when scholars seemed to be 'operating in a world . . . hermetically sealed against outside developments' (D. Cohen 1989: 82). It is not just the subject alone, the intersection of law and social status. We should note too the wide range of interests of those taking part. So, for example, Cynthia Patterson has just published a book on the Athenian family (Patterson 1998); Edward Cohen writes extensively on the Athenian economy (e.g. E. Cohen 1992); David Mirhady works on Dicaearchus and Theophrastus (Fortenbaugh and Mirhady 1994; Mirhady 1995); Robin Osborne is an authority on Greek archaeology and art and their relevance to social history and on the Greek countryside as well as being the author of a standard history of archaic Greece (Osborne and Goldhill 1994; Osborne 1987; 1996); Stephen Todd's masterful account of Athenian law is meant to offer something interesting 'for comparative lawyers and social anthropologists' (Todd 1993: vii). Noteworthy too are the titles of two recent collections: *Nomos: Essays on Athenian Law, Politics and Society* (Cartledge et al. 1990) and *Greek Law in its Political Setting* (Foxhall and Lewis 1996). All this amounts to compelling proof of the revitalization of the study of Greek law, a redefinition so well established that it has even provoked a mild counter-reaction (Crook 1996).

David Cohen's work has had a lot to do with this resurgence of interest in Greek law and the sophistication which characterizes it (see especially D. Cohen 1991; 1995). In particular, Cohen has developed most persuasively the view that Athenians were actors

This commentary has benefited from the legal expertise of my colleague Craig Cooper.

and agents in respect of the law, capable and even skilled in using the law's provisions and procedures for their own purposes (and ignoring them when it suited them to do so). This has been one important trend in recent work on Athenian law and its relation to social reality. I will point here to three other leading tendencies, identify some traces of these tendencies in the chapters of this book, and suggest some questions pertinent to each, in the hope of provoking further study. My three trends are of course interrelated. They involve treating (1) law as parallel discourse, (2) law as productive discourse, and (3) law as permeable discourse. I caution that in what follows I make no attempt to supply a comprehensive account and that I illustrate my remarks with works in English only—though the view that the courts, along with the army, offer the most accurate insight into any state finds one of its most famous formulations in the German of Goethe (*Dichtung und Wahrheit* 3. 12). One excuse for this is the fact that the social context of Athenian law has mostly engaged those writing in English.[1]

LAW AS PARALLEL DISCOURSE

What I mean by this is simply that law does not necessarily provide an accurate portrayal of social reality. We often find what Crook calls 'bad fits' (1996: 35). An example, well discussed in Virginia Hunter's *Policing Athens*: though Athenian women were legally always under the *kyrieia* of an adult male citizen, the orators sometimes allow us glimpses of women who acted as heads of their households (Hunter 1994: 31–3). (What David Cohen stresses, personal choice and individual temperament, must often have entered in: see Foxhall 1996: 148–52.) In this vein, Patterson argues here that the apparent legal protections of metics were in practice of little value. Hunter notes that the fact that slaves who lived on their own (*khoris oikountes*) possessed the wherewithal to pay fines did not exempt them from public whippings. Edward Cohen urges the essential irrelevance of juridical distinctions (citizen, metic, slave) in accounting for individuals' real social and economic roles and rewards. Similarly, Cheryl Cox has demon-

[1] Cf. Todd and Millett 1990: 10–11. Among exceptions, see in particular the pioneering work of Louis Gernet (including his editions of Antiphon, Demosthenes, Lysias, and Plato's *Laws* in the Budé series and the articles collected in Gernet 1955 and 1968) and the studies of torture by Gerhard Thür (Thür 1977; 1996).

strated that the difficulty of establishing that a legal marriage had taken place, combined with their residence in the household, allowed *pallakai* (concubines) and their children to encroach on its property despite laws explicitly excluding them from a share (Cox 1998: 170–89).

Questions

We need not take every instance of the disjuncture between law and social status in classical Athens at face value. Some indeed may send us back to our understanding of law or society (or both) and lead us to modify our views (see Crook 1996: 35–6). But the phenomenon is real enough. What then? Is this a significant finding or trivial? Is it true cross-culturally (see the discussions of problems in dealing with law as a category cross-culturally in Todd and Millett 1990: 11–18 and Foxhall 1996: 133–40)? Is it the product rather of a certain definition of law, of law as the sum of a set of statutes or a code? (By this reckoning, such a disjuncture could not be true of Sparta, where custom and law may, as David Cohen argues (1989: 100), be much the same.) If it *is* true cross-culturally, do the same mechanisms operate and the same explanations work everywhere? We are familiar with laws which remain on the books long after they have become obsolete. Archaic language is a feature of some Athenian laws (see e.g. Lys. 10. 15–21), and such outmoded statutes may have existed at Athens as well. They are invoked here in Todd's account of throwing condemned criminals into the pit. Our own obsolete laws often concern sexual practices such as sodomy; our politicians hesitate to advocate their repeal in fear of being labelled as supporters of sodomy (or whatever) and so they remain undisturbed in our statute books to trap consensual couples with flimsy curtains and a neighbour with a video camcorder. This kind of explanation might apply to the Athenian laws forbidding citizens who sold sexual services from active participation in the democracy—a law Edward Cohen calls a dead letter (though capable of coming to life under Aeschines' care). Is it applicable to other leftovers too?

Virginia Hunter explains the whipping of *khoris oikountes* as a marker of their status and compares their liability to torture, from which the free were exempt. This brings us to my second heading, law as productive discourse.

LAW AS PRODUCTIVE DISCOURSE

It is also true, of course, that law creates and reinforces social differences and hierarchies. It does these things in two ways. (1) Laws may apply equally to those who are different and so foster varying outcomes. This equality under the law is often represented as fairness. An example comes from Patterson's discussion of the legal position of metics. The polemarch's role in legal cases involving metics is formally identical to the archon's in citizens' cases, notwithstanding the real difference in rights and privileges between the two juridical statuses. (2) Laws may replicate hierarchies by treating those who are unequal differently. For example, within the Athenian community, metics could be seized and imprisoned before trial (unless they produced sureties), unlike citizens (Hunter); the murder of a metic was handled differently than the murder of a citizen (Patterson). Such distinctions do not merely mark a difference and establish a hierarchy; they represent it—the practice of seizing and holding metics marks them as rootless cosmopolitans, likely to leave their adopted home (though in fact, like Lysias, they may have lived and made their lives there).

We may observe the law operating in this way in relation to those outside Athens too. Osborne draws attention to the regulations imposed by Athens on the members of the Second Athenian Confederacy in the fourth century BC. While slaves were restricted in their ability to bring accusations against alleged wrongdoers in Athens, they were less hindered among Athens' allies. There is no obvious practical explanation for this distinction. Its motives must be symbolic, to underline a hierarchy of status which placed Athenian citizens above citizens of the allied cities.

Questions

We are left to wonder why these particular measures were chosen to signal and make differences. The focus on the body as a marker of the non-citizen—metic or slave—is remarkable: whipping, seizing and imprisoning, the *metoikion* (an unusual tax in that it was levied on the person and not on his or her property). There is clearly something to Bruce Robertson's reading of the young Athenian's *dokimasia* as an attempt to ensure that he was fit to enter what we still call the citizen body; in fact, it created the citizen body, in both senses of the phrase. To be sure, Edward Cohen challenges this line of thinking. For him, all bodies (of whatever juridical status) were free to engage in prostitution, just as all were protected against *hubris*. Prostitution, then, is not the arena for the display and denial of status but a simple matter of sex and money. As Freud said, sometimes a cigar is just a cigar. Now, it is certainly possible to stress representation at the expense of reality. One of the most productive discussions at the 1997 conference which gave rise to this book centred on the execution of Socrates. Why hemlock? One intriguing answer, originating in a comment by Jutta Raithel, was that the democracy did not choose this method *despite* its associations with The Thirty Tyrants but precisely *because of* them. In other words, Socrates' death was meant to signal the covert cause of his prosecution, his links with leaders of The Thirty. Persuasive as this may be, however, such symbolic speech is only incidental to the main and incontestable result of the trial—Socrates' death. So too the torture and beating of slaves, whatever its conceptual content, was a source of real suffering for the victims. But we should also recall that Freud—who smoked cigars—died of mouth cancer: things are indeed often more than they seem.

Cohen's case is based in part on the view that the household, like the city as a whole, made room for slaves. This is overstated. Rome offers a telling contrast, slaves and freedpersons connected by name, and often buried, with their masters (Pomeroy 1997: 21). But just as Cohen denies important distinctions between slaves, metics, and citizens, the concentration of other scholars on juridical status may (as Hunter observes) elide significant differences among adult male Athenians. Equal before the law they might be. But the costs of bringing a suit and the financial consequences of losing one weighed much more heavily on the poor (see Isoc. 16. 47 and the convenient account of fees and fines in Scafuro 1997: 41 n. 66). The Athenians could have met this problem head on, using a system of costs and fines graded according to wealth, as they did in establishing different dowries for *epikleroi* of the four Solonian census classes. They did not. Instead, the demos had more recourse to imprisonment as a punishment, on the grounds that this afforded equal treatment for rich and poor alike (Allen 1997: 126–35). It did so, of course, by separating prisoners from other citizens and assimilating them, in respect of their lack of freedom of action, to metics and slaves. Statuses might be fluid after all—the cue for my third tendency.

LAW AS PERMEABLE DISCOURSE

A number of recent writers have stressed that Greek law was not a separate sphere with its own concepts or ideology but rather integrated into and strongly influenced by other areas of social life (Carey 1994 offers a good outline). For example, Marilyn Katz has explored the conceptual links between laws governing homicide committed by non-human agents and stories on the origin of animal sacrifice in Greece, Mesopotamia, and Israel (Katz 1993). This permeability must occur anywhere, of course; it is the extent to which it was true at Athens and the particular areas of interrelationship which are of interest here. Osborne puts the case forcefully and at the same time identifies a characteristic linking Athenian law with other realms: 'Athenian courts were places in which social standing was contested.' Contests, rivalry, competition. The law overlaps with warfare in that the legal officer charged with responsibility for metics was the polemarch, the war archon (Patterson). Another competitive arena with links to the law is athletics: Robertson discusses the *dokimasia* in the context of methods of allocating competitors to the proper age class. But many recent students of Athenian law have been most struck by the parallels between the courts and the plays presented at Athens' competitive dramatic festivals (e.g. Garner 1987: 95–130; Hall 1995; Slater 1995: 143–6; Scafuro 1997). Stephen Todd's contribution to this volume is itself structured as a play (Todd 'sets the scene' and so on) and both he and Virginia Hunter emphasize the public nature of trials and their outcomes. (Hunter speaks of the 'moral degradation ceremony' in which slaves were whipped in public, Todd notes that condemned criminals suffered *apotumpanismos* in a public place, with other citizens, including the prosecutor, as a kind of audience for the spectacle.) If tragedy (as Patterson notes) could present Antigone as a metic, litigants could invoke passages from tragedy 'as pieces of evidence like any other deposited in the courts' (Wilson 1996: 312).

Questions

Does this tendency underestimate the extent to which Greeks, and Athenians in particular, had developed legal principles, in practice anyway (Harris 1991; Crook 1996: 33)? May it also (once again) overlook necessary distinctions between different marginal groups (slaves, children, women) and between different contexts of competition? It is true, as Osborne observes, that neither slaves nor women could testify in Athenian courts, just as neither group competed in athletics or drama. His explanation is that they had no honour to gain or lose, and should not affect the status of those within the charmed circle of honourable men. Cases of impiety test the rule but do not contravene it, since gods too are outside the calculus of honour, exalted above it rather than unworthy. (As John Updike said of baseball immortal Ted Williams's refusal to tip his hat to the fans, 'Gods do not answer letters.') Mirhady points out, however, that Aristotle thought free women had the deliberative faculties slaves lacked and some such belief may underlie provisions of Athenian law, both positive—allowing free women to swear oaths—and negative, in reserving torture for slaves. Furthermore, some prosecutions, like Neaera's, clearly use women to attack and dishonour men connected to them, and 'many disputes which become court battles between men seem to have begun as quarrels between, involving, or even generated by women' (Foxhall 1996: 143). Finally, boys, though excluded from testifying in court, made up an important class of athletic competitors; their victories were much sought after and celebrated (Golden 1998: 104–12). In another particularly prestigious pursuit, equestrian competition, women could strive for honour and slave jockeys and charioteers could assist both men and women who did.

The parallels between the theatre and the courts which are presently so prominent may prompt the most interesting queries. As Adriaan Lanni's title asks, were Athenian trials 'spectator sport or serious politics' (Lanni 1997)? Lanni's own answer emphasizes the hubbub of an Athenian court, the frequent interventions of onlookers (including Athenians of every social class as well as—significantly?—metics and foreigners), to whom litigants played; they in turn influenced juries. (So too in the late Roman Republic trials in the Forum were political by nature in part 'because they were exposed to and much affected by crowd reactions and . . . were often disturbed by outright violence' (Millar 1998: 88).) Jurors themselves might react like an audience, appreciating a fine piece of characterization (Scafuro 1997: 50–67) or laughing in delight at ridicule and abuse (Halliwell 1991: 292–4).

Does this go too far? For Edward Harris, the rule of law was paramount at Athens, and jurors took the law, and their oath to uphold it, very seriously indeed (Harris 1994: 132–7). Should it go further still? Students of Greek society have made something of the physical and vocal mannerisms of speakers in court (e.g. Hall 1995: 46–9, 53) but less than, say, Amy Richlin, who argues that similarities between speaker and actor at Rome might result in some confusion about the ascribed gender and so the social status of an advocate (Richlin 1997). Implications for our own attitudes towards statements made by the orators are among the most important. There is no doubt that much that we read in our texts of forensic speeches is misleading or wrong, from grossly exaggerated caricatures of opponents to garbled accounts of historical facts. Ian Worthington identifies the problem, adduces instances, puts forward an explanation: the speeches as we have them were revised for publication—no jury could have swallowed the fabrications we find (Worthington 1994: 109–18). But it is daunting to contemplate revision on the scale Worthington has in mind. Are we to imagine that Demosthenes (to Hellenize Housman's famous example) wrote *o* but said *Buzantios*? The more the courtroom resembles a theatre, however, and the more jurors act as an audience (even an audience made up of festival judges), the less we need appeal to such solutions. A juror who was persuaded by a litigant's persona or amused by a speechwriter's wit could also persuade himself that he was remaining true to his dicastic oath (cf. Slater 1995: 153). There are modern parallels. Tenure and promotion committees made up of rational and judicious academics often ignore the contracts which set out criteria for their decisions. If modern parallels are out of place (as Harris insists, 1994: 136), we may notice an ancient Athenian one: the return of Pisistratus, staged as a festival procession with Athena in the leading role, the tyrant as her side-kick, and the demos joining 'in a shared drama, not foolishly, duped by some manipulator, but playfully, participating in a cultural pattern they all share' (Connor 1987: 44). If this is on the right lines, it will not affect our judgement of the Attic orators as sources for just law, life stories, and historical events. Even the arguments from plausibility favoured by social historians—such as Robertson's 'to claim a jury cannot know that which they believe they can know is dangerous indeed'—will be at risk. A jury's judgement will largely depend on what else it has been told and how (cf. Todd 1990). Twentieth-century studies of Athenian law and society may end in the scepticism where they began: only fools rush in where Wyse men fear to tread.

References

ALLEN, D. 1997. 'Imprisonment in Classical Athens', *CQ* 47: 121–35.

CAREY, C. 1994. 'Legal Space in Classical Athens', *G&R* 41: 172–86.

CARTLEDGE, P., P. MILLETT, and S. C. TODD (eds.) 1990. *Nomos: Essays in Athenian Law, Politics and Society*. Cambridge.

COHEN, D. 1989. 'Greek Law: Problems and Methods', *ZRG* 106: 81–105.

—— 1991. *Law, Sexuality, and Society: The Enforcement of Morals in Classical Athens*. Cambridge.

—— 1995. *Law, Violence, and Community in Classical Athens*. Cambridge.

COHEN, E. E. 1992. *Athenian Economy and Society: A Banking Perspective*. Princeton.

CONNOR, W. R. 1987. 'Tribes, Festivals and Processions: Civic Ceremonial and Political Manipulation in Archaic Greece', *JHS* 107: 40–50.

COX, C. A. 1998. *Household Interests: Property, Marriage Strategies, and Family Dynamics in Ancient Athens*. Princeton.

CROOK, J. A. 1996. 'Legal History and General History', *BICS* 41: 31–6.

FORTENBAUGH, W. and D. C. MIRHADY 1994. *Peripatetic Rhetoric after Aristotle*. New Brunswick, N.J. (Rutgers University Studies in Classical Humanities, vol. 6).

FOXHALL, L. 1996. 'The Law and the Lady: Women and Legal Proceedings in Classical Athens', in L. Foxhall and A. D. E. Lewis (eds.), *Greek Law in its Political Setting: Justifications not Justice*. Oxford. 133–52.

FOXHALL, L. and A. D. E. LEWIS (eds.) 1996. *Greek Law in its Political Setting: Justifications not Justice*. Oxford.

GARNER, R. 1987. *Law and Society in Classical Athens*. London and Sydney.

GERNET, L. 1955. *Droit et société dans la Grèce ancienne*. Paris.

—— 1968. *Anthropologie de la Grèce antique*. Paris. (Translated as *The*

Anthropology of Ancient Greece by J. Hamilton and B. Nagy. Baltimore, 1981.)

Golden, M. 1998. *Sport and Society in Ancient Greece.* Cambridge.

Hall, E. 1995. 'Lawcourt Dramas: The Power of Performance in Greek Forensic Oratory', *BICS* 40: 39–58.

Halliwell, S. 1991. 'The Uses of Laughter in Greek Culture', *CQ* 41: 279–96.

Harris, E. M. 1991. 'Response to Trevor Saunders', in M. Gagarin (ed.), *Symposion 1990. Vorträge zur griechischen und hellenistischen Rechtsgeschichte* (Pacific Grove, Calif., 24–6 September 1990). Cologne. 133–8.

—— 1994. 'Law and Oratory', in I. Worthington (ed.), *Persuasion: Greek Rhetoric in Action.* London and New York. 130–50.

Hunter, V. J. 1994. *Policing Athens: Social Control in the Attic Lawsuits, 420–320 BC.* Princeton.

Katz, M. A. 1993. 'Buphonia and Goring Ox: Homicide, Animal Sacrifice, and Judicial Process', in R. M. Rosen and J. Farrell (eds.), *Nomodeiktes: Greek Studies in Honor of Martin Ostwald.* Ann Arbor. 155–78.

Lanni, A. M. 1997. 'Spectator Sport or Serious Politics? οἱ περιεστηκότες and the Athenian Lawcourts', *JHS* 117: 183–9.

Millar, F. 1998. *The Crowd in Rome in the Late Republic.* Ann Arbor.

Mirhady, D. C. 1995. 'Plutarch's Use of Theophrastus' "Peri tous Kairous"', in I. Gallo (ed.), *Teoria e prassi politica nelle opere di Plutarco.* Naples. 269–73.

Osborne, R. G. 1987. *Classical Landscape with Figures: The Ancient Greek City and its Countryside.* London.

—— 1996. *Greece in the Making, 1200–479 BC.* London and New York.

Osborne, R. G. and S. Goldhill (eds.) 1994. *Art and Text in Ancient Greek Culture.* Cambridge.

Patterson, C. 1998. *The Family in Greek History.* Cambridge, Mass., and London.

Pomeroy, S. B. 1997. *Families in Classical and Hellenistic Greece: Representations and Realities.* Oxford.

Richlin, A. 1997. 'Gender and Rhetoric: Producing Manhood in the Schools', in W. J. Dominik (ed.), *Roman Eloquence: Rhetoric in Society and Literature.* London and New York. 90–109.

Scafuro, A. C. 1997. *The Forensic Stage: Settling Disputes in Graeco-Roman New Comedy.* Princeton.

Slater, W. J. 1995. 'The Theatricality of Justice', *CB* 71: 143–57.

Thür, G. 1977. *Beweisführung vor den Schwurgerichtshöfen Athens: Die Proklesis zur Basanos.* Vienna.

—— 1996. 'Reply to D. C. Mirhady: Torture and Rhetoric in Athens', *JHS* 116: 132–4.

TODD, S. C. 1990. 'The Use and Abuse of the Attic Orators', *G&R* 37: 159–78.

—— 1993. *The Shape of Athenian Law*. Oxford.

TODD, S. C. and P. MILLETT 1990. 'Law, Society and Athens', in P. Cartledge, P. Millett, and S. C. Todd (eds.), *Nomos: Essays in Athenian Law, Politics and Society*. Cambridge. 1–18.

WILSON, P. J. 1996. 'Tragic Rhetoric: The Use of Tragedy and the Tragic in the Fourth Century', in M. S. Silk (ed.), *Tragedy and the Tragic: Greek Theatre and Beyond*. Oxford. 310–31.

WORTHINGTON, I. 1994. 'History and Oratorical Exploitation', in I. Worthington (ed.), *Persuasion: Greek Rhetoric in Action*. London and New York. 109–29.

Index of Sources

A. LITERARY SOURCES

B. INSCRIPTIONS

C. PAPYRI

General Index